Don't look for a lover. Be one.

—James Leo Herlihy

In the Flesh

undressing for success

by

Gavin Geoffrey Dillard

BARRICADE BOOKS
New York City
1998

An extra *thank you* to Tom Kellie, Michael Michaud,
David Dalton, John Preston, Richard Labonté,
Matt Sartwell, Ian Young, Christopher Schelling,
William Barrett, Terry Anderson, Armistead Maupin,
Steven Gaines, and David Burns.

Portions of this book have appeared in:

FLESH AND THE WORD – John Preston, *Plume*
BAD DATES – Carole Markin, *Citadel*

Front cover photo by John J. Krause.

First Edition

ISBN: 1-56980-118-5

to the living

JO

Experience is the only teacher;
the heart, the only preacher.

My beloved dad deposited me, in a frigid February rain, on the Asheville, North Carolina, west-bound on-ramp for I-40. His deer eyes were teary as he cautioned me about the dangers of the road, drunk drivers, and "funny people." We had never been close, Dad and I, but somehow this parting became a critical connection. And I knew, and he knew that I knew, that in spirit and in desire he traveled with me, as me, for I was now the only part of this staid southern gentleman that could still seek adventure and freedom.

"I love you, Buddy," was all he said.

"I love you too, Dad. Don't worry about me."

I stuck out the thumb that had already taken me across the continent six times. This time I planned to not return; I had just turned twenty-one and was no longer the reckless gamin I once had been. It was 1977, the hippies were fading, life was getting serious, and hitchhiking wasn't as benign as it used to be. Beyond that, I had absolutely no further use for the stifling traditions of North Carolina; I was going to find my adult self in Los Angeles, Hollywood, the Promised Land. The Center of the Universe.

I had come west the first time to attend the California Institute of the Arts, Walt Disney's semi-successful attempt at a thriving arts community some forty-five minutes north of Hollywood proper. I had pals from high school (North Carolina School of the Arts) who had ended up there, who then harbored me and showed me the ropes. It was my first exposure to non-southern culture, and left a taste for worlds-yet-unexplored. Worlds that I was certain existed beneath Southern California's swaying palms.

California was also the farthest English-speaking land that I could get to by thumb, be warm year-round, and get away from my mother, my roots, and my bitterly estranged first husband, Dalton. My life thus far had been entirely within the web of Mom's random moral etiquette, augmented but not replaced by that of the twenty-four-year-old Dalton, whom I moved in with when I was sixteen. I now sought to escape both their clutches.

Besides, LA was the home of both Lily Tomlin *and* Christopher Isherwood, my only two living heroes. Yes, I was looking for the roots, *and* fruit, of my ill-positioned sexual identity, but I was hoping that through this exploration there would be provided an appropriate niche for my soul. My spirit was bold and restless, and though by this time I had already published two books, I felt as though I had really done little more than survive the debacles of growing up. I was little more than a reaction to someone else's morality—that is, a reaction to a reaction to a reaction... Somewhere there had to be the truth behind the mores; somewhere there had to be the possibility of pure spontaneity.

Over the next twenty-some years I never found what I was looking for, as a poet, as a romantic, as a spiritual pioneer. What I found instead were all the layers of belief that I could ultimately shed and live without, unfettering my steps toward that unseen goal of freedom and peace of spirit. This is what I am exploring in these pages, the gradual undressing of that little beast, Gavin, that has brought me to this quiet mountaintop near Yosemite—the Naked Poet, spontaneous and alive at last—in the flesh...

On this trip were the usual number of wino drivers, my heart thumping madly as we wove along the freeway at ninety-five miles per hour. There were the usual number of frozen toes and fingers. And truck drivers who, like Mac (named after his truck, I presume), at three-o'clock in the morning on an icy lone highway decide that it's an appropriate time to pull over and have their dick blown.

"Weell, I'm reel tired, fella. Why don't we just crawl up here in the berth and rest a spell. You look like you could use some shut-eye..."

I can't say that I was ever happy to oblige. I had always *hated* sucking dick, had steadily refused to even through my five years with Dalton.

On the other hand, it was eighteen degrees outside on an unfamiliar side road, and Mac was not a bad sort, pleasantly chatty, frightfully white-skinned and hairless, but otherwise not an unattractive dude, for a thirty-two-year-old. He rambled on about his girlfriend back home and how much he'd like to watch me corn-hole his fifteen-year-old daughter.

I gave it the old college best, gagged and swallowed—for want of alternative hygiene—and we resumed our amnesic banter of road-talk, expletives, and related heteroisms as though nothing had just occurred.

"Say," he said as he dropped me off in front of his favorite piss-hole hotel in downtown Topeka, slipping me six bucks to pay for the room, "you ever been to a Wesson oil party?"

"Can't say that I have," I confessed, stifling a yawn.

"Well hey, call me up next time yer comin' through."

"With your girlfriend and daughter?" I mused.

"Hell yeah."

Though he never gave me his number, Mac was just one of the many road-signs along the dim and closeted terrain of White Trash America. I knew that I would never pass that way again.

Two days later I arrived, body, if not sanity, intact to the Beechwood Canyon door of Jo and Peter.

Jo had been the dorm mama at Cal Arts. She was six feet tall, gorgeous (but never quite sure of this and always plugging for strokes), dressed like a man, longed to be a fag, and was at that point arguably my bestest friend. At Cal Arts she had been married to a delicious grizzly of a tattooed biker named Chas. Chas and I spent hours painting each other's fingernails black with tiny white skulls and racing stripes. He would hug me to the point of threatening my ribs; his waist-length black hair defied the comb, and his disdain for clothing had been the bane and the delight of all the ladies and queers on dorm-block D. I loved him. But now after one bike crash too many, scars across her brow that had cut off all possibility of returning to her professional modeling gigs, Jo had become tired of being the eternal moll. She left Chas and Cal Arts with a hunky young design student named Peter.

Peter was an ex-hustler from St. Petersburg, Florida—half Jew, half WASP, blond, blue-eyed, with the legendary "dick of death." He was the perfect mate for Jo; they shared a charming two-room basement apartment just below the Hollywood sign.

It was much too small for three, but nevertheless I moved in and became instantly at odds with Peter, jealous of me jealous of him, with Jo delighted by the contention of her two favorite males. She could be fey with me, straight with Peter, and always have someone to play with. We played while Peter was at work. Jo was as ecstatic with the company as I was at being young and alive in Babylon. Mostly we shopped, mostly the secondhand and rag shops on Melrose, this being the era before Melrose became *Melrose*-fashion-capital-yuppie-arama. We bought fatuous outfits and costumes that could have only been worn back in the days of dorm life; back at the apartment we had continual weekend garage sales of the costumes and bric-a-brac that no longer struck our vogue.

Evenings, then, we went out dancing. Always the gay discos—hell, there weren't even any straight discos in this time before *Saturday Night Fever*, heterosexuals (white heterosexuals) hadn't learned to dance. I was mortified, trembling, yanking endlessly at the wrinkles in my tanktop. Still I was all eyes and gawking mouth, sucking in the stench of sweat, British Sterling, sawdust, and spilled beer as though it were the freshly-tilled spring earth. For me it was.

And black, wolfish eyes glared back at me. Not only in recognition and acknowledgment—another man of ambiguous sorrow, another lily in the shadows—but in lust! Titters accompanied catcalls; low growls as well as the occasional falsetto "Ooo *girl!* Look what the Twinky Man just dropped off!"

Horrifying! Tawdry! Exultant! Passionate! This was Oz, with all its demons, witches and wizards. This was the land beyond the pale: something at last that felt like home.

"Why don't *you* guys dance?" I would goad, desperate to explore the darkened walls on my own.

"Ohhh," Jo would whine, "I wanna see you and *P* dance."

"I don't *feel* like dancing," Peter would counterwhine, sitting impatiently with a tepid beer while Jo and I moseyed off to work on our swingsteps.

The nights that Jo and I went out alone didn't work for long either, as Jo felt so miserably guilty and worried about Petie at home that she was unable to hang loose and have a good time anyway.

One definitively whiny evening she got the great idea to introduce Craig.

Craig had been Jo's best fag friend at Cal Arts, once I had left to pursue a young man I'd encountered in the summer program. I didn't remember Craig, though we had overlapped a semester or two, but we connected instantly this time around. We immediately dumped Jo and sped out on our own to make the rounds of all the less trendy homo bars, the old vampire haunts, the hotbeds of essential human perversity, even the seedy bathhouses that struck terror and delight into the bowels of my half-virgin soul. Jo and Pete got to stay at home and fuck while I was out and about, and *I* no longer had to listen to them rattling and cooing under their breath in the dark of the night. And Craig—shit, Craig was the best! He was my height, though very thin, drove a ratty old Metropolitan convertible whose roof never came up, and was the world's most anal-compulsive and brilliant graphic designer. We didn't even think of being anything other than comrades-in-arms, girlfriends, as it were.

Now *Jo* was jealous.

Fuck her, she had Peter!

Now I had a partner in crime, and I was ready to delve the undergrounds of Los Angeles and vicinity, therein to begin to traipse the uncharted jungles of Baby Gavin's psyche. Craig would be my guide—my first guru.

CRAIG

*Corruption
purifies the innocent.*

As that spring of 1977 fed into summer, Craig and I became inseparable. And though we never actually lived together, every single day was spent in being as religiously worthless as we possibly could. We had determined to live as wild and dangerous a life as we were able, even if it killed us.

Craig's granddad had once owned some significant portions of what is now prime Wilshire Boulevard real estate, the site of many of Beverly Hills' flashier and most definitive businesses. We didn't know how many millions he was worth, but the bank that was built near his West LA home was constructed largely to house *his* money.

Craig banked there; they treated him like The Prince. Craig had been given his first credit card upon leaving Cal Arts, and had discovered that no matter how much he rang up, the bank simply upped the limit each time.

"Shit, Gav," Craig announced to me, "we got it made. Free money!"

Which meant free food, free entertainment, anything that we could pay for by plastic, was at our disposal.

For some seventy years his Gramps had built an empire out of the dust, and now he was a miserable wretch. Craig's dad had done little in his life but kiss up to his father and try to recoup his own investments. But dear Craig saw himself as the end product of the three generations, with no sentimental or emotional attachment to the money whatsoever, a profligate, the ultimate spending machine: he considered it his duty to eventually whittle the family wealth *back* into the dust. He had no intentions of ever seriously working— that made us compatible playmates, caught up as we both were in the artistry of discovering what youth and flesh could do and what money could buy.

So we ate. And played. And became accustomed to a pattern of going to *this* restaurant for breakfast, then heading straight over to *that* one for an extended outdoor lunch, then killing a few hours in the park before it was time for dinner, a set of Lina Wertmuller or Fellini flicks at the Nu Art and it was time for snacks at one of our favorite all-nighters. With the exception of my needing to escape Jo and Peter's petite domain and Craig's semi-regular car crashes, life was perfect. Only drugs eventually became a bit of an issue, since few dealers accepted credit cards—but we would discover ways around that too.

We set about the sightseeing task of apartment hunting for me. I wanted a cheap, vintage place where I could have a garden. Nothing fit the bill. We cruised every street in every neighborhood that Craig recommended as predominantly white and English-speaking, yet ethnic enough to have some flavor other than Methodist. We became authorities on the architecture of West Hollywood, Hollywood and vicinity. We had had it.

We were cruising up the last block of the last street we had mapped out, when we passed a glorious Twenties Spanish courtyard complex. *Mi Casa de La Ronda*, the pediment proclaimed. It was obviously out of my price range, but there was a sign for a single.

Through great iron gates we walked into the bosom of a grove of massive rubber trees. The large yellow leaves crunched beneath our feet, the air was cool, and the quaint-to-grand Mexican bungalows peeked out here and there from behind coruscating walls of ficus and eugenia.

We were immediately accosted by a chubby whitehaired gentleman in an obviously hand-tailored leisure suit. Maury. "How may I be of service to you?"

"We were interested in your single," Craig spoke up.

"For both of you?"

"No!" Craig laughed, "Just for my friend here."

Maury held out his hand and I took it. I introduced myself. He was sizing me up. I presumed him to be a queen—he looked like Jonathan Winters. I flexed one knee and thrust my groin forward.

"I like your haircut" was all he said.

My hair was in a crew, not especially fashionable at that time. And the white cover-alls that I wore stated the simple rubric *vivatorium* over the left breast pocket. Maury liked my look. He led us in, testifying about the historic old building.

The room he showed us was just that, a white-painted adobe brick room with a simple, uninsulated wood-slat ceiling, French doors along one side leading out to the patio which was as large again as the room itself. A tiny bathroom with shower, toilet and sink jammed in together. No kitchen. *But* it had a yard, private enough to wander around naked, and complete with a couple of aged banyans, a canopy of bougainvilleas, and lots of sand in which I could plant whatever I desired. Perfect.

The room had been the quarters for Clark Gable's maid. Clark's apartment was directly above. This building, you see, had been a counterpart to the famed "Garden of Allah," that torrid monument to the Hysterical Hollywood of the Thirties where Tallulah and Bette ran about butt-naked and instigated continual brawls that invariably involved the entire complex.

Maury had been the resident manager there, prior to building his own version down the street. I would become inured to his sedulous and lengthy recollections of the decadence and splendor of ancient H'wood.

"How much?" I asked, quivering.

"Two hundred," Maury smiled.

"I want it."

"It's yours."

I had my own home. In Babylon!

Being in the center of West Hollywood, which was, by my psychic calculations, the *center* of the Center of the Universe (the gay mecca set the trends for all of Hollywood and consequently the world), La Ronda immediately became *our* center of operations.

We staked out The Source (a tony outdoor vegetarian restaurant on the Strip—a block and a half away) for both our breakfast and our lunch menus, often combining the two, sipping iced herbal teas and ice cream desserts in between. This was not only ideal food, sun and pretty people, but an excellent vantage point for cruising the world's finest cars, a fave pastime of ours, as they sped the narrow gulf between Hollywood and Beverly Hills.

Craig taught me the subtle points between years of Avantis, Citröens, the early Vettes (the 1961 and 1962 models being *my* favorite years, with Craig preferring the 1958/1959 styling). Now, with a perfect place to live, and a life in the red hot center-of-it-all, I was living a life I could not have even dreamed before.

At night we hit the happening West Hollywood bars—The Stud, The Eagle, the Rusty Nail—rank, stifling pits fraught with desperation and unquenched desire. We would cruise through each without emotion or commitment, like dolls on a float in some nightmarish parade, stopping only long enough to play a favorite song on the juke, get a second look at some chubby little imp in his weekday flannels and fresh denim. All simply a tease, a rev-up, a few Perriers, then on to the other side of Boy's Town and Studio One, where the fey fantasies of the planet worked their febrile tits and pressure-sealed baskets in a gyrating ritual of animal lust. Dionysius save us!

The air was veritably flashing with advertisement—and it wasn't from the tacky neon wall motifs.

"Shooo-eee!" Craig would yodel in his finest *Hee Haw* yell, and we would set immediately to the practice of dancing and pretense of being oblivious to the rest of the raffish carnage swirling around us. Donna Summer's "Love to Love You" had just come out; it was the dawn of disco.

We discovered drugs. I hated marijuana and would always turn it down, but from out of some dark medicine cabinet appeared the first Quaaludes. We were in love. I didn't drink. I simply didn't have the stomach for the stuff. But the Quaaludes put the *Yes* in my *Maybe*. For despite one repressive early marriage and two or three dismally oblique affairs, I really hadn't had much sex yet—bein' from Jesse Helms Country, the buckle on the Bible Belt. At twenty-one I was a storehouse of pent-up feelings and suppressed desires. I was horny, or lonely, or something, but sex had always been elusive and tinged with a touch of "nasty," so infected was I by my mother's own puerile sense of guilt and dissatisfaction.

Sex was *dirty* to Mom because she was getting it from a man that she didn't love. But wasn't that what good Christian marriages were all about? It was certainly the scenario that *I* started out with as I teased and taunted Dalton through five years of holding back, putting out silently in the dark of night, feigning indifference in the morning, and bragging about the girlfriends that I rarely got past first base with, while he mutely supported me through my last years of high school and several years of rural poetdom.

Leaving North Carolina hadn't made the difference. I went on to torment my suitors at Cal Arts. I spent a couple of less-than-sexual summers with a straight bud in Seattle, along with a winter in New York with Ian Young, Ginsberg, and all the Christopher Street poets. Everywhere I went I was an uptight wretch. All the fabulous sex I *could* have had!

It was a scenario that I intended to get over. Libertine LA was just the place to do it.

A half a 'lude and people started getting friendly. *Real* friendly. My hands would freely dance their way through the steamy isles of bedenimed flesh. I smiled at people and they smiled back, surprised.

Sex still eluded me, but it was crawling into my reality at the baths.

West Hollywood's chicest bathhouse was the 8709. You entered through a battered, untitled door near a back alley of Cedars Hospital, up a narrow stairway, past a window where the homely got carded for more picture IDs than anyone carries and the cute got smiled right into the fecund depths of bronzed bodies, white towels, the clouds of amyl nitrate, Crisco, and decomposing feces. It was more than anything I could've envisioned on even the most sultry of southern evenings; I felt as though I had just been given sensory perceptions never available to me before, like I had awakened for the first morning of my life, to this paradisiac womb, this Inferno, this Hellenistic heaven with a disco beat.

Craig and I spent many sleepless nights probing the faceless gloryholes, the seductive mirrored maze, the circulating catacombs that opened to ever-changing and rearranging bedmates. Men with no names. Men with no past, no future, no careers; men who were just turgid fantasies, sacraments, dark recesses that tasted of life and death and angelic visitations.

My pastime, I confess, besides eventually learning to sodomize the denatured bodies that greeted me butt-up in shadowy little cubicles, was holding vigils in some alcove where the colored track lights edged my budding form with high-lights and shadow. Seldom speaking, moving, or acknowledging the glances of another, I found it as satisfying to say *no* as to actually oblige an encounter, often more so (more vestiges from Mama's closet).

But sex *did* happen. Of course I started out slowly, often completing the evening without as much as a nibble. But it was amazing how rapidly a tad of pharmacological engineering began to dissolve those well-honed garden walls. One night a hirsute blond stranger gripped the towel around my hips and used it like a slingshot to launch me into his rented lair. He didn't kiss me—not until afterward—but yanked me down on top of him, without words, conditions or prerequisites. We were two bodies; sex was aerobics, a dance of virility and technique. His became the hands of the mother confirming, "Yes, my precious boy, you do this like no other ever could!"

He made it so easy for me. A little peck goodbye and a slap on the rear to let me know that he thought me a sexy dude. *You did good.* After that my training wheels just naturally fell away.

I was shy, but perhaps only for effect. I was vain. This was the place that validated both my feelings of social isolation—common to most every homo male that I've known, that aloneness that is both our torment and our strength—and my need for male companionship. It was camaraderie of a blind sort: the smell of wet male bodies, semen, urine, the sickly colognes of the ethnic queens, even the drugs. A testosterone highball with a Lemmon twist. These were all the things that my mother had denied the existence of. These were the things that weren't *nice.* These were what I would have hidden under the mattress as a child.

The baths were a regular affair for us, as with many of the queer elite. They were rather like what gyms have since become—very few had pumped-up bodies in those days, slim was all that really mattered, along with proportion and attitude. For Craig and me the baths were sacrosanct, our religion. We were safe there.

These bodies, these beds, and these experiences became so customary and so ritualized that Craig and I could eventually recall from memory the various room numbers at the 8709, the person or type of person who frequented each room, the names of those who had them, peculiar smells, sexual preferences, those who would lead you to the urinal, genuflect, and glut on your pee, the supine gentleman with the disembodied toilet seat over his face—it was as easy as recalling Mr Buzbee's English class with friends at a high school reunion.

Only once did Craig and I actually cross our personal taboo against sex. It was some obscure bathhouse in the Valley where there was an obvious paucity of even remotely familiar faces, or any within twenty years of our own age. We were listlessly involved in our favorite argument.

"Assholes are made for shitting, and that's what they do best," Craig asserted.

"But sex *is fucking.* You think that throats were made to have dicks shoved up 'em, or down 'em, or whatever you do? Sucking's just a vile and vulgar form of foreplay. Who wants to have a nasty old dick in their mouth?"

"Well *nobody,* after it's been in some *shitty butthole...!*"

We chalked our disagreement up as another reason we were such inviolable pals, that if someone wanted a blow job, hey, Craig was always ready. And if they wanted a good fucking, well...

But somehow this particular night, tired of swatting off the liver-spotted hands of the locals, we ended up locking ourselves in a room with a large lighted two-way mirror, facing in. We began mocking sexual play until without much ado Craig had me in his mouth and I was dancing to the music— he certainly wasn't about to let me *fuck* him—and a good, compensatory, time was had by the octogenarians in the hall. I suppose it answered some question in Craig's mind about what I would taste or feel like; it was the closest to sex that we ever got. We washed up and went home.

One night we gave up on the pretty boys and headed east toward Silverlake, the "other side of town," stopping at the first bastion of lined-up motorcycles and bearded hunks in black leather vests. As we slogged through the bodies inside the bar, our path was soon blocked by a mountain of Budweiser cartons, across which was a living bas-relief of gentlemen affecting vague conversations, but with peculiarly glazed looks in their eyes. Another row of balding heads could be viewed just at waist height in front of them, the sounds of zippers and slurping coming from the shadows, an occasional gasp appearing merely as punctuation in the discourse.

"Right here in front of God and *every*body!" Craig camped. "I—I think I'm gonna faint!" He yanked me by the hand and thrust us deeper into the sylvan gloom.

A naked bottom pushed by, squeezed shut within the window of a pair of chaps, and we both gasped. Amyl nitrate was the cologne du jour. Nipples brushed against nipples in the meat-tight aisles. A bored-looking boy in a hanging basket swung his butt to and fro, his brandy curls backlighted in a saintly nimbus.

We tittered in the corners like blushing schoolgirls, and I must admit that I was quite taken by the ingloriously exposed hineys, the gruff beards and the darkly shaded chests and armpits. Craig, however, was infinitely more attuned to the preppy/surfer look—taboo here—it was a genre to which he had always aspired and ever felt evaded by.

We drove back to the West Hollywood bars, where a game of pool would be the most action that an evening would embrace. There the boys languished in brand-name shirts, Levi's (the scourge of designer jeans hadn't yet descended), perfectly coiffed and sprayed short hair, perhaps a tasteful touch of eyeliner and Indian Earth, ostensibly applied to cover the zits.

The preppy bars were exciting for the intensity of the cruising game, which was like a well-thought round of chess, eternally subtle, all played in the eyes (mouths never smiled or spoke). A nod might be the closest thing you'd get to a *Yes, let's fuck*, but often the sexual contract was merely telepathic, one man leaving discreetly, the other following at a safe distance. These were the bars for the legal secretaries, the bank tellers, real estate sissies and waiters after work. Lawyers, doctors, and tax specialists all preferred the seedier, dimmer leatherette establishments; they were the pierced nipple and Wagner crowd.

We still spent most our evenings at Studio One, *the* disco. Eventually other discos came into being—Odyssey, Circus, Probe—but Studio One was the first, the Mother of Disco. Studio One was magic. Casablanca and organized crime hadn't yet destroyed dance music—though Summer was strong on the scene—and the songs still contained primal elements of rhythm and blues and traces of some individuality. The singers were "stars" and we knew each one.

The discrimination practices at the door were rigorously hierarchical and warlike. The only women allowed in were tried-and-spoken-for fag hags; white-mannered or almost-white-skinned blacks were the only ethnics (there were only one or two accepted Mexicans and *no* Asians).

We didn't approve of the discrimination, but we allowed it; we liked the pretty-boy crowd, and *we* always got in on my good looks.

Here Craig and I were especially inseparable. We both loved to dance, and all that gorgeous music without a dance partner could be quite depressing, though I would often go myself during the stints that Craig had with a date or one of his little Mormon boyfriends. Eventually we learned to dance by ourselves, but not until we had escalated the drug ante and lighting had become far more sophisticated.

And eventually I came to buddy my way in with one or more of the commissars of the club, allowed an occasional backroom chat and blowjob, the bartering of intoxicants, and gained the leverage to guarantee prime seating at the Back Lot cabaret shows, marching through the door guards with barely a nod, even receiving free drinks from the "knowing" bartenders. I was home.

We had leather if we wanted it, we had pretty-boy Hollywood all the time, and we even had drag.

My first drag ball was an affair the likes of which this tarheel child had no preparation for.

I had seen drag queens before: my suitemate at Cal Arts would go on to become Pee Wee Herman, but at that time was greatly identified with the persona of Carmen Miranda. Paul was ever in front of the bathroom mirror doing her hair, mud packs and makeup, and would attend all classes, meals, and parties in full fruit.

But I had never conceived of the pomp, the majesty, the *attitude*. The theme was "pink."

Craig and I spent two weeks shopping. Our gowns were both vintage prom dresses. Rather than wigs, we went for more pert, Fifties styling done with our own short hair.

I believe I was basically comical—being a novice, I didn't understand my options, besides which my shoulders *were* broad and my cleavage *was* beginning to leaf-out, albeit slightly. But when I saw the finished product, Craig, I understood the possibilities: Craig *was beautiful!* He was straight out of a Suzi-Sweetheart magazine circa 1961, with a tiny epicene waist, a long graceful neck, and white button earrings. He wasn't gaudy or silly—this was Craig's magic, his finesse—but genuinely, subtly lovely.

The ball, hosted by a rather large and caustic hairdresser named Ronni, was terrifying. *This* was what the Goddess created Quaaludes *for*. I must have downed a half-dozen en route (and I wasn't even in heels yet).

Ronni's "studio" was a grandiosely capacious Victorian salon/theatre that went on to become La Cienega Boulevard's famous Court Theatre, where I would design sets. The walls were richly ornamented in Georgian columns, gargoyles, and fleur-de-lis-gone-ga-ga. Ten-foot French doors opened on every side to a lush and tropical brick patio hosted by dozens of bartenders and pink-tuxed waiters. Clouds of pink balloons concealed the dim Hollywood sky, and inside, vast arrays of Land-of-the-Giants-sized pink crepe and feather flowers leapt out of gargantuan Egyptian urns.

Adither at the door, Ronni and his beau du jour shouted out the names of the arriving guests. Of course they awed over Craig (at last, I had an opportunity to be jealous of *his* looks). Ronni was a tragicomic pink amalgam of Lucille Ball, Joan Crawford and Totie Fields, many tucks and bustles, beanbag tits and natural hips.

"Oh, uh... of course!" he forgot my name.

"I can't remember either," I assured him.

He motioned his ostrich-feather fan into the room. "Yes, well, welcome!"

"You're very well-hung too," I said cattily, skirting by. I was getting the hang of it, pinching her adipose falsies as I passed.

"Bitch!"

We were ushered through to the bank of photographers who posed every guest against apple-blossom satin curtains, wielding balloons, ribbons, feathers and assorted color-integrated props. I was peeing with excitement.

The jostling dance floor was more my element. I've always been able to forget anything when dancing, as though the motion itself were some sort of etheric security blanket. But the faces! the outfits! the endless jewelry and attention to nuance! These were the queens who designed *America*, via Hollywood, via Lucy, Liz, Cher, Barbra; here they all were, I had fallen into the heart of them; they were *wearing* Lucy/Liz/Cher/Barbra's clothes! Had the Quaaludes not eventually erased my consciousness (I shudder to think how we arrived home), it would have been the time of my life. But what a time it *was*!

I always considered it pitiable, once "gender fuck" became no longer the fashion, once fags started co-opting into the roles of Amerikano-Rambo-Republi-trash, that it was only at Halloween that these ersatz femmes fatales were able to come alive. Which is, I suppose, the nature of Halloween, that the devils, sprites, witches and goblins get to emerge for their annual festive haunt, before being tucked firmly back into their closets once again by the prayers of good girls and boys everywhere. All those boas and sequins gathering dust in the dark until they can hatch out afresh on the following year.

But drag gave way to drugs and the Madison Avenue dream male. Even Ronni, as the years went on, became "Ronny." His drag salon turned into a gymnastics studio as Ronny and his "partner" turned into *the* trendy men's apparel boutique, both sporting crew cuts, black leather Italian-ware, an open black Jeep. In their West Hollywood world were no more tears, makeup or screaming, just pathological social drugs, attitude and occasional—though pharmaceutically controlled—depression.

Still, Halloween weekend 1977 found Craig and me tricking and treating as the "Beauty Contestants": "Señorita Costa Rica" (Craig, with his mounds of gooey black wig, anchored in place by a petite diamond tiara) *y* "Señorita Jalapeño" (my large-shouldered blonde version), both equipped with form-fitting black one-piece bathing suits, title ribbon/sashes, two dozen long-stem roses apiece, five-inch custom spikes from Frederick's of Hollywood, matching gloves, and layers of nylons to disguise telltale leg hair.

The following Halloween, our girls appeared as roller-skating carhops. The same wigs grew bigger, though considerably less formal, and the outfits were authentic, the legs longer, and the takeout trays (from LA's one remaining drive-in, Tiny Naylor's) were epoxied with dishes, glasses, french fries, snubbed-out cigarettes and copious napkins and utensils, all siliconed to the point where the trays could be turned completely upside down with only the napkins fluttering. We parked the car and sped from one side of town to the other, practicing our pirouettes and taking orders.

Next year we were back as the "Smart Shoppers," the same girls (hair *more* casual, this time flopping in curlers and nets—these wigs had been through it!), still on roller-skates, now in tiny Sixties mini-skirts, dime-store Peter Max earrings, bigger, looser tits, as we pushed around two mini-market-sized shopping carts stuffed to the sky with Wonderbread, Pampers, maxipads, Ruffles, TV dinners, and other essentials of modern housewifery.

Studio One and Odyssey judges alike gave us first place and swore we were the funniest things that they had ever witnessed on wheels. We didn't listen, we were determinedly chewing gum, smoking cigarettes, drinking Tab, eating potato chips, pushing our carts and reading the *Globe* and *TV Guide* simultaneously. Paul Lynde fell to the dance floor crying. Waylon Flowers, Charles Nelson Reilly, and Allan Carr all jumped out of the judges' box to shake our hands (we had none available).

The final Halloween of our reign of terror the girls had slid back socially: "White Trash on Wheels." The hair was short and only briefly concealed with scarves and barrettes, the outfits went from Twiggy to LuLu, and the shopping carts turned to baby carriages assailing the crowds with matching African-American baby-dolls, the Tabs turned to six-packs of Coors, which were stuffed under and around the brats along with the cartons of Viceroys and boxes of Little Debbie's. It was the decline of Western Civilization, such as it is.

By that final Halloween, Craig and I finally began to drift apart and find independent interests with boyfriends, husbands, different strata of drugs. Over the course of our friendship he watched with interest as I began falling into the world of the movie star set, and he even had his own mini flings with a couple: Tab Hunter out at his daddy's stables, Princess (Tom) Lasorda.

But something had changed by 1981. Quaaludes had gone off the market and I had discovered a powerful hypnotic powder known then as TT1; Probe was the new disco and the crowd (myself included) was all muscle-pumped and affectedly macho.

Jo and Peter turned into mega-yuppies, replete with matching Beemers, real estate licenses and their own "income properties."

Craig moved in with a gang of coke-dealing lesbians at the beach and only rarely touched base with "our side of town." He remains the best friend that I have ever had.

But our lives would change, all of us, as our pleasures became marketable and industrialized, and our drugs became as deadly and as serious as our loves.

SAL

When in doubt, just say yes;
the future's anybody's guess.

One of the givens in coming to Hollywood is to rise to stardom. Or at least a good American try.

That meant I'd need "head shots," proper head shots, the type the studios, agents, commercial agents, managers require. Who am I? What do I represent? What is my commercial appeal? I just knew I wanted to look in my teens, fetching, yet unavailable.

After I had been banging around the scene for a few months, someone recommended me to someone who recommended me to a gentleman named Oscar, who I was assured would take my photos at cost simply because I was young/male/attractive.

He lived in a supermarket-sized loft almost all the way downtown, so it took me half a day to get there (I didn't drive, and when Craig wasn't around I took the bus, which in LA can be slower than walking).

Oscar was a burly Scottish redhead, in his mid-thirties, must've been six-two, was chubby in a sexy mountaineer sort of way, and, from what I could discern around the edges, extremely hairy, which always gave me a delectable, warm-all-over feeling. One of the more amicable cameraheads I would ever meet, he greeted me with verve and flattery; we did our shoot, there was nothing to it, and he ended up with a few rolls of nudes for his own purposes. I was excited to oblige, even disappointed at his professionalism.

"Gavin," he said when he phoned me in a couple of days with the proofs, "I hope you won't mind, but I did take the liberty of showing your shots to a good buddy of mine, a movie producer and director—and, well, he'd like to discuss with you about a film he's putting together..."

(But of course, isn't this just what we anticipate from Sin City?)

"If it's okay, we can both drop by your apartment. His name's Sal."

Sal was an elfin-sized Italian-American, balding, bearded, roundish but cute. He *was* a movie director—his big feature to date was the B horror classic, *Frogs*. He was currently assistant-producing what was to become another inadvertent horror classic, Mae West's *Sextette*, though he eventually got fed up and quit long before the film wrapped. He was one of the funniest men I have ever encountered, making it very difficult to carry on any kind of reasonable business discussion. He immediately put me at ease.

It was not, however, the sequel to *Frogs* that Sal had in mind. He was producing/directing a porn film designed to capitalize on the film *The Front Runner,* the coming-out novel by Patricia Nell Warren that was supposed to have been made into a movie and yet never has, to this day. His film was tentatively entitled *Track Meet* (possibly *Track "Meat"*—he hadn't decided) and demanded an exciting young new reasonably athletic type. He came over, then, to see, in fact, if I could *talk*, if I was interested, willing, and how I looked hard.

I was intrigued by the prospect of doing porn. I had spent the previous summer in Seattle; "gender-fuck" was in. I marched all over the place wearing nothing but my Capezio dance skirt, getting myself arrested with lesbians for removing our shirts in public places. Marching for gay rights, I was a "radical faerie." I had been a hippie since I was fourteen, my brother had been the first drug bust in my hometown, I repeatedly got sent home from junior high for not wearing socks, for wearing the first bell-bottoms; I had gone away to art school and at least tokenly experimented with every drug made available to me.

I didn't want to do the flick for the money. I *wanted* to make a porno movie simply because *it was radical*. This took no deliberation at all.

Sal even ended up taking the opposite side. "It could *ruin* you for 'legitimate' films, people will recognize you all over the city. I plan to make your name a household word..."

"Yes yes yes!" I effused. It's radical. It's conceptual. It's art: *Life as art. Be art now*. I had already had two volumes of sexual verse published by Catalyst in Canada; my name *was* known (at least in some minute cliques); I had buddied with the Ginsberg crowd in New York; at Cal Arts I was famous for wearing nothing but boxer shorts; I had uncut hair, long fingernails, and submitted nude self-portraits for design projects.

Yes, porno, *yes!* It was the natural next step. I ripped my clothes off on the spot; I was already hard.

The filming didn't start for over a month, but Sal and I became Siamese twins. I was fascinated by the whole process (I had majored in film for one quarter at Cal Arts, even made a film or two there, but this was a *real* film— or, *almost* a real film). We went to sporting stores to buy my attire, the rest of the cast's attire; we bought props, film supplies. Most fun was going to a porn-star-turned-porn-agent's house and hawking through a book of mugs to select the people that I would most like to "perform" with. I couldn't wait! The costar was already cast—I was assured that I would be pleased. I was, when I finally met him at the shoot. Though Mike was far from my type, he was a charming and attractive well-groomed Frisbee champion from somewhere near Santa Cruz—slim, defined, lightly freckled and green-eyed. He smelled like salt air and could've been anybody's brother. His dick was as smooth and hard as lacquered soapstone.

The rest of the cast was *my* pick. I went for body hair, brawn, and that doleful basset-hound look that always melted my heart straight down into my stomach.

Craig was even more ecstatic by all of this than I was; he went along with us everywhere, abetting us with his classic tastes and vigilant critiques of men, costumes, and scenarios. And he was assured an assistant's role in the film-making process, the choicest positions, holding the fill-light ("Excuse me, sir, could you spread your legs a little bit wider, wouldn't want to singe anything we might need later...") and "fluffer" (he who keeps the actor "aroused" between shots, which was already Craig's specialty).

The actual filming took a little less than two weeks. I was unprepared for how excruciating a procedure it was. The never ending fear of not being able to get it up is, alas, never ending, especially since I was more than aware that I was not by industry standards graciously-endowed. In fact, we discovered that under pressure I have an unnerving ability to climax without even being hard. I believe that I never really did get it up completely—at least not in *my* scenes, though I did wonderfully in the substitute shots, when my own member replaced other members in the cast. When certain of the "talent" had difficulties with that essential cum shot, I moved in for the close up. Never mind the change in hair color—as Sal put it, "If they're looking at *that*, then something *is* wrong!"

Don was my favorite and I was breathlessly anticipating our time together. We had met on the set the evening before our scene on the ladder, when he would seduce the young track star who was helping him paint. We were, of course, strictly forbidden to leave together, lest any of the magic rub off prematurely.

"What's up for tonight?" I whispered.

"Oh baby," he panted back, handing me a simple card for house-painting services with his name and number upon it.

We rendezvoused at his house, Gavie quivering like a quail in the hunter's breast pocket. This was the biggest and the hairiest thing I'd ever touched—he had tits, real man tits, a thicket of black mustache, and a smile to rival John Aston as Gomez Addams. And I was the *star*, and he wanted *me*.

"Hey there Stud," he urged me into his simple lair, "*look* at those *lips!*"

We pawed, drooled, and chewed on each other like reunited puppies from the same litter. His clothing simply came apart in my hands as we dissolved into the filthy carpeting of his diningroom floor. *This* was sex at last, without drugs, disco music, or the cloak of anonymity; the lights were on full and I could discern and fondle every follicle of this man-beast.

I fucked him, with very little ado, pounded my way onto his back and ground him into the floor with spit and pure chutzpah. He alternately purred and growled beneath me, his arms flayed out on the carpet. A cursory round of Pepsi and potato chips and he was on top of me, my legs framing his panting face and that devilish Gomez grin. We rallied all night, sumo style, and still had a marvelous scene the following day.

Sal wasn't terribly pissed. Don and I went on seeing each other for, oh, a good week or two.

One hideous scene of the movie took place in the back of the car as the coach drove the team to a competition. I wasn't part of the sex scene, just a shot of my shocked reaction from the front seat. Problem was, the chosen road wasn't deserted, *and* one of the chums in the back had a time getting it up and out. I eventually filled in for the spill, after three unrelenting hours of seven people trying to be patient and cool on a 95-degree *not*-deserted desert road.

The funniest scene, believe it or not, was the rape scene. In it I am bound and gagged with white towels by the black hotel porter. Trouble was, the towels just wouldn't stay put, and the poor actor, "TC," was so nervous and afraid of possibly hurting me that he couldn't even begin to get aroused. When Sal wasn't looking I kept slipping him Valium fragments. It was all I could do to get a decent plunder!

And after the filming came the editing, which Craig and I also sat in on, the convivial Sal invariably taking us both out to eat afterward, then on to bizarre Valley bars and bathhouses that we had never even heard of. It was a festive time, and all the admiration was encouraging to me. People did make fun of the way I ran when we did the running footage at UCLA. It was bad enough with all those *real* college jocks staring us down, but I had to listen to our own crew telling me I jogged like a duck.

Then the release. The *LA Times* at that time still advertised porn. I remember one Sunday edition featuring three gigantic full-page mugs, Barbra Streisand in *A Star Is Born*, Laurentis's *King Kong,* and Gavin Geoffrey in *Track Meet.*

We premiered in a prime-time theater on La Cienega Boulevard. Sal designed a marquee that had two eight-foot blow-ups of my face and shoulders jutting out over the street on either side. (Craig and I got drunk one night toward the end of the run, dragged out a ladder at four in the morning and cut one down. It was my headboard for years.)

Everyone in West Hollywood knew the face. I was chased through supermarkets and down streets in the middle of the night while out doing my shopping. Not that anybody was ever rude. They would simply walk fast behind me, or stand somewhere in my path and continually clear their throats. Bolder men would ask for autographs, or let me know how genuinely touched they had been by the film.

One evening I was dining with a classy trick at a fairly schmaltzy Sunset Strip restaurant when the waitress asked, "Say, aren't you that guy on La Cienega in that movie?"

"Uh-huh," I nodded with a mouthful of rice pilaf.

"Oh." She caught herself, remembering that it was a fag sex film. She smiled nervously and left us; we had a different waiter for the rest of the meal.

The film within weeks became the top grossing gay film ever. Because it had dialogue, believable characters, and a coming out story, it was a *movie* to people, not just a sex flick. *I* didn't get that and started pushing it all behind me. But now, years later, friends still "in the business" or connoisseurs of this particular genre all assure me that *Track Meet* is one of the finest fuck films we've got.

Someday I must see it.

I didn't have much interest in making further films. Performing in porno is not the most comfortable of experiences, though working with Sal was by far the easiest that I would encounter in the biz. The joys of having to get it up and keep it up on demand in front of a dizzy and ogling crew, inclement lights, a tempestuous director, and the panting queens who have provided the location—well, pardon the pun, but it sucks. And of course, when you finally *are* on a roll, hot, hard and ready, your partner invariably has a vehement case of flaccidity, the runs, or suddenly remembers his religion at the last minute.

Once, it was my turn to be chosen by the lead, Jack Wrangler. I was flattered by the offer, and turned on to Jack. Though I was less interested in his famous lance than his handful of fleshy bum. But as soon as he started doing his schtick, choking his chicken and contorting his face as if a rusty Volkswagen were shifting gears in his colon, it was all I could do not to guffaw. I was so desperate not to crack up laughing that Daddy's little soldier just wouldn't march at all. They paid me anyway, I was a star.

I did have one final pleasant film experience in those years, though. The producers had a brilliant idea: they held a small party of porn stars, and we were all asked to submit the names of the two men that we most wanted to have sex with. Three of us chose each other—Grant, Robbie and me—and we came back the next night to film. Twelve hours of sucking and fucking on a lighted carpet dais—I believe I came six or seven times: it was magic, easy to be hard, and hardly problematic at all.

The film was dissolved in a bad batch of developing fluid, but Grant and I went on to enjoy many an evening together, me tucked naked into his grizzly carpenter's arms, eating my cup of yogurt while he sat chewing his plate of raw hamburger meat and onions. The wan face of a sea-wearied sailor, elastic white skin stretched over the most invincible wooden form.

I didn't fuck this one, he fucked me; *this* was a true carnivore!

I was crushed when he moved back to San Francisco. But I was busy, thanks to *Track Meet*. I was a star, relishing my fifteen minutes. The offers were coming in daily.

SAM

*The key to perception
is one's own reflection.*

One day, while the film was still rolling on La Cienega, there was a period of about fifteen hours (from morning until closing time at Studio One) in which I was accosted by some dozen different people, all with the same message, that there was some *very* rich and *very* famous person from "the industry" who wanted to meet me.

It started in the morning with a limo that actually stopped for me on the street. Its driver had, I suppose, been given a copy of a *Track Meet* ad from the *Times* and set out to cruise. The day ended with a half-dozen bartenders, and eventually the manager and owner of Studio, letting me know that this mogul had seen my movie and absolutely *had* to meet me.

"Well I'm flattered—I guess..." Flattered enough so that I would agree to an encounter with the gentleman.

I refused an arrangement of the limo in the early part of the following evening, instead employing Craig as my personal chauffeur. We were given a Beverly Hills address. I still did not know whom—or what—I was going to encounter.

I didn't ask further questions, figuring that my fate was already sealed and that it would all be made apparent to me soon enough. I was riding on my new persona, I was a star of sex, I had no need of money, and my face was plastered all over the papers and La Cienega Boulevard. What had I to fear? Ah, but so much yet to learn! I was cool, but excited.

We entered Beverly Hills and then the hills above, snaking up past the visible estates into an area where the houses were obscured by gardens, walls, and private forests behind Gothic electronic iron gates and up winding driveways that led straight into the imagination.

The gate that opened for us was the baddest of 'em all, the drive trailed up through trees and neurotically manicured plantings, opening eventually into a clearing with a vista of the whole of Los Angeles and a mansion fit for the Beverly Hillbillies.

"Thanks Craig," I said grinning. "If I'm not back in three weeks, you'll know I'm living on my own estate in Bora Bora..."

"Right. Send me a card, okay?"

An aged butler opened the door and led me through the entrance hall, a ballroom-sized livingroom, and into a niche in which sat, on a fox-fur-covered settee, my mysterious pursuer.

I'll call him Sam—Sam was small—say five-six—about ten years my senior, nice-looking, dark-haired, Jewish, but no one to die over. He looked strangely frightened and lost within the grandiose and pretentious surroundings.

I hadn't the vaguest idea who he was, but he held out his hand nervously and smiled sincerely, though he was clearly put off by my biker's jacket, torn jeans, and dirty boots. It was not the innocent and preppy image that the movie conveyed.

We exchanged only brief amenities before he asked me if *I* was nervous.

"Not especially nervous," I said, "but this house gives me the creeps."

"I love this house—what do you mean?" he asked, smiling.

"Oh, it's real... pretty... I guess. I'm sorry. It's just so fucking *big*."

"Follow me," he said, bemused, after a moment's pause. He was more intrigued than pissed, I'm sure, but feigned a trifle irritation nonetheless. He led me through the foyer, across the cobblestone courtyard, into the carriage house and one of three black Porsches.

We left the house and grounds and headed west, barely speaking.

His beach house was much more to my liking, and I told him so. He was clearly pleased. It was exquisitely fashioned out of a classic Twenties structure, with walls of curtains that at the touch of a button disappeared to disclose walls of solid glass and the spotlit surf not a hundred feet away.

For privacy, Sam had purchased the houses on either side of his, had them removed and trees and walled gardens planted in their stead. With the noise of the tides drowning out the sounds of Highway 101 behind us, the garden vistas to either side, you would presume that you were all alone in the world, just you and the sea in this taciturn Beach Club of Eden.

Fresh flowers overwhelmed every table and counter. Bowls of expensive-looking chocolates and mints danced around every vase—I helped myself, pausing only briefly to reflect whether or not the candy was to be eaten.

"Go ahead." He grinned. (They were real.)

"Do you like Linda Ronstadt?" he asked me casually.

"Oh she's my favorite!" I responded with a mouthful of mints, and added, "but I liked her best when she was doing country. I wish she'd forget about the rock 'n' roll crap and just do country."

"How about Paul Simon?"

"Well, I respect him. He's a brilliant songwriter. But that's the problem, just brilliant; he has no heart, he's all cerebral."

Sam looked displeased. Had I failed the test? Then he smiled. Well okay, he could see that I was very opinionated, and he liked that. He could see that I wasn't easily manipulated. And he liked that.

He motioned me to sit down with him on the banquette. He had put on the latest Joni Mitchell album; "I thought she was dead," I said. He kissed me.

He kissed me again. It was an excellent kiss.

"I love your lips," he said, "you have beautiful lips."

He would say this to me again and again. I thought it was funny; my lips were just like his! Perhaps that was what homosexuality was all about: mutual admiration. *He* had beautiful lips. I kissed him.

"I love your lips," I said back.

We made out, carefully at first, but genuinely, no overt agendas, we reached through shirts, knocked off shoes, but quietly for many minutes before the couch became obviously uncomfortable. He invited me upstairs.

The bedroom was the entire top of the house. The bed, immeasurable, with a massive solid chunk of crystal for a headboard, lighted from beneath so that it glowed an amber green. The only other light was an aura that bounced off of the crunching surf below and reflected back against the ceiling. Sam hit a button and the ocean went dark. Now there was just the headboard, and the moon. We removed each other's clothes thoughtfully, savoring what we both knew without speaking would be our only "first" undressing.

"Cocaine?" he asked, commenting on my inch-long baby fingernails.

"Naw! Something I learned from an old Filipino man in Seattle," I said, "I never cut'm. They make indispensable tools." I mimed picking my teeth, my ears, my nose.

He smiled. As he led me onto the turned-down bed, I noticed a pair of ladies shoes jutting out from underneath. "What size do you wear?" I jested.

"Oh." He looked bothered and embarrassed, a child who had just been caught with his hand in his pants. "Those are Sandra's. She's in New York making a movie."

"Sandra Williams?" I squealed.

He nodded.

Wow! She had been my favorite actress as a child. I was sworn to marry her (somewhere between Shari Lewis and Elizabeth Montgomery). Now I was going to steal her lover!

Sam was pale, petite, though comfortable to hold. His genitals were just like mine, which I always considered a bonus—thick, well shaped, not big enough to be cumbersome in action, but big enough to be reckoned with. His butt was the thing, smooth as a powdered baby, the definitive bubble. I would have it.

"You know," I said, "they wouldn't let me fuck anybody in the movie, I was supposed to be too naive, or not really a fag or something. But fucking is what I do best."

"Well," he laughed, throwing me back on the pillows, "I hope you like to get fucked as well!"

"Oh sure," came my knee-jerk response, "I like that too. It's just that I *really* like to fuck."

"Well, I've never been successfully fucked," he told me, "but we can try it. Maybe you're the one."

Yeah, I thought, *I'm the one.*

"But you have to go slowly," he added, "and stop if I tell you to."

"Promise." I grinned, and held up two crossed fingers.

With little fuss and only the obligatory amount of foreplay I was on top of him. We had both remained hard from our first kiss. I always had this ego thing that I had to screw my partner *first*, to prove something or other—once that was out of the way I could just relax, anything could happen, it was okay by me. And the kissing and all that stuff I figured could continue later, if we were still awake and into it.

But he was tense and fought me. He let me progress, yet it all felt very clinical, an experiment that he was conducting with me as the—*er*—tool. I was determined to break through, and held myself forcibly in him until he let go of the vise on my prick. But going slow was not my usual, youthful MO, so I started feverishly building my tempo. I wanted to find his threshold.

I could tell that he was pleased that it was working, that he had conquered this barrier, this essential frontier—maybe he would ditch Sandra, hide *my* heels under the bed. Then he pulled off, breathless; he had started fighting again. But he was excited, exultant, radiant with this newfound pleasure and acuity.

"Let's rest for a while," he breathed.

"Was I hurting you?"

"No! Yes. I mean, I really *feel* it. I like it!" He was laughing, catching his breath. But it was only a second of smooching before he threw me over onto my back. "I want to fuck *you* now."

So he hoisted *my* legs up and entered me brusquely, clumsily. I was amused—he was so cute, just a little boy with a new bike that he hadn't yet learned to ride. I winced, but took him in, not wanting to thwart his momentum. Then *I* pulled off. And entered him without a fight this time. And back and forth through half the night. We were excited. It was beautiful; dark, young, innocent. Romantic and mysterious. What he lacked for me in physical attributes he made up for by his sweetness, his power, his élan, the exquisiteness of the locale. He *felt* good, and for me tastes and aesthetics always follow feelings. Besides, the parts that I was focusing on were all just about right. And our kisses were intoxicating, like my dad's as he'd tuck me in each night, wet and full.

I don't think that we slept much. In the morning when he finally pulled me downstairs there was a complete breakfast laid out. A butler lived there, I discovered, but he would never be seen. It would go on this way for three days. The butler shopped for me—I didn't eat meat, loved fresh exotic fruit, and there came back worlds of papaya, guava, avocado, mango, berries, fruits that I didn't even know existed. And we never had to leave the house.

We never put clothes on, except for our brief walks along the tideline. All dirty clothes disappeared down a drop in the bathroom floor. Sheets mystically changed while we ate or walked. Flowers were freshened and rearranged; cocaine manifested itself in toothpick-thin lines across the black marble veneer of the majestic bathroom counter; the caviar mints that I attacked at every passing refilled themselves as if from an eternal source—it reminded me of my favorite film, Cocteau's *Beauty and the Beast*, though in the most splendid shades and colors. How would I ever return to my barren little room in the city?

I did, and it was okay. I loved my quaint palace. And it was always good for me to be by myself, in my own element. To reflect, write poems, gossip, and revivify my life with Craig.

But we continued to have a great relationship, for a time, Sam and I. It wasn't love, but it was a pleasant enough mix of other things.

We rarely went again to that big house. We would usually weekend at the beach, but most normal working nights were spent at yet a third home, his "office," not far off the Beverly Hills end of the Strip.

It was an aesthetic enough house, though nothing like Malibu; it grew to be a comfortable second home. I became accustomed to waking up there each morning, yawning while Mr Mogul attended to his array of early morning phone calls. It amused me no end to lie there teasing his sensitive parts while he schmoozed and cavorted with Paul McCartney, John and Yoko, Paul Simon, Rona Barrett, Cher...

Because I had always wanted to sing professionally but had never had the wherewithal to pursue it, Sam sent me to a voice teacher/therapist in the Valley, Warren Barrigian, who had various radical techniques for releasing the blockages in "the instrument." I daily brushed elbows with the likes of Jane and Peter Fonda. I don't know what it actually did for my voice, and Sam regularly quizzed me about this—the sessions cost over a hundred bucks apiece, and Sam, for all his millions, was not one to toss his pennies into fountains.

By the time we had been together three or four months, I was growing restless at trying to fit into what was in fact a very rigid society of self-possessed professionals and not-quite-public homosexuals and their "knowing" associates. I wasn't especially good at the do's and don'ts of social etiquette, at least not for such long stretches of time. I enjoyed the times that we *were* together, but was offended by the times that I was *not* allowed around, accusing him of being closeted, leading separate lives. And Sam, of course, *never* attempted to submerge himself into *my* reality with Craig, my friends, the poetry that was my constant.

He was paying for my voice lessons, but I steadily refused to sing for him. Okay, Jackson Browne I was not. And I covered for my own feelings of inadequacy with a censorious repartee directed at Sam and *his* world. He gave very legitimate critiques of songs that I had been writing, and I obdurately dismissed his comments as "only concerned with commerciality..."

"You will *never* be a songwriter!" he cursed me. He veritably spat when he came to such deductions. Had I brought him to the point where I had left Dalton just a year before? Or to the exasperation that my dad would experience as I sat before him defiant without acknowledging his authority or hearing a word he had to say?

One particular morning I heard Sam scream from the bathroom. I ran in to find him flushed with anger and confusion. Did I know if I had the clap? I said that no, as far as I knew I was clean. Sam stated that in *my* case, how could I ever be *sure*, and that *he* couldn't have gotten anything from anyone *but* me.

"Still," I said, "I'm pretty certain that I'm clean."

He took me home without another word exchanged. I only much later found out that he had experienced a passing of blood, which actually proved to be a product of some benign something-or-other. He was treated, successfully, and apologized to me at a later date still. But the romance was dead.

Over the several months of our affair, Sam introduced me to a few of his "in the know" friends. We most regularly attended the informal screenings of almost-finished films at the house of his good buddy, "the Bear."

Bear was the head of a major studio, which he had taken over some years before and dragged up out of a fiscal slump. He was hailed as the industry genius, the Golden Child.

One evening Sam gave me a call and told me that Bear would like to see me alone, if I was so inclined, at his house that evening. I gathered that to mean that Sam and I were finished, at least for the time, and that was fine. I knew that I was being "passed on," but I never felt out of control. Even pawns can take kings. That is, it was a willing move, and no matter how base the motives of these men might have been, my own moves were clear to me—I felt it was a step up. And besides, someday these would all be poems, and chapters in my memoirs...

The Bear was a big sexy thing, slow, thoughtful, deep-voiced, and as hairy as a bear. He was certainly as wealthy as Sam, and his secluded Beverly Canyon home was as deliciously endowed as the Malibu beach house. Besides, I love movies. I cheerfully accepted.

LUIS

*The only loves I now regret
are those I never met.*

Life went fairly smoothly around La Ronda. Quiet, when Craig wasn't about. Sam was only weeks out of my picture and I resumed the déclassé life of impecunity and basic maintenance. I walked regularly to the local health-food store, the bars at night, and the Source when I had some cash.

Bette Davis had purchased the penthouse of the chateau-gone-condo next door. I would wave at her in the mornings from my patio as she peered out through her black windows like the crippled Blanche in *Whatever Happened to Baby Jane?* Occasionally she would respond with a nod or a wave—never a smile.

Maury waived my rent in exchange for gardening duties. In no time I had the court dripping with hanging baskets full of geraniums and fuchsias, every square inch of ground deployed with mosses, impatiens, and colorful bloomers. Maury was ecstatic. While I was out and about, in my usual bare feet and boxer shorts, I would be the first to encounter the barrage of home-hunters and looky-loos who came to check out or just ogle the Ronda's majesty. An occasional aged star would wander in to reminisce about the grander days of Havenhurst Drive.

One day a sexy little tyke accosted me from behind, seeking out the manager. Luis Furey was a dashing French-Canadian and was clearly willing to be friends. He had a provocative smile, but it was the cleft in his open white shirt, exposing a virtual garden of fur, that truly put a twist in me knickers. Luis was just finishing the cutting of his first album. He was living in the infamous Sunset Tower, the city's first skyscraper and most famous classic Deco building which, after having been tastelessly revamped during the Sixties, was now full of wanna-be musicians, prostitutes and drug dealers—not to necessarily lump them all together.

"Why don't you join me for dinner," he suggested after a leisurely ramble through the grounds with Maury.

"Be delighted," I said. "You buyin'?"

"A&M's buying," he chuckled, "we write it all off! By the way," he added while acknowledging the open rift in the front of my shorts, "don't dress up."

I dressed in my normal repressed black, of course. Luis, Euro-Canadian sophisticate that he was, was charmed. After a luscious meal in the stuffy little wine bar across the Strip from Le Chateau Marmont he entertained me for hours back at his ninth-floor cubicle, as we sat side by side upon his piano bench, performing his entire repertoire in between witticisms and my bratty, nearly imperceptible shows of affection. Luis wanted me and I wouldn't have it. He was a beautiful young man, probably twenty-five at the time, furrier than any I'd met, and a great butt by most any standards.

"What's wrong?" he asked me.

"I don't know. Can't we just be... buddies?"

I truly liked this fellow. I was attracted to him. He was going to be a star; he was living just five blocks from my house. Yet I was reduced to being a cock-tease. Why? I wouldn't admit it, but it was because I had something at stake here. This wasn't just a matter of the courtesan being swept off her feet by an industry dynamo, nor was it as simple as a quickie squeeze from a porn-star compatriot. Besides, Luis had already admitted that he was mostly straight, that he had a girlfriend back home in Quebec. I froze up. His fires remained stoked.

Luis's album was just about ready to be released. He invited me to a pissy bash the following night at the jaunty hillside home of his manager, Barry Krost. The party, actually, though partly to introduce the nascent superstar to the patricians of Hollywood, was in honor of some famous playwright or another. The crowd was largely English, exotic, famous, and I stuck very close to Master Luis's wing, as though we were in fact more than just "buddies." Luis was complicitous, pleased and no doubt challenged by the unrequited affair. I was soaring; here at last were all the faces and names that Sam would never allow an encounter with, and Luis casually took me by the hand as though we had just borne each other's children in the back bedroom.

Krost immediately took a liking to me, as did *his* young companion— Luis's *ex*-boyfriend, Doug, whom I was much too cautious to bat more than a lustful eye at. I was whisked around on the official tour, shown the art (mostly the work of England's Mr Hockney, which I found to be rather simplistic and undeveloped for *my* sophisticated North Carolina tastes. I was discreet enough to not provide this critique to the artist himself, but merely on the sly to Luis, who would wrap his hand over my mouth and reproach me with a *shh-shh!*).

I was introduced to many favorite stars, whom Mr Krost managed, among them, Elizabeth Montgomery, my number one childhood witch, and my own mother's fave stud, the statuesque Mr Chamberlain, and his well-heeled lover.

But as I've said, I had two distinct goals in Hollywood: to meet Lily Tomlin and Christopher Isherwood. Needless to say, when I spotted the adorable little man in the dining room, surrounded by a bustle of covetous industry adorers, I yanked poor Luis out of a critical conversation and asked him if, in fact, that was the beloved Mr I. When Luis assured me it was, I promptly insisted on an intro. I should mention that I had never actually *read* any of Christopher's books at that time, but I had seen the movie *Cabaret* exactly thirty-three times and worshiped the *fact* of the man (whose books I would *someday* read).

Luis took me over, I held forth a trembling hand, and Christopher immediately (to the great interest of the crowd, I might add, and the complete devastation of me) said, "Oh yes, I've read your books." He smiled so sincerely, as though thoroughly considering me an equal among literary peers. He was referring to two now-extinct chapbooks that had been printed by Ian Young's Catalyst Press when I was nineteen and twenty, hardly editions that had been touted by scholars worldwide. Luis was delighted and laughed heartily. I was speechless, and embarrassed for no obvious reason.

We chatted awkwardly, properly, the senior writer and I. He was subdued but quite forthright, asking about my work, possible future books. When my boldness had returned, I asked him if I might see him again.

"Why certainly," he assured me, "I would be absolutely delighted."

"How can I get a hold of you?"

"Why don't you give me a call," he responded, simply and without guile.

"Can I have your number?"

"It's listed," he said, as though stating the obvious.

Luis and I saw each other off and on. I soon discovered that my withheld sexuality was as much of an attention-getting ploy as it was a self-protecting device. I found myself playing Luis against his manager for favors and social solicitations, finagling luncheon dates, and evening rendezvous with both. It wasn't a smart thing to do, and it didn't ultimately work very well; the tide began turning against me. It was just as well, because Luis became actively involved with a French actress whom he would eventually marry. I was of course predominantly involved with trying to pry my lyrics onto Luis's next album. My manipulations didn't work.

Luis has since moved to France and begun a family, he has become the most famous for the scoring of all his wife's films. Though as the years and music progressed (or at least changed), I would come to hear Luis's work revered over and over again as the first New Wave or "progressive" rock albums. And though Luis's albums never made it past the elite of the industry, people like Deborah Harry and David Byrne would profess Luis as the progenitor of their genre.

He had such a beautiful chest.

It was actually quite some time before I cleared the headspace I needed to give Christopher a call. I was worried that he might have misplaced my memory and our brief conversation.

"Hello," I yelled, after securing his number from Information, "Christopher, this is Gavin. You might not remember me, but..."

"Oh yes," he stammered, "Gavin. Of course I remember." And proceeded to recite:

"I don't want to know you
but just want to blow you,
don't mean to control you
just roll in your skin;
take off your britches,
show me your stitches,
oh scratch me, it itches:
come on, let's begin!"

It was a poem from my first book, *Twenty Nineteen Poems*, perfectly rendered, in its entirety.

"That's my favorite poem," he reiterated. "Of course I know who you are!"

Again I was flabbergasted.

We set a date for the following Thursday and he actually drove himself over in his little blue Volkswagen. I had asked him if there was anything special that he would like to do and he said, "No, talking is fine." I asked about dinner and he said, "No, I can eat at home."

I paced nervously in the front until he had arrived. He said he knew the building well from days long past, parties, perhaps secretive encounters—I didn't inquire.

"I am so... thrilled that you have come," I babbled.

"Of course I have come," he assured me. "I don't get asked out on as many dates as I once had."

I flushed, directed him back to my little patio where he fell into one of the two butterfly chairs that were my only furnishings. I wanted to rap on the doors that we passed, and shout out, "Look, I'm taking Christopher Isherwood back to my pad!" and yell up to Bette next door, "Yo, Miss Davis, look! Christopher Isherwood!" (But her windows were dark.)

From there it went downhill. I was such a wreck, and Chris was so hopelessly British, terribly polite, not volunteering anything at all. I found myself intermittently interviewing him for I-didn't-know-what, careful to conceal the fact that I had still read none of his books.

I made him tea, clinking the pot and cups self-consciously to fracture the silences. I didn't know whether he expected a blow job or a performance or if he was perfectly happy just reposing and occasionally striking up a short-lived dialogue.

Much later I would learn that my hero was notorious for his Mr Hyde side under the influence of alcohol (which I didn't have to offer him); I would eventually encounter him quite rude and inimical at dinner parties where he downed wine as though his liver were a pest he was attempting to drown. I would hear stories of fistfights and brawls initiated by the acerbic-tongued Chris whilst inside the bottle.

Our date was tragic—or perhaps it was just fine. "Well," he offered by and by, "I must say that at my age I no longer stay up quite as late as I once used to do."

I helped him from the depths of his chair and made some asinine remark about the great many years he must have left.

"Oh dear," he said, wincing, "I do hope not. I see no point at all in dragging on and on with what has been a good thing. It will soon be time to pack it in, and I will be ready when that time does come."

I saw him to his blue bug parked underneath the giant date trees out front of our villa and he rolled off into the void of Sunset.

It wasn't until close to ten years later, after encountering Chris and Don Bachardy (his lifelong, younger lover) on numerous occasions at the parties of friends, that I again found my way, albeit briefly, back into Christopher's life.

I began sitting regularly for Don, infamous just then for his radical official-state-painting of Governor Jerry Brown, which had shocked dreary-assed old Sacramento. Don's studio was built into, on top of, and out of an old garage at their Santa Monica Canyon home. The entire south wall of the studio was glass and looked out over the splendid canyon, with the mountains behind and the ocean and Santa Monica Beach to the extreme left. Chris would always be present when I arrived to sit, invariably in his cushy old brown terry bathrobe and his little paddler slippers; his hands were always cold and he kept them shoved into the pockets of the robe. He would offer me tea (black currant with sugar and cream) while Don went out to prepare his paints and paper. Conversation was stilted at best, though the master was obviously more comfortable on his own turf, and he would occasionally grasp an idea that he thought might be of particular interest to me and blurt it out as if it had stung him in the throat. Don had this peculiar affectation of speech as well, along with a very pronounced stutter, and, although California born, a significantly stronger British accent than Christopher's.

Once in the studio I sat endlessly staring back at the myriad Christophers that hung all about the walls above me. There were also portraits of Stephen Spender, Bette Davis, Louise Fletcher, and other recognizables all about us, and dozens, perhaps hundreds of drawings of other nameless nudes, like myself, reclining awkwardly across a large canvas-covered divan.

I sat, assorted body parts falling painfully asleep, staring horrified at the monstrous faces that the maestro would make while studying his *objet*, noting the times that he would dip his brush into his coffee instead of his paint jar, wondering if he ever knew.

Christopher never entered the studio while Don was working. He spent most of his time in their bedroom at the back of the house, surrounded by a lifetime of collected and personalized art, by his heater keeping toasty and often reading, sometimes my books so that he could bid me farewell with a comment or a quote.

One day I showed up with my old-fashioned Yashica double-lens camera to cop some as-casual-as-possible portraits of the two.

Christopher came to greet me in a pair of English-pressed Levi's, a proper cashmere sweater, and clean white tennis shoes. This was not how I knew him or wanted to photograph him. "I remember you in your bathrobe," I exhorted, "your slippers, with a cup of tea."

He sauntered back into the depths of the house like a scolded puppy and returned some minutes later in the garb I'd requested. I fixed him a cup of tea and moved him gently around his element, struggling for some degree of spontaneity; and eventually posed him with Don, out on the patio with the canyon as the backdrop. They were not an exciting pair, these two, and getting any kind of smile, grimace, or other semblance of personality or emotionality took more creative wisdom than I was able to conjure.

Nevertheless, the setting was interesting, Christopher was Christopher, he and Don were history, and an occasional canyon breeze created some minor reactions about the hair and collars of the two.

The photos proved to be the last that were ever taken of Chris, and the only ones in the final years that had been taken of the two of them together; Christopher died two weeks later.

VINCE

Faith and patience take their toll,
but passion stirs the soul.

It became quite the norm, even before *Track Meet* had made its appearance, to find myself being pursued down our local streets by mature gentlemen in their slow-moving vehicles. I was always on foot, and usually out and about at least once a day, strolling around in loose-fitting shorts and almost invariably shirtless. A car would slow to the same pace as my walk, occasionally passing, glancing over at me, then circling the block only to do it one more time. At first I assumed that someone needed directions. Then I hipped to the fact that these were always and only solo men in the mid-age range. A pattern had developed.

One fine autumn day a car actually stopped, rolled down the window and asked me where I lived. This I thought to be rather forward, but not wanting to be rude (I was right outside La Ronda) I said, "In the neighborhood."

"Would you like a ride?" the poker face asked.

"No thank you, I'm very close. And I enjoy the walk."

"I'll give you twenty dollars."

Well, twenty dollars to take a ride seemed slightly inflated by even Republican reasoning. Yes, I could certainly *use* the twenty. But I had the smarts to suspect sexual commerce.

"No, thank you," I said, and wandered *away* from my current home, cataloguing just how many yogurts and Tiger Milk bars I could buy for twenty bucks, and feeling like an idiot for heading away from my destination.

"Well," he said as he passed me, "if you change your mind, I'll be at Theodore's Cafe."

Fine, I thought, *I'll be in my garden.*

This became a common occurrence, and though the concept of prostitution was nothing new or obscene to me (I had marched many times alongside the Coyote ladies in Seattle, and in fact had befriended prostitutes as far back as junior high, much to my mother's horror). I suppose it was simply the fear of the unknown, and I was too shy (or vain) to ask for it all to be spelled out ahead of time—not knowing then that that was certainly quite my prerogative, in fact usually prefered by the paying party.

One afternoon, while I was returning from the health-food store five blocks away, another fellow pulled his car near the curb and politely offered me a ride. His smile was more sincere than coercive, and his manner seemed especially trustworthy and dignified—he could even have been a wealthy Hollywood producer or casting agent!—and I said *Yes*.

For the lust of me, I cannot recall what made this gentleman so unusually persuasive, but he in brief time parked the car and helped carry the two bags of groceries into my tiny Eden.

"I really haven't much time, just finishing up a sequence of poems and I haven't even watered the garden today..." I rambled as I found my clothes being taken from me, folded and placed neatly by the single mattress on the floor.

His clothes remained on and I began to delight narcissistically at his praise and the touch of mature hands.

There were no drugs involved, no sordidness, it was a bright and lovely afternoon with the veranda doors flung wide to the music of the birds, and I was being orally and digitally maneuvered into a state of complete arousal. Then, in one epochal instant, I realized that this "businessman" had his entire hand within my barely-explored colon, something that I didn't even know could happen, and which would certainly never occur again without great ado, massive drugs, and the "right" person. And yet here I was, like a lolly-pop on the end of this stranger's arm.

When he left, having never removed his clothes or implied his own needs (I believe I even *asked* him if *he* wanted to come) he gave me a rolled-up twenty-dollar bill.

I protested, even though I needed it, on general principle (I can't remember *which* principle), but he insisted and I woodenly reneged. It was my first Hollywood score, and it would mark the beginning of a long and at-times painful career/lifestyle.

One morning, shortly after this discovery, and right before Christmas 1977, as I was on my way back from the supermarket that I visited most every day (usually just wandering through the aisles, pushing a cart and noshing on items that I would leave in the basket and never pay for—I was broke) I encountered another gentleman smack on my corner of Fountain and Havenhurst. He was coming from the other direction wielding his own bag of groceries, sporting a testicle-tight pair of Levi's and the biggest blackest mustache I had ever seen. He smiled at me and I smiled at him and I guess my balls were beginning to develop, for I hastily offered him my hand and my name.

"Vince" he said his name was. "Romano." He lived a half-block away; I lived a half-block the other direction.

Vince was small, thirty-three, dark, grotesquely hairy—where he shaved he made a sweater-line around the base of his neck—bright-eyed, full-lipped, with this dense shelf of a handlebar mustache that engulfed half his face, curling up his cheeks into a permanent smile. He was the most beautiful man that I had ever seen. A hirsute daddy-dude—yet small enough to be manageable. I was in love and told him so on the spot.

"Say," he said, "we're having our annual Christmas party tonight, starting about seven, but you can get there anytime, we'll be cranking as long as everybody's stoned enough to wanna hang around. Come on by. It'll be mostly my lover Stuart's business queens and I'll be banging around in the kitchen trying to avoid them. My mother just sent her yearly box of Christmas cookies. You ever had Italian Christmas cookies?"

No I hadn't, I confessed, but I certainly could see where I would like to start munching, Stuart notwithstanding.

"I'll be there. Thanks. Sure is a killer mustache."

He beamed broadly, unabashed, and catcalled low under his breath as we passed. We pivoted to find each other turned for one final glance at the important aspects, smiled and ambled on. I continued to smell him all the way home and struggled desperately to remain unaroused within the flimsy security of my shorts.

He and Stuart, his spouse of three years, shared an exquisite built-in-the-Twenties Spanish unit in what was probably La Ronda's closest sister. A rustic garden courtyard, less formal, filled with wishing wells, fish ponds, wild jungle plants. The spacious beam-ceilinged apartment was aflutter with tinsel, colored lights, candles, cookies, presents, tree, intoxicating kitchen aromas. The walls were garnished with charming nudes and macro-photos of plants and flowers—Vince was a photographer. I was at once jealous and wanted to trade places with Stuart, marry Vince and wake up beside him on Christmas morn. I swore to myself that not another holiday would pass without him.

The party was spuriously polite, though occasionally humorously bitchy. It was *too* decorated; so were the guests, Stuart's associates and assorted (homo) family holiday regulars. I was dressed in my normal inappropriate cocktail attire of leather biker's jacket, cowboy boots, dirty black-dyed jeans; everyone was a trifle put-off (which I suppose was my intent) though fascinated, as though I had stepped in by mistake from the back alley. But Vince liked it.

When I engaged Vinnie in an earnest conversation about his exotic plants (he shared this avocation with me) pheromones were already flying. He invited me up the circular stairway to the loft/sunroom/bedroom where the bulk of the exotics were wintering. We toured the plants briefly, sharing this intimate botanical foreplay in subdued but passionate tones. We were all alone.

"May I kiss you," I breathed.

"I wish you would."

This could be described as the first kiss of my life; and now, over twenty years later, must still be among the best.

Vince's lips were as soft as the petals of a lily, only endlessly wet under their canopy of densely-manicured black bristle. His breath tasted of Christmas, a hint of marijuana, and of generations of Italians.

Our kiss grew to encompass more than just our lips. Where my boldness came from I don't know. I do know that in a flash I had his handsome jewelry in my hands, and in the second instant in my mouth.

His dick was beautiful. As I've said, I am the most comfortable with genitals that are essentially like my own—anything too much bigger *or* smaller inevitably presents competition and ego problems in bed, besides the inherent difficulty one might have with regards to sexual function; and while I have come to prefer uncircumcised penises for social and aesthetic reasons, there is much to be said for familiarity; and extreme curves, bends and dips I have always found to be distracting, if not entirely awkward.

Vince's fond member was virtually identical to mine, fat, round, wholesome in length, a perfect mouthful (and most any other orifice). The one difference was the Mediterranean tone, olive in hue, which made my little WASP weewee look positively pink by comparison. And his testicles, though similar in structure to my own, had the extra bulk and the added distension of his additional decade—they were a man's balls, and enveloped in their own little cardigan of the most ethnic Latin wool. I *was* in love.

Vinnie proved to be an easy cum on nearly any occasion, though never as swift as in this dicey moment, with his lover and guests downstairs. In fact Stuart, at the height of our oral-digital frenzy, called up the stairs to ask if we were all right: "Yes!" Vince croaked between gasps, "W-we'll be right down!"

With that his teeth clenched, his hands tightened on my hair, his legs went into spasms, his juicy distension doubled in its breadth and coughed its opalescent ecstasies into the bedroom of my throat.

Remember that oral sex was *not* my forte, and semen to me was something to be wiped up and rapidly flushed down the nearest toilet. But Vince was different, it was as though I already *owned* him, as though he were my child or a puppy I had raised from birth, nothing about him was ever vile or disgusting, even when he was ill, and there were no taboos or limitations between us (at least not in body).

He nervously yanked up his trousers and took only the instant for the obligatory post-coital kiss before heading back to the stairs, frenetically repreening his moustache as he moved.

I carefully rearranged my own jeans to leave only enough of my waistline askew to give Stuart the hint of what had happened. I was certain that they were on the skids, and though furious and envious that I would not be unwrapping my own Italian cookies beneath *our* erect and bedecked tree, I was determined that the man *would* be mine.

"Vince, it's Gavin," I accosted him by phone the following morning. "Thanks for the—uh—party. When can I see you again?"

"I'm busy. I'm, well... we've got company coming over for dinner. Um, maybe... I'll call you in a coupla days."

"I'll call you Wednesday," I said, persistent. "I really want to see you again. I'm sorry if I created problems. I *have* to see you..."

"I'll call you." He trailed off.

We communicated more than a few times over the next couple of weeks, mostly at my insistence. He was alarmed over Stuart's suspicions and our improprieties in his cushy love nest. He was, after all, Italian and conditioned to the belief in marriage and home and family and the other familiar myths that have seldom applied to but always haunted our peculiar species.

Not long after my encounter with Vince, however, on the other side of a firepit in the back lot of a cowboy bar in a seedy section of Hollywood (is that redundant?), while I was hanging out with Craig I caught sight of another older dude who assaulted my equilibrium. He was fully bearded, probably six-foot-three, wore an elegant black cowboy hat (to conceal his scalp) and had a smile that would warm a Baptist. He was obviously musing over the train of men who were ambling by him oh so casually, or ogling from across the pit, beers in hand. He was not Vince, but he was spectacular. And Vince was, after all, not available. And if perchance some waft of another interest made its way back to precious Vinnie... Well, perhaps it might fan the flames.

I undid the next button in my vivatorium coveralls that were already undone significantly past the navel, meandered over and introduced myself.

"Frank," he said back, having already noticed me and smiled back at me smiling over at him. "Frank Drummond."

I immediately got the distinct feeling that he would have felt more comfortable with some surly leather sap, but that he was nonetheless completely intrigued by this saucy young goober.

"That's some hat you got there," I declared. "Some beard! some eyes! some smile!"

"Some lips you got there yerself," he drawled, shit-eating grin on his face, "and it looks like yer not wearin' any underwear."

He peered down my frontside, blowing a ring of smoke off my bare chest that somersaulted down into the pubic nest.

"Don't blow smoke on anything you wouldn't put in your mouth."

"That your buddy over there?" He barely nodded in Craig's direction.

"Best friend."

"Why don't you tell him yer busy fer a spell..." He gave me a delicate and smoky kiss as I felt the crowd grow turgid around us.

Frank spirited me off to his humble flat for coffee, conversation, and Boz Scaggs. "I'm a psychologist," he confessed to me as we sipped our sodas on his kingsize bed/sofa, "work mostly with delinquent teenagers. I suppose it comes from my own growing-up years. Lived on a cattle ranch down in central Florida. My dad used to take me out in the barn and throw me over the feed trough and fuck the daylights outta me. Kinda created a strain, too, between Mom and me. Guess it was pretty shitty all around. Rotten thing to do to a kid, without any words or explanation. So now I'm listening to other kids' horror stories. Keeps me busy..."

I wanted to cry at this dolorously analytical and guilt-filled giant. But I had never felt such desperate lust before. He was gorgeous, I couldn't take my heart out of his smile, his silky gray eyes.

I leaped on him, dragged him under me, embedded myself in the carpet of fur that was his chest, his face, his arms, his thighs, his beer and smoke-infused armpits, and proceeded to slice my way dry into the great white buttocks beneath him.

He was amused, flattered, perhaps aghast, but he was only putting up with my blind pumping into his recesses; I'm certain that he had enjoyed our conversation a great deal more. His kisses were polite, bitter, his breath a distillate of alcohol, cigarettes and coffee that only the love-infected could find desirable. Still, I was enraged. This was *my* father, and *I* was *raping him*. Sex took on a new meaning. This wasn't just cleaning the pipes with a bud, this was Psychology 101, and I was in another world. So was he.

I pulled out before coming. My dick stank. I plied my lips on his penis and began the grueling task of drawing forth this daddy's own juices, which filled me with the taste of wet ashes, coffee, beer (in spite of my amateur status, I was already hip to the fact that a man's semen invariably tastes like a liqueur of his saliva), and that peculiar emptiness of unrequited passion. I, who ostensibly hated blowjobs, had done it again. Was I to become like organist Craig? Or was I just teetering on the brink of something much more encompassing, expanding my repertoire, my boundaries?

"Hey, good meeting you, Sweet Man," he waved as he dropped me back off at the bar.

Marry me, let's run away together! I wanted to scream, but all that came forth was "Call ya..."

We met again, though Frank always preferred talking to fooling around. I prayed for Vinnie's rapid divorce that I might be freed from this gorgeous monster. One afternoon Frank dropped by my cell simply to inform me that my emotions were too hot, that he was personally afraid of commitments, it was *his* problem he knew but *that was the way it was*, that he loved me and *goodbye*.

I hit him.

He didn't hit back or even act surprised. In fact he smiled, after a second or two.

I couldn't talk at all.

"I know," he said solemnly. "I *do* know."

I was shaking, it was all I could do.

"It may not be worth much now," he said, "but when the air has cleared, just know that I love you, Sweet Man. As best I am able."

He left. I cried for days.

We continued to stay in casual contact. Eventually an excited kiss, grope, and verbal compliment accompanied our barroom encounters; he even came over one day to cry about another relationship—I was disgusted. But I did love him, as I did Vince, and I would always have done anything for this gentle, rueful soul.

He was an early AIDS death some years later (I was in a monastery at the time and found out only later) and only his smile remains with me, and the regurgitated memory of wet ashes...

It was some weeks before Vincent finally came to the realization that his relationship with Stuart was blown (pun intended). He was moving into his own apartment just over Laurel Canyon in North Hollywood, and he claimed he needed some time alone.

There are no busses over Laurel Canyon, so I hitched.

He was cold, but I kissed him; he struggled, but I pulled his dick out; he said that he needed to be alone and I moved in for the kill.

I took him there, on the living room floor, amidst all his recently arranged plants, stones and artifacts bargained for in the divorce. He saw the tide coming; it didn't make sense to him, but he didn't get out of the way. It was the beginning of the most passionate time of my life.

I was with him almost every night. Craig and I became all but strangers, coming together for occasional lunches or shopping sprees, only to have him deliver me in the early evening to Vince's doorstep. By now I was already learning to support myself as a working boy, which I did during days when married businessmen could take lunches off and run over to get their flabby asses spanked or their squeaky little pricks jerked. Craig and I had moved headquarters out of La Ronda and into our own design studio/art gallery on the corner of Robertson and Melrose. It was a feeble attempt at a business. I lived in the back; Craig's credit was finally running dry and I supported our exorbitant rent and obsessional redecorating ideas with a daily parade of gentlemanly tricks. These came about through an assortment of means, some street-walking, some referrals, but mostly through an ad I had placed in the *Advocate*, stating: "Athletic young porn star..." or even "Star of Track Meet..." It was a job, an occasional joy, and it was rapidly becoming a lifestyle.

Of course I didn't tell Vince. But through his own devices or the meddling of a friend, he came to the realization that I was supporting myself in a very non-traditional (though very Italian) manner.

His rage, as we sat on the end of his bed in a sweat of repressed action, hung like a noose around my neck. I couldn't think, couldn't breathe, hadn't the wherewithal to manipulate him as I always could.

He asked me how I acquired these "tricks."

"Through the *Advocate*," I sighed with remorse, "I have an ad."

"I know," he said, "I saw it." He turned livid and smacked me across the chin. "God damn you," he spat, tears spewing down his face, "just get out of here. Go home. Leave me alone!"

It was the only time I ever allowed anybody to get away with hitting me. I gladly accepted the punch. I worried that it might be the last.

"Vince..."

"Just get out of here."

"I'm sorry. I'm sorry."

"Get in the car. I'm taking you home."

But my magic started working in the car. I had every wheel whizzing in desperation. We made it to the gallery, but I had made every promise from absolute chastity to getting re-baptized in the River Milano, and by the time we arrived I had him talked up the stairs, into the door, between my legs and on my pillow asleep. That was our closest call.

The one thing that Vince and I always maintained was our sexual heat. Looking back on all my past lives and past loves I cannot recall a single soul before or since who has touched me in quite the same manner. One look, one breath, one pinch, even a passing smell would be all that the two of us ever needed to consolidate a riff, to forget about even the most pointed insults, to yank out the arrows of complete social and intellectual incompatibility.

Of course I kept being a prostitute—I was already hooked, financially as well as emotionally—but in the wake of our détente I was more discreet. We spent three to four nights a week together. We stuck to our routine of pasta, a couple of joints, *Laverne and Shirley* on Tuesdays, rabid sex, and sex again in the morning before he delivered me home on his way to work.

Life would've been bliss, except for the fact that I got so blastedly bored. Love, yes, but there was little or no other stimulation. We had plants in common, and sex, lots of sex, but that was almost all of it. I even found Vince's photography hopelessly pedestrian, so I rarely commented on his work, with nothing positive to say, except for fishing around for reasons as to why Craig and I wouldn't show his prints in our gallery (I blamed it on Craig, although I never even asked him about it).

I loved the man. Our lust was just the means for that love. Vince was as good-hearted a soul as I've encountered. But Laverne and Shirley we were not, and as our conversations waned, so did our patience. One evening sticks out, some nine months into our ceremonies, me half-naked at one o'clock in the morning, screaming from out in his courtyard, on my way home, that he was *stupid, ignorant, we have nothing to talk about...!* I pounded on the door, embarrassed everybody in the complex, burst back in and raped him on the kitchen floor.

I was becoming *so* Latin! We made up, but he never forgot my comments, and it was the beginning of the end of the "lover" era of what would be an enduring relationship.

We struggled to keep it together through Christmas 1978. *That* had been my fantasy and *I would have it!* Vince, believing dearly in such things as holidays, families and other Italian essentials, needed me in *his* life at that time as well. We had friends over; Vince made his traditional holiday eggplant parmigiana. I baked desserts, worked the party with my fly undone. It was a marvelous Christmas. The next morning, opening our cache of presents beneath the tree that I still have (twenty years later) planted outside my current LA studio. We took lots of pictures. We both knew that this would be our first, last, and most splendid holiday.

But we grew apart, found new lovers—I went back to hustling full-time.

We always said we were "the right people at the wrong time." But it wasn't that. Vince was a very conservative Catholic–at–heart–lower–Chicago–Italian–boy. He loved his mother, made obeisance to the Catholic god, and maintained his position in the status quo. I was an arch-radical, a social pariah; I hated my mother, disbelieved in God, and would opt for any road untraveled or forbidden me.

Still, for years, in between lovers or simply behind their backs, Vinnie and I would come together for a torrid night, with no more expectations than our own connection.

During the course of my writing this chapter, Vince died. He had been struggling with AIDS for well over a year. He had tried both traditional approaches and, at my insistence, alternative methods. The message was clear: he was ready to split. His roommate said he was at peace, content, tired of fighting, appreciative of his forty-six years.

That was the difference between us: that he was able to believe in and give himself to the system, to allow the doctors to poison him, desecrate and ransack his body, humiliate him, and leave him for Death. And yet that was the nature that I had come to rely on Vinnie for: that stability, that expectedness, that fundamentalism, whether blind, stupid or simply unconscious. He was Vince. And I loved him.

I called to console his mother, who still considers me her son-in-law. An avid fan of my poetry, she lived in LA for the better part of a year doing nothing but alternately taking care of Vince and his also-dying ex-boyfriend/roommate. I will stay in touch with her, as long as she is alive, as I would a relative of my own.

I will stay in touch with Vince also, when the libido rises, and mortal lovers fail. He is always with me.

FLIP

The truth is never hard to find,
it's telling lies that takes our time.

When Craig and I moved the Center of the Universe from La Ronda to Robertson Boulevard, life transformed: chichi fags and designer everything, we were "uptown" now, and had to find some way to keep the ball rolling. But first, naturally, we had to redecorate.

We painted everything 000-white, with gray industrial carpeting, ripped out all the interior doors and had chicken-wire-glass shower doors installed in their stead. I had my bed, desk, and all my belongings shoved in the back room with my *Track Meet* headboard, a sink, a tiny apartment refrigerator, and myriad potted plants spilling out onto several balconies and roof gardens.

It *seemed* like a step up. Done-up and petulant designer-fairies hobbled about from showroom to showroom with their gold-embroidered clientage. By night the street got heavily cruised for its proximity to Studio One on the one side, and the 8709 baths on the other, both institutions operating in their heyday.

I saw johns daily, as many as six a day. It was a natural progression from the attention I had received from doing porn—fans of the movie, friends of friends, men encountered about town, at the disco, were all willing to pay for a piece of the action. It was exhausting, but it was addictive as well.

So was the money. At fifty to a hundred dollars a pop, I was sitting pretty, so to speak. Of course our rent was exorbitant, as were our tastes, but it was only money, it was only time, it was only sex.

Actually, it often wasn't even sex. There were many men, like Lester, who came to see me regularly, merely sat next to me on the bed for an hour. Lester was fifty-something, lean and dignified, with brushed back salt-and-pepper hair and lips still sweet and full. "It's worth it to me," he would croon, "just to be close to you, without having to feel guilty, or afraid that you'll reject me."

"But you don't want to have sex?"

"*This* makes me happy," he said as we sat upright, arm in arm, he in his boxers (I never saw him without), me naked, pliant, and available.

"I just don't fit into the club scene," he went on, "and a bathhouse, I'm sure, would scare me to death."

"But they're not scary at all, Les, you should pop by one night."

"They probably wouldn't even let me in."

I realized he was right and shut up.

"*This* is all I need from life. I can spend twice as much with my psychiatrist and not get half of the satisfaction. And you're *much* better looking than he is!"

He laughed and I went on to pontificate about everything from modern psychology to faggot disco-ology. I only charged fifty bucks for the non-sex encounters like this, and I came to rely on them as they did on me. It was innocent, and I felt that I was performing a worthy service. I saw Lester for several years, and was sad when he moved too far to comfortably bus in to see me.

I was performing an essential service to the others as well. Though some were grotesque, many were quite charming and simply needed a friend, someone to take dominion over their bodies for a while, roles that were clearly delineated. So many dollars buys you so much time. You can have my ass, but not my face. And don't expect me to be available for lunch afterwards—that's extra. Prostitution is a blessing that way: once the demarcations are set and sequenced, they are rarely challenged, so you always know exactly what will transpire as well as what is expected of you.

Then there were the scary ones, like the foot doctor. Jim shaved every hair on his body, was probably thirty-three or -four, rather nice-looking if he had only allowed some fur for contrast. He'd have me rub him all over with either talcum powder or baby oil and would climax while I pummeled his feet. I wasn't allowed to be naked. I never asked him why; it was enough simply to have him skulk back in week after week. Maybe this enabled him to go home each evening to his wife and kids and function without anger or anxiety.

Burt, a lumpish eunuch, paid royally to lick my butt by the hour. It seemed like an easy gig: he liked all-nighters, I figured I could snooze. I was wrong. After about three hours in his bleak Wilshire condo I came to understand such things as Chinese water torture, solitary confinement, the village stocks. One man was a borderline freak, with eyes so far apart that one would immediately presume him an alien. A third nostril, he informed me, had been removed through cosmetic surgery. Another man was so massive and hairy that he might easily have been shot if sighted out in the wild. Both of these were timid, querulous, apologetic to the point of bringing tears to my eyes. "I wouldn't ask you to have sex with me," I recall one of them whispering. "I don't even need to take my clothes off, just let me look at you for an hour."

"Please," I responded, "I don't mind, make yourself comfortable, we can do anything you'd like. Honest."

I meant it. While I steadily refused giving oral sex to any of my suitors, I found it remarkably easy to proffer my ass. I learned that when I needed to not "be there," I could maintain friendly eye contact, yet put my mind far away into the arms of a fantasy or the embrace that I knew I would receive that evening from Vince, or future lovers. It was cheating, this professional prowess, but I believe that the clients rarely felt that it was. And while the work could be occasionally taxing on my mind, my nerves, or various parts of my body, I took ample strokes from the attention, the client's satisfaction, and my own feeling of being ultimately "in control."

My "athlete" ad brought in some major hunks, like the jocks from USC who were simply terrified of sex, had never had it with a man, didn't know what to do, and didn't even know whether they were queer or not.

Rick only came to see me once. He was everybody's idea of a good time and I was astonished—and a bit embarrassed—that he was wielding a fifty in his hand. I would've gladly paid him! Young, dark, football-scholarship, solemn soft voice, chastening hazel eyes...

But he never even took off his briefs, merely sat there touching my naked extremities as though they were ephemera that might vanish without warning. We kissed like two does in a forest; I had to refrain from engulfing him—it was *his* dime.

"So, do you think you might be queer or you're just not sure?" I asked him.

"I don't know." It seemed like he would cry.

"Does it matter?" I suggested.

"Maybe it doesn't. Well, maybe it does in the locker room at school."

"You kiss very sweetly, like a sensitive man. I think that's great."

"You have a beautiful body," he said, and blushed.

"*You* have a beautiful body! Don't you wanna slip out of those nasty ol' briefs?"

"No!" He laughed. "I think I'll keep 'em on."

"Suit yourself. God *knows* what might happen! Be comfortable..." But I wanted him, in me, on me, all over me. I was aggrieved by our abortive tryst. Strangely, the most difficult "tricks" in my book were the ones who wouldn't let-go-and-let-Gav.

Jasper was a drop-dead gorgeous black child who was dying to fuck someone but never had, and was completely disgusted by fags and fey life (imagine that). He was so gentle (as well one might be with twelve inches of weapon at one's disposal), so polite, that he let me lead him through the entire regimen.

"Doesn't it hurt you?" His brows bowed with concern, discovery.

"Well, I'm enjoying you enjoying yourself. Yeah, you're *big*. How do *you* feel?"

"Oh, this is... great. Thank you."

"Hey, thank you. It's a pleasure."

He came as quietly as a mouse.

"Why don't you stay the night," I suggested as he was yanking up his chartreuse socks, "no charge."

"I can't. I live at home. I'd love to. Thanks. My mother..."

And there were the studio execs, a representative for Cartier, the vice-president of a classical record label, a minister from UCLA, all thoughtful kind men who took me regularly out for lunches at Le Restaurant, Chasens, Le Dome, shopping at Maxfield Bleu, Brooks Brothers; we had gentle and warm sex that became as familiar as a favored wine. I placated these friends for years, even mingled anonymously at parties with their clients, their wives or lovers.

There were also annoying jack-off calls. Breathers. Murder threats. Times when I would leave a window open in case I might need to scream for help. But I never did get into trouble; a phone voice indicates so much. I never made housecalls for people that I didn't know, and there were only a handful of maladapted gents that I suggested not pay a return visit.

Much later in my life I would undergo past-life regressions. In those sessions I would have profound experiences of a war in which I had killed all of these men, all of whom, in this lifetime, were coming back for a completion, a healing, as it were, to take back a piece of me, to relinquish this attraction/animosity/lust/karma that we shared. And it did come to exhaust me, to leave me feeling deleted, pillaged, like there would soon be nothing left for *Gav*. Though to me it seemed that there was nothing different about my life than there was in the enervating routines that every working soul experiences every day in an office or a factory. There were ups, downs, some people who fill you, and those who leave you quite empty. And besides, I rationalized, I was only at it a fraction of the time, when I felt so inclined; the rest of my time I could marshal for writing, painting, acting lessons...

But prostitution *is* an addiction, like a drug or so many other behaviors that balance darkness and danger against occasional peaks and thrills. And like a drug, while you might be able to control the flow and the supply, you cannot always control the quality or predict the effect.

Nevertheless, it never stopped my romancing, though it certainly impinged upon any serious interactions. I would stalk down the street most every night and either drag home a bimbo from Studio One or hit the 8709 and fuck a half-dozen men there. Perhaps this was just my way of shaking off the vibes from the afternoon's visitors, reaffirming my faith in honest lust, taking back something that had been taken from me, or merely giving myself a more pleasant visage with which to fall into slumber.

It was a wonder I had the sperm. It was a wonder I could still walk.

Occasionally I would get invited on a mini-trip, a weekend or an overnight drive. One week I went to a fag resort in Palm Springs with Michael, a famous photographer and testy queen who instantly grew as bored of me as I did with him. We stayed completely inebriated on 'ludes and Valium just to be able to stand the heat—and each other. But while sliding into the pool the first day, I noticed an especially inviting blue bikini sticking up out of a half-submerged rubber raft.

The face was not as attractive as the butt, but there was a walrus-like mustache that reminded me of my Vincent, and frightened blue eyes. The Quaaludes swam in my head. When my partner was indisposed, I slipped the sprite my number and suggested we do this trip *together* sometime.

He called me immediately in LA. His name was Flip (*Mervin*, actually, but that was verboten), from Chelsea, Michigan, a wiry, nervous little creature, bristling with sexual energy. He had money, a video deck (playing what seemed like an endless loop of *Hello, Dolly!*), a huge old flat across the street from the tar pits and County Museum, and he drove a gaudy new LTD or something that I was equally humiliated to ride in. Oh, and Toto, too, a yappy little schnauzer.

"You want some coke?" he chirped, on our first encounter at his flat.

"No, thanks, I don't drink... Oh, you mean... well sure, I mean, I—I've only done it a couple of times—um, sure."

He chopped out six joint-sized lines on his glass, living-room coffee table and lined up a half-dozen Grace Jones and Shirley Bassey discs on the turntable.

Flip took much of the load off my hustling racket. He was awash with cash and easily covered all our entertainments. And yet, stoned as we were, Flip was much too unconscious to even recognize what were blatant signs of my extant career (the second phone, the all-too-often swollen and tired cock, my occasional disappearances).

He loved to get fucked but continued to pretend it was not something that he normally would allow. He had an endless supply of cocaine, which I rapidly learned to inhale. We did videos most every night. *I Love Lucy* and *The Addams Family* during the day. And we took lots of trips—as far as San Juan—restaurants, Studio One on weekends, all the distractions of the emotionally ill-equipped.

We *seemed* happy. I spent many a night there; came running over in the middle of one night to deliver Toto's litter. Flip was beside himself, trembling; he couldn't light cigarettes fast enough.

Yet he was endearing, this skittish frailty with the scrawny butt and the dick of a man three times his size. I would ridicule him for his nervousness, his coffee, Pepsi, and nicotine compulsions, then throw him into his waterbed and pork him while he salivated over the pillow, Lucy and Ethel in the background.

We even formed a business. Knocked off the "I-*heart*-NY" design for LA. Made T-shirts, sweats, et cetera, and made a bundle, even got into the big department stores.

But we got bored with the business and stopped delivering orders. Flip, it turned out, was doing some major coke dealing, which was why we had a seemingly endless supply. We were each packing in about a gram a day, shoving it up each other's asses because our noses were stripped bare, then screwing it in until our dicks grew numb and ceased to work.

"You're a liar," I would accuse him, loftily, "you're fucking sleazing all over this town. I know you hit every cha-cha bar on Pico when I'm not here. I don't want to smell your filthy cock or catch your fucking diseases. You're a fucking drugged-out mess!"

"Me? Sister, you got your boots on inside out! You're the one that lives at the 8709. And it seems to me that you've been packing down some major grams of *my* coke. And by the way, seems I'm missing some hundreds out of my desk drawer."

"Well! You fucking piss-queen, wire-assed fruit! I don't need your mother-fucking drug money."

"Damn right you don't," he fulminated, "all the tricks you been turnin' over there on *Robertson!*"

It got gruesome, this Lucy-and-Ethel-do-West-Hollywood routine. Everything that Flip told me at that point was a lie, obvious lies, silly pointless lies, paranoid lies, when I realized, *Hey, I'm doing the same thing to him!* It was the coke—it had to be.

"No more drugs, Flip. No more coke."

"No more for you, girl, you're a fucking mess."

"No more for you either. I'm serious. I'm tired of this paranoia, this bullshit."

"Eat shit. You're the one who can't handle it!"

The results were uncontestable. I had to extricate myself from the whole mess—Flip and all his friends. So I left him, hating me but still snorting up. There was no way to reconcile a relationship that was systemically rooted in deception, paranoia, fantasy, cocaine.

I started dead-bolting my door.

(None of this, incidentally, is to say that I am "against drugs." I am not. I merely discovered, *for me*, and *through my own experimentation*—"abuse" if you will—and consequent reappraisal, that cocaine, like marijuana, is a stupefying and non-productive substance. If there is anything that I am "against," it is the grandstanding *against* drugs by people who have no personal experience with their use—this is like receiving sex education from a nun. Life is *not* theoretical.) Things got ugly.

There had been alleged, for some time, death threats made against Flip because of me (a wanna-be relationship, an ex, maybe, an irate fan...); phone calls, pinned-up letters on his door. One day (so he said) the back door was jimmied open and a dead cat left in his washing machine.

Then he got mugged by a hit-man in his driveway.

"It's the coke, Flip, you gotta get it outta your house."

"It's you, you fucker. It's one of your tricks." His terrier eyes were two shimmying splats of terror.

"Get rid of the coke, Flip, lock your fucking doors."

The letters on the door and the phone threats did all stop once I was cleared out. But then Flip started getting regularly burglarized, the coke and huge sums of cash. He always seemed an inch away from death, endlessly frightened, shivering. Was *I* really that way too?

My time with Flip was a year spent in that maelstrom, with a man that I never loved, on a drug that was destructive and anathema to consciousness. It was a year that almost *wasn't* (it is difficult now even to recall) and yet it *was*. I quit coke altogether, except for the most obligatory of social instances.

Other drugs would seduce me later on. Still, I had the opportunity to reflect on chemistry, relationships, and the effects both have upon my consciousness. I was learning when to say no.

I resumed the semi-fulltime routine of hustling. And I never missed Flip. I was thrilled it was all behind me.

And his little dog, too.

BEAR

*Is there anything greater
than the ability to be small?*

As I have mentioned, the Bear and I were introduced through Sam, perhaps as a means to get me off his (Sam's) back, but I suspect more as a goodwill gesture toward Bear, whom even Sam kissed up to.

Our first encounter, in the spring of 1979, was a trifle tense, predominantly due to Bear's surprising shyness, but also due to the fact that I was genuinely in awe of this one. This was not simply a fixation for Jewish patriarchs—this *was* Mr. Hollywood. But even more, this was a man who actually *did* impress me, with both his intelligence and suavity *and* his size, hirsuteness, daddy-hood. A hug from him was like the embrace of the entire Prussian army. His kisses were timid, but direct. He was elegant, commanding, yet, I was sure, yearned to become putty in someone else's hands. Doesn't every corporate executive?

That first evening was terse. Once again Craig dropped me off at a set of great iron gates, where the voice of a British butler asked for my name; I was flagged into a long hall crammed with brand-name artwork and an extensive array of Tiffanys and rare sandwich glass urns, vases and lamps. And I noticed how much smaller the Master seemed without the accompaniment of gaggling fans.

"Hullo," Bear stumbled, blushed even, "um, there's a full bar there." He waved at an entire wall encrusted with mirrors, bottles, glasses and hand-carved wood.

"Pretty," I said.

"Thanks." He blushed again, looking down into his chest. "Well, um, what can I get you?"

"Tequila tonic, lime if you have it."

"Of course. I have everything. I think."

He scurried behind the bar and ducked out of sight in search of the appropriate glass.

He was an obvious rookie at this—not at bartending, but dealing with the likes of me. I believe the whole setup offended him—but there I was.

We had an affectedly casual, though cautious, interview in the lodge-sized living room (the one where one entire wall could change miraculously into a full-panoramic movie screen and an invisible yeoman in a room behind the bar would roll whichever flicks were soon to be released and needed to be at least scanned). "Would you like to see a movie?" he asked me.

"I don't care. I love films. I'm here to see you."

Blonds can turn so much redder than dark-haired people. "Well, follow me then. Let's go upstairs. We can watch films up there as well."

"You got a jacuzzi?"

"How about a steam?"

"Bitchin'!"

We headed up the central stairs to the grand-but-treehouselike bedroom that covered the entire top of the house, built in and around the grounds' ancient desert oaks. After a brief run through the steam, with only token pets and kisses, we dried off and lumbered onto his overstuffed four-poster. I hardly had time to enjoy the thick and furry presence that surrounded me before he dropped, exhausted, a stranger on top of me.

Bear waited nervously for me to bring myself to satisfaction. I would've gladly abstained but felt as though it was expected of me, didn't want to appear rude, as though I hadn't enjoyed myself, and wanted to protract my time there as long as I could.

But Bear wasted no time in escorting me into the Jag and back to my gallery/home. I thought I had done something wrong—I wanted to spend the night there, amid that beauty, to wrap myself in those masculine arms, snuggle into the rug of a chest, marry him, move right in.

But there was much silence between us. I attempted to turn down the fifty-dollar bill that he pushed into my hand. We hadn't discussed money, it had never been an issue with Sam and me—but he insisted, and I frankly needed it. I hoped that that didn't preclude a further visit. I wanted to be Bear's friend, his lover, his wife, *not* his *whore*.

Two weeks later he called again. This time I took a cab up to his estate—he gave me twenty at the door to cover the ride. I didn't resist it. This might be the only way that the demigod would be comfortable with my presence. I mean, money-as-control was his expertise—and a splendid way to avoid commitments. For now, a hustler was what the man wanted (he already had a girlfriend!).

I came to learn that Bear lived both in New York *and* in Beverly Hills. In New York he was seen publicly with a fashion mogul; she rarely came out West.

The next visit, it was not just the two of us. I had arrived to see a movie, as I used to do with Sam. But Sam was not present. Instead there was a gentleman named Randy, a Hollywood manager, one of the biggest, and Bear's best friend. Also present was Randy's boyfriend, Jim, an obstreperous tyke with Bette Davis eyes and mud-colored bangs. Jimmy was taller than any of us, svelte, and bounced about from Randy's embrace to the Master's lap and back again with the grace and verve of the dim-witted. He was smart enough, though, to avoid any physical contact with me. Also there was the famed director John Schlesinger and *his* friend, Michael Childers, and a couple of other miscellaneous boys who seemed well acquainted with the bar, where the intoxicants were stashed, and the whole progression of the "scene."

I'm not sure what that first film was; during my time with Bear, I would view all the major films some months before anybody else had the chance, often in an uncut or unscored state considerably different from the final version (those that I ever saw the final versions of). I do remember the viewing of Polanski's *Tess*, largely because the version we saw was some four hours long, and especially because Bear's New York consort was there, soused on the couch with everyone else, skirt up to her navel, flashing her beaver like a box of popcorn, as oblivious of my position in the house as I was *aware* of hers. I didn't get to stay that night—and yes, *that* made me feel like a whore.

The biggest thrill was the viewing of *The Incredible Shrinking Woman*. You could take all the Liz Taylors in Tinsel Town and not impress me as you would with one glimpse of Lily Tomlin, whom I considered not only one of the funniest people in the world, but one of the most intelligent, and one of the most politically right-on. This evening was sprung on me. Bear, knowing of my deep fixation for the comedienne, simply insisted that I come up that evening (I rarely needed coaxing, but rather lived for the nights when the Bear was in town and his "boy" was an appropriate fixture). And there she was, that face that expressed a hundred other personalities through its mercurial eyes and those lips that have to virtually force themselves closed over a mouth and teeth that always seem ready to explode with laughter. Would she be cool enough to be polite and show some modicum of interest in Bear's Boy?

We were barely introduced before the film was rolling. But I realized one thing, *she was nervous!* She was nervous here in the company of the Titan. Funny: *I* would spank his bottom that very night!

The film was only a rough cut with entirely unfinished and often inaudible sound. So what we got that evening was a version performed by the star herself, complete with side comments, sound effects (that we all came to contribute to) and the voices of innumerable Tomlin characters that were, of course, not in the final edit.

After the film the actress was bustled out with the rest of the group, as if to politely leave Bear alone with his evening's prey.

"Well?" Bear asked.

"Funny lady. Funny film. I would've liked to have gotten a chance to really talk with her. I wanna sleep with her!"

"Fat chance!" He laughed. "But you'll get plenty of opportunities to get to know her. She's a marvelous woman, a very talented lady."

Bear and I by now were getting quite comfortable as boyfriends (or whatever we'd call it). I had asked him to stop giving me the fifties, in part to provide *me* with the illusion that I was more to him than simply a trick, *and* in the hope that by eliminating this petty exchange, greater rewards might come my way. This technique proved effective; as our bonding continued, occasional "allowances" were made available to me. When taking taxicabs got cumbersome, my favorite model car was presented (I then had to get my first license—I was twenty-four). We occasionally hit a first-class men's store and stocked up on cashmere. I had a custom blazer fashioned for me by Maxfield Bleu, and I was simply allowed to pick through the stacks of elegant basics that lined the walls of Bear's immense dressing closet— clothes that were merely created and delivered *in case* he should ever desire that item, that color, that fabric.

Drugs were an inevitability. I don't recall ever seeing Bear do cocaine, and I was over the stuff, but with a toot toot here and a toot toot there, many of his guests were not quite so restrained.

Quaaludes were *my* gig, having by then acquired a doctor who would prescribe a hundred for me every few months (Bear covered my medical bills); and my pockets were kept ever stocked with bona fide amyl nitrate, and a variety of classic American uppers and downers. I was beginning my days with TT1, the mysterious hypnotic powder that appeared on the scene one year, kept me fully addicted for three, then vanished as mysteriously as it had arrived—this Bear only dabbled in at my insistence—it was certainly stiff stuff.

As for sex, once I concluded that this industry giant most needed a strong-willed young dick who would throw him on his back, we were fully on our way. When the act was established as not only desirable but *possible*, there was no turning Bear around. *I* came to miss the penetration of that great vasculous calabash, the pounding of his balls against my spine, his weight pinning me into the luxury of his massive bed.

And as my sexual persona turned into that of aggressor, so also my verbal and psychological abuses grew. It was a game I knew all too well from my mother—humiliate, manipulate, castrate—and I played it even in front of our friends and those business associates with whom I was allowed to mingle. For Bear it was a relief to take the passenger seat and pretend he was mortal from time to time. Granted, he still *was* who he *was*, still paid all the bills, still received the curtsies and prostrations of the Streisands, the Beattys, the Nicholsons. Yet he was *mine* in bed.

I had been invited to dinner at Randy's grotesquely excessive canyon estate after his psychic had told him I would eventually earn him more money than he had ever dreamed. Since he was already vasty rich, this was a most charming concept for both of us—though we never established exactly how, or unfortunately *when*.

After a sumptuous vegetarian meal prepared in my honor by the Sikh chefs, Randy escorted me through a maze of halls past a room in which a radiant be-wigged blonde was propped up in bed reading, a sheer peignoir only barely camouflaging her goddess-dimension breasts.

"Well howdy!" she greeted us with a smile that reached both ears and set in motion a rash of genuine dimples.

"Well howdy indeed," I responded as Randy nodded out the door and abandoned me to the southern hospitality of this mistress of song.

"Well there he goes!" she laughed heartily, if defensively at Randy's sudden retreat. "Pull up a piller and make yourself comfortable."

I cozied up next to her in the high-backed bed and sought frantically for something that would seem appropriate. "So you're from the Tennessee mountains," I asked.

"That's right." She winked.

"Well I'm from Asheville, North Carolina—just spittin' distance I bet from where you're from."

"Well, you sure are. Bless yer heart." She began unraveling the tales of her mountain childhood, the evolution to the Opry of Nashville and on to Sin City to play Carson and become a household name. "Say, you wanna hear some new songs?"

"I'd love to!"

"Well just scoot over a skooch... no, not over there! just to make room for my guitar..." She reached under the bed, pulled the sucker out, and proceeded to play for me an entire repertoire of songs that I would later applaud at her concerts at the Roxy, Tahoe, and Universal.

Dolly Parton is one of the most fluidly gracious divas that I have ever encountered in the "industry," and certainly one of the most naturally beautiful women (under the affectations) I have been so close to.

I asked her if the hair ever came off.

"Only *after* the lights go off!" She giggled.

I longed to be comfortable the way I never have with a woman. Her breasts were hangin' right out there like fruit displayed for any guests who might've ambled by; she was so smooth and easygoing I got the impression that I could've played her as easily as she had strummed her guitar. But I'm being presumptuous; she was simply being hospitable. Was that all? I detected no sign of disappointment or expectation on *her* end, and when Randy returned to pull me from her bed, *I* was sad to bid a goodnight.

Dolly and I became quite chummy. And although her desire for the Bear became all too obvious, there was never a trace of resentment or discourtesy allowed toward me.

One evening I bumped into her unexpectedly with Randy in the upper hall of Bear's home.

"Hiya Toots," I said cheerily.

"What did you say?" Randy guffawed.

"I said hiya *Toots*."

"Oh!" he jested, "I thought you said *Tits*."

I blushed and assured her I had not said "Tits" but "Toots."

"Never mind him." She graciously took me by the arm. "You can call me *Tits* anytime you like..."

One splendid evening was a double date between Dolly and me, Bear and Lily. We attended an outdoor Melissa Manchester concert at the Greek Theatre. Lily has the ability to pass relatively unnoticed, but not so with Dolly, already on the covers of women's magazines, whose grandiose coif turned every head in the amphitheater as we shuffled late into our front-row seats.

And even greater still was the opportunity to attend Dolly's Vegas warm-ups in Tahoe. I was employed along with Lily and Jane Wagner to sit through both shows each night and scribble down jokes and suggested changes in the patter. By day I was touring around with Bear, Rand and the ladies seeing the mountain sights, checking out the real estate.

"You're really funny," Lily insisted.

"It's the drugs," I assured her, smitten with such an ultimate compliment.

"Well write some of it down for me."

"How 'bout I just give you the drugs?"

In December 1981 we all rendezvoused in Aspen for the New Year's weekend, flown in by a fleet of privately chartered and catered Lear jets. Although I disdained going anyplace that had *snow* for *fun*, I was ecstatic at being invited to travel with Bear, this being the most time I would ever get to spend with him, sleep with him, and socialize with him.

Bear had rented a commodious cliff house not far from town belonging to the late Ed Wynn. He and I, Randy and Jim, Calvin Klein and a couple of other gentleman all had our own suites (Bear and I, of course, the master). The town rested under a moderate layer of snow, neatly manicured of course, and the tasteful cold only gave us one more reason to do more intoxicants. Straight shots, hot toddies, coke, dope, 'ludes, amyl and my own private stock of TT1 were wafting through the house in denser clouds than the snow that would fall that evening. While Bear (rarely interested in even token drug usage) discussed business-related matters with Randy, my confrere Jimmy and I (in our skivvies and armed with bottles, vials and joints) made the rounds from bed to bed offering solace against the season and the death of the old year. It was the first chance that he and I had ever had to be buddies, not just fellow accouterments, guarded as we ever were of our respective positions. And it was the first time that I had really been able to play with the notion of being Bear's Boy, freed at last around other hierarchy of the jet-setters.

As for Mr Klein or any other potential suitor: I, of course, was strictly off limits—*nobody* "fucked" with the Bear—and though I was 90-percent sure that most anything that I did would be okay by him, I was cautious nonetheless. But I never detected any snobbery about my role in the game. I was treated, at least by all in our household, as a real live person. And though Young Jim was my age and sexy in his own right, there was no one that I would rather be bedding with than the one that I had. That didn't preclude Jimmy and me from toying with each other's panties, however, or shamelessly flaunting ourselves and teasing the other members of the household. "Nice little butt you got there."

"You want it? You gotta catch it!" We chased each other over beds full of jet-lagged guests, through closets, around the icy balconies. After all, any attractive young man will confirm that the fun is infinitely greater in the flirting and the "being desired" than it is in the consummation.

So, we partied, until Jimmy, being a bit of an alcoholic, passed out on the livingroom settee. I believe he and Randy were getting a trifle bored with one another by then—hence Rand's flirtations with me. I covered him with a comforter, and tucked a pillow under his pretty head.

The next day was a doozer. We saddled up with the appropriate ski equipment and took the lift up to the ski-slope home of Marsha and Neil Diamond, where we hung out and drank until the entire junta showed up, including Barbra Streisand and Jon Peters, and a lovely young dancer named Debbie Allen with her Motown-producer husband.

A potentially awkward situation developed. It seemed that the only ski novices were Babs and myself. But being bolstered on a mega-dose of TT1 (the only thing that could've gotten me onto a ski slope in the first place), I offered that I would be delighted to take Ms Streisand out on the baby slopes.

Barbra was clearly not happy when Jon and everyone else went off, leaving us in the hands of some geeky-but-charming young lady for basic starting-and-stopping direction.

One of the advantages of TT1 was that fear simply did not exist—neither of Barbra nor of the slopes themselves. One of the disadvantages was that I couldn't focus on a thing the poor instructor had to say and was obliged to rely on my intuition, lack of fear and basic beginner's luck. Fearlessness, I believe, was the key; that plus the fact that my body really couldn't feel a thing anyway, so there seemed no potential for getting hurt.

Ms Streisand's terror in itself gave me courage.

"Hang on, baby," I told her, "we'll survive this day yet. They're probably not expecting us back alive."

"They're probably right," she scowled.

"Come on, what's a few bruises among friends. We'll get drunk tonight and not feel a thing."

"I can't feel anything now..."

I didn't know which was colder, the snow or Barbra. Not that I blamed her for feeling pissed at being dumped on this stoned-out vixen. But I just let her smolder—in my psycho-pharmacological sang-froid, I was clearly in my own world. And the entire downhill was spent largely yanking the woman by the skis from out of drifts.

Barbra was rather chubby at the time, dressed in a dowdy plum-colored knit suit, the matching sock hat pulled down low enough to conceal hair, ears and half of her un-made-up face. She looked like any frumpy middle-aged housewife. But *everyone* noticed her, flailing her arms and screaming in horror, as she stumbled past. It was as though she were hailing a neon banner which flashed *Look! I'm Barbra Streisand!*

Perhaps it is just that New Year's in Aspen is such an infamously star-studded event that star-*gazing* is half of the experience for the vacationing laypersons. But I suspect there is another element, something like a pheromone—some unseen, unconsciously detectable particle that exudes out of these mega-stars that does in fact turn on that neon sign. I had noticed this once before when coerced by Sam into dating Bianca Jagger for sushi and dancing at the Studio—*I* would never have recognized this tiny black-draped figure with head turned down; it was as though I were dancing with a slab of pork in a river of piranha, it took all my attention to keep hands away from her and prying faces from hounding her with questions and requests for autographed biceps.

We made it to the bottom, Babs and I. I was sure that the lady was entirely too sore and humiliated ever to speak to me again. We survived, and she was almost congenial to me that evening for New Year's brouhaha.

Bear and I spent our afternoon at the casual mountain lodge of Jack Nicholson. After the tour (I was most impressed by the heated Olympic-sized swimming pool, steaming amid the leftover drifts of icy snow), we settled into the cushy sunken livingroom floor, where Jack dipped liberally into the cereal-size bowl of white crystal powder as though it were a heap of pretzels. I abstained and attempted conversation with Jack's beautiful and pristine teenage daughter, visiting for the holidays from her home in Hawaii.

Jack, I must say, is one of the more chummy and unaffected stars that I have encountered, seeming as comfortable and as graceful with his unnatural societal position as Dolly is. "So *welcome* to Aspen! *How* in *hell* do ya like it so far?"

"Well," I recalled, "I didn't die on the ski slopes my first day, no thanks to my company. I suppose that's a good sign."

"Gavin ended up in charge of Barbra today," Bear interceded.

Jack doubled his grin, "Well, if the slopes don't getcha, the fucking *stars* will!"

"I'll try to avoid them," I smiled back.

"*You* stick close to the Bear," he assured me. "*He'll* protect your ass!"

I believed that was meant as an "in" joke. I took it that way as Jack rambled on with Bear about this and that movie or director. And I swiftly noted that he was one of the *only* individuals that I detected no nuances of need or greed with Bear.

The evening was another story. An entire restaurant had been procured (I believe by Peters) for the New Year's Eve party. I was seated with the Diamonds at one large round table, the Streisands were at the table directly beside us and behind me was a table that included Cher and whatever bimbo rock-star-burn-case she was enamored of at the time. That entire table was about eight sheets to the wind, though Cher, in a nipple-tight black ski jumpsuit that Emma Peel would have frowned upon was beyond participation in any earthly celebrations. I don't recall all the faces of the night—I remember a brief conversation with John Denver, one of the Gibbs or other, downing a drink or two with parrot-head Jimmy Buffett,

Burt Bacharach and Carol Bayer Sager. It's a wonder that I can recall anything at all.

The moment of New Year's was cacophonous, though unimpressive, and I swiftly escaped with errant Jimmy to stagger our icy way back to the house, where we continued our own bacchant reveries in the dark of the livingroom, only the dim light of a gas flame burning in the fire pit, necking tentatively, wryly through the cloying vapors of booze and party breath. I would have had him, had such a thing been possible, or permissible (it *may* have been), but that was the closest that we ever got. He and Randy soon grew tired of one another and Jim Boy went on to invent some little hardware gadget that grossed him several million dollars practically overnight and moved with a new lover into a posh Malibu condo. I had most loved to listen to his beautiful voice sing cowboy songs a cappella with that charming, if affected, "sh" sound to his *S*'s that characterizes the voice of Loretta Lynn and so many other country singers.

Besides that, he had a lovely butt, and any lovely butts missed during that period were sorely lamented.

Then Bear stormed in past me. "What'd I do wrong?" I asked. I was afraid he thought I had buggered John.

"You did just fine."

"No no no, come on, what's up?"

"Well where the hell were you? Why'd you leave so early? How do you think that makes me look?"

"I don't know, Bear. I was tired. Drunk. Stoned. I wanted to be here. It was so smokey."

"I brought you as my guest. You don't just leave on me."

"I didn't *leave on you*. Besides, you weren't exactly *with me*. I mean, where was my New Year's kiss?"

"Oh fuck you! Don't go into that Bear's Boy shit!"

"Bear, if I was with you, why couldn't I sit with you at Ms Streisand's table? It's not like everyone doesn't know we're here together. What *am* I, your fucking poodle?"

"We were talking business with Jon. They're fighting like siblings. It was boring..."

"So was the rest of the party!"

"You were very stoned."

"*I* was stoned! Cher was standing on her fucking ears—you kissed *her* Happy New Year!"

"Okay, let's not go into it. I'm sorry."

"I love you Bear. I'm sorry this is so difficult for you. You want me to sleep in the living room?"

"No, don't be stupid."

"I'm sorry. I'm sorry it's so awkward for you."

"It's not awkward..."

"Well it's awkward for me! I love you and I want you to love me. But how can you love somebody that you can't even be seen with?"

"Just stop."

But the riff continued, and always would as long as I remained an alien to that society, Bear's Boy, a half-person.

The more and more I became acquainted with the whole group, the more and more vapidity I came to experience. Which isn't to imply that this hollowness applies to all the denizens of H'dom, or to demean the extraordinary talents and contributions of the Streisands, the Nicholsons, the Partons. As I've said, there was often a surprising amount of genuineness found among certain of the nobility. But keep in mind that I was largely dealing with a set of emotionally inert people for whom relationships are essentially sub rosa, at best a show.

Even among the liberal matrix of drug-crazed vacationers in Aspen, Bear and I could not hold hands, clasp each other, kiss and say *Happy New Year darling!* And Bear was continually aware of my increasing fury at the fraud. And *I* was increasingly aware of the fact that nothing that I would ever do would change that situation for us. This was not to be the romantic tale of a king leaving his dominion to marry the peasant's daughter. For even if I were to achieve such fortunes as these gentlemen had, I would still, by and by, be traded in for a fresh and less opinionated model. I was a toy, a fancy for a man-who-had-everything-else.

Which is what eventually pulled me away from that whole ballgame. That plus a hard-hitting change of direction that would ultimately send me into the halls of my quest for spiritual identity. I had seen the famous and the rich at their height, and it was not enough *for me* (even if it had *been* me). I was after something else. And other winds soon began blowing that carried me far away from that golden shore.

Bear and I, I should say, have remained friends. He became fascinated by my assorted spiritual quests, vicariously thrilled to see me grow and change. I believe he was, like my dad, envious of the freedom and the anonymity that I was still able to enjoy. Money, he always asserted, was not what life was about, and fame was hideous (he avoided it where possible). Still, his position remained fixed, and mine was amorphic. So after several years of our relationship, I split.

But when I check in, Bear is always delighted that I am well, nimbly surviving AIDS hysteria, the swill of the Hollywood charlatans, the fascist majority; and I believe always most impressed by the fact that I continue to love him sans money, fame, or even further romance. *Mon Petit Bear.*

PUSS

*One good cat is
worth a thousand lovers.*

Bear and I continued to "see each other" regularly for three years, then waffling off-again/on-again for almost a decade. We met in the late Seventies, and, although Master Bear's world was sedate by comparison, it was the height of the disco era, the apex of wanton homo culture, and I found more than ample occasion to participate in the decadence of the concentric realities of West Hollywood, San Francisco and New York.

As I've noted, Bear was in New York as often as he was out here, and while out here he was usually involved with work-related projects that I was seldom privy too. He did not expect me to be faithful—*he* certainly wasn't about to be. AIDS did not exist yet, and all that could possibly go amiss was the occasional clap, which either of our respective doctors could easily sew up in an office visit. So the fields were wide open.

Once I was comfortable with my secured status as "head boy," and once the honeymooning was clearly behind us, I ended up dating an occasional ancillary friend to the inner circle—usually someone that was in town from New York and Sam wanted to make sure was properly entertained. I invariably proved a flop, torn between my desires for further conquests, yet prideful and ever mindful of my all-important association with Bear; I had made it to the top and felt as though I were now merely reaching down. It was clear that I would never become Bear's spouse, but just how much of a strumpet was I willing to present myself to be?

On one occasion I was asked to entertain Larry Kert, in town for the LA premier production of *Side By Side (By Sondheim)* in which Larry was starring, along with Hermione Gingold and a couple of other famous Broadway broads that I had never heard of.

I sat with the cast at a one-woman sideshow that one of the ladies was doing at the Backlot Theatre. Hermione was absolutely charming, if a touch sopped, and Larry wouldn't have been bad himself had he not been walking around with such a chip on his shoulder. I guess starting out soaring (the original Tony in *West Side Story*), and then coasting steadily downhill since, was not an especially attractive haul—rather the way I felt that evening. His patter was terse and queeny.

"Sam said you *would*," he wheezed querulously when I had refused to invite him up my stairs for the night.

"Sam ain't paying for this."

"Oh... well, how much do you want?" he reached for his back pocket.

"I don't want anything. You're drunk. Go back to your hotel, let's talk tomorrow..."

He was soused. And even though he was starring in this new production, I felt as though I were going out with an all-time loser—I was already *much* too spoiled for that.

So even though Larry set me up with front row seats at opening night, and even though he winked at and greeted me during the performance, and even though he was *still* attractive, through the puffy skin and the frightened eyes, I simply couldn't follow through on our encounters. My turn-down made it back to Sam, who was pissed, and Bear, who thought it hysterical and couldn't have agreed with me more.

I really liked Hiram Keller, drop-dead-gorgeous star of *Hair* and Fellini's *Satyricon,* except again for that chip (the star who was-then-wasn't). He was also so coked out, I eventually ascertained, that there was little of any honest beast worth relating to. Still, he was beautiful, if somewhat overweight; we dated a half-dozen times over a few-week period, had a blast going out with his hysterical landlady, Susan Tyrrell, to Fellini and Wertmuller movies where the two of them would contrive their *own* versions of what the English subtitles *should've* been.

But Hiram, of course, also got put out with my lack of sexual response. We tussled more than once on one bed or another, stripped down to our briefs, leaving teethmarks and hickies in our frustration. I could suck on that famous smokey lower lip of his for hours (as he did on mine) but I'd stop there.

"Just fucking give it up!" he'd scream.

"Give it up, Gavie!" Sue-Sue would holler back, laughing outside in the hall.

I tell you, by then it was easier to perform with someone that was holding out a hundred-dollar bill than with someone who was ostensibly attractive and allegedly a "friend." Or was I simply afraid of what Bear might say if he heard the braggings of one of his coeval elites? Certainly, I was still bopping about the bathhouses and allowing myself to be boffed by profligate familiars within the porn and hustling biz. But that was de rigueur.

Some almost-stars knew I was Bear's Boy and thought I might be a vehicle to the higher heights. I became lionized as "Mr Hollywood-by-Proxy," and opted to enjoy several of these for what they were worth.

Among them was Paul Jasmine, trendy photographer and adopted son of Judy Garland. Paul latched on to me at a party at his girlfriend Marrissa Berensen's house and coerced me (it didn't take much) into letting him do some photos. We had a blast; I introduced him to TT1 and he told me all about the two years that Nancy Davis (pre-Reagan) had lived as "Judy's Girl" in the Malibu beach house, as well as about his friend who used to accompany the smarmy governor's wife on her monthly excursions to Hong Kong to purchase bulk-rate narcotics. These stories jibed with landlord Maury's tales of Miss Davis's weekly appointments with Mr Gable.

On my one unsuccessful date with Randy (the evening that we attended Elton John's birthday party and I told Rand that some smart agent or manager should snap up Tina Turner and Patti LaBelle because they were the two greatest voices in the industry and both were out of contract and he laughed at me and did another toot), he made a token call to a gentleman named Bruce who was an already successful songwriter/composer and would be willing to read through my lyrics. I was aware that this was a potential sex set-up, but I used the opportunity to actually write with Bruce and we eventually sold our first song.

Bruce lived with Herb Ritts and did the best Streisand and Midler imitations that I had seen prior to Kenny Sasha (who did both divas better than they do themselves). It helped that Bruce knew and worked with them personally. We avoided sexual confrontation with only a few cursory run-around-the-bed episodes, and enough flirting on my part to keep sparked enough interest to get out at least one song.

That was about all that Bruce and I ever got it up for. But that one song, "The Rescue," was eventually recorded by Sam Harris and Janis Ian on Sam's ill-fated second album, *Sam-I-Am* (which the vice-president of Motown, in a later moment of passion, assured me was deliberately killed by Berry Gordy because they didn't want a "little blonde fag" on their label). The single rode to a 54, nationally, with years of air-play on the beachside K-*MUSH* stations...

So I socked in about six-grand, got in the songwriters' union, and was able to legitimately call myself a lyricist.

Bruce also introduced me to *his* best friend, Bud Cort, whom I buddied around with for some time with no real strings or discomfort on either's part, double-dating on occasion with the sultry porn star Al Parker. Bud was gentle, funny, ebullient, and though hopelessly neurotic about his appearance and career, genuinely pleasant to be with.

With Bruce and Bud I chop-chopped with Gore Vidal (I had had only one dinner with him before, with Bear, and sat in complete awe—he is still one of my few secular heros) and a variety of singers including Donna Summer, whom Bruce had written a number of hits for (though who was recently Christianized, married and simultaneously on the outs).

And somewhere along the line there was a date or two with Divine—I think I was porking her manager. There's little now I can recall of the diva, except how surprisingly shy and nebbishy she seemed—perhaps they kept her sedated between gigs.

On the profane side, among the "real" people, my life became a disco.

By 1981 and 1982, when I had reached the ripe old age of 25, Donna Summer and the scourge of Casablanca musak/disco-sound-alikes, combined with ritual drugs and the "new" sexualité that they stirred, took us all to a bizarre and wonderful mystical primitive state of homo-mass ecstasy. Singular relationships were less important than ever before and drugs began teaching us many things that we didn't even want to know, and certainly had no preparation for.

Oh, these weren't the creative and mind-exploding psychedelics of the late Sixties, but they were powerfully seductive meditations nonetheless, which, in a tight and overpopulated social microcosm like West Hollywood, Frisco, Fire Island, became like unto a religion in which the penis was the god (not an unfamiliar deity, herstorically). I am happy to say that I was at the forefront of this *a*-morality, dancing my pinched titties off at Probe three nights a week on TT1, nonstop movement for every song for twelve-hour stints, until *I was* communing with the dolphins, the "saucer-people," speaking in tongues. So much so, that even sex ceased to exist as mere sex. The ritual of the dance became our sex (not the watered-down version of disco that the breeders would soon adopt in imitation of their fey sisters, nor in fact the milquetoast version that the fairies of today adopt by rote) and sex was our ritual. If sex occurred, it was often on the dance floor or along the side walls of that steamy black arena. But as often as not the sex was the endless bumpings and embraces that pervaded *during* the ritual of the dance among all the members who had made it until the wee hours of four-through-ten o'clock of the following Sunday morning. We recited song lyrics like credos. The dance was our liturgy, and orgasm; sex was merely the fore—or aft—play.

We drove home transparent. Often alone. And if not, just to crash in someone else's arms, bathtub or bed. And miraculously, thank Goddess, we *did* arrive home—unable to focus, unaware that all the world did not see as we did. It was an aesthetic that was ours, a culture, a cosmology.

Eventually Hollywood stepped in and attempted to capture some of these moments. My likeness has been preserved, I am told, on celluloid in *American Gigolo* (starring Richard Gere) on my usual platform against the wall of Probe, in ripped black attire, a bottle of amyl in one hand. I'm glimpsed as well in a movie called *Partners,* which I also haven't seen. And eventually some rock videos.

One afternoon, somewhere in 1981 or 1982, I encountered a middle-aged gentleman named Bernie.

Bernie was a charmer, a polite, soft-spoken, and sincere man, one of the only legit encounters that the streets of Hollywood would ever offer me. He flattered me; he had seen *Track Meet* (and so had recognized the... face) and affirmed that he felt I had a certain *je ne sais quoi*, a "naturalness" that would lend itself to the screen.

"Why don't you come by for dinner—and I mean dinner!" he said, immediately squelching any suspicions. "Perhaps I can point you in a direction or two."

Bernie, I discovered, had been a *very* successful manager, some time prior to having a substance-related nervous breakdown and "retiring" at an early age. He had been married for many years to my all-time fave character actress, Nancy Culp (Miss Jane Hathaway of *The Beverly Hillbillies*). He had managed the lady, along with such other clients as Marilyn Monroe, James Dean, Lee Strasburg, the entire Actor's Studio in New York, and a young man who had lived with Strasburg, Monroe, Dean—a lad named John Sarno, who now taught acting in Los Angeles, something called "The Method." With nothing more than a skillfully executed dinner, pleasantly jocular conversation, a positive appraisal of my acting ability (if *Track Meet* had been acting), and a ride home, Bernie and I ended the evening with my promise to attend an acting class the next night.

John Sarno was astonishing to watch, a genius, as much of a showman himself in teaching as he was a *teacher*. I found his energy explosive; he was quite sexy in a slight, pompous, intimidating sort of way. Although not especially petite (about 5' 10"—my own height) he seemed to suffer from what I later came to refer to as small-person's disease, something which Sal had dealt with gracefully, but which plagues so many—the need to act as though they are that much *bigger* than anyone else.

John had suffered as a kid from a degree of palsy or rickets or something that had made his legs a bit twisted and frail—he always wore baggy trousers to conceal this. Through his childhood, he recounted endlessly, he had lived through many sexual and other violent abuses. Or perhaps it was growing up in the shadows of such giants as Strasburg, Dean, Hoffman, De Niro, himself never achieving quite the tenure.

I would seduce him and become a star.

"Bernie's recommendation is all *I* need." John smiled at us both. "Anyway, with your looks you'll have no problem at all getting the jobs; it's my job to make sure that you can *keep* them! You can start this week if you're ready."

I did. I never saw Bernie again, though John would occasionally recapitulate a conversation they had had. Eventually Bernie got a gig managing a restaurant in Dallas and moved out of town.

"Welcome," John shooed me into the room with a handful of other students flitting about, securing their scattered seats. He personally seated me in a center chair, his hand remaining on my shoulder for over a minute as he rattled off the instructions for the opening exercise. I didn't know whether or not I truly wanted to be an actor, but Sarno sure as hell had me intrigued.

Classes were two nights a week and one afternoon, from four to six hours long. We began each session with a relaxation exercise, our chairs facing John at the opposite end of the studio. All summer long I made certain to wear unseemly, loose-fitting shorts through which my genitals could be sporadically viewed from where the teacher sat. I wasn't acting, I was acting out. Why did Mom travel with me wherever I went?

As we focused inward, relaxing muscle after muscle, groaning to dispel unwanted tensions, Sarno would walk the room and spontaneously grab a body part and shake or revolve it until finding a nuance of resistance.

"Release that!" he'd bark, and I'd feel my limbs go limp and my gonads wax hard. Other times he would manipulate my jaw or neck and linger for two raw seconds, his parietal hand on my thigh as he instructed the girl beside me. I can't honestly say that I ever received any special fondles that everyone else *didn't* receive, but I always imagined that I did.

From the relaxation exercise we would go into upright postures with all mouths moaning and chirping and limbs revolving and falling—resembling, I'm sure, a coven of zombies from *The Day of the Dead*. And on into the assorted Stanislavskian "sense-memory" methods designed to engender and enliven a role.

I didn't give a whit about enlivening a role, I simply wanted to be a star. But what I came to love the most (besides the endless subtle flirtations and possible reciprocations from John) were the inner workings of my own psyche. This seemed a follow-up to the aborted Barrigian voice sessions begun under Sam's auspices, and brought up images and memories of childhood that I had long-ago lost altogether.

I stuck with these classes for six years and they became a principal outlet for emotions, for the developing of my incipient sense of self, my awareness of myself as a feeling, loving, hurting and passionate homo sapien animal/spiritual being. Eventually I came to master certain techniques with such suppleness that John would stand me up as an illustration for new students, screaming off his rapid commands of "a smell," "bitter taste," "intense heat with a cold external object," as I jumped about, folded over, chuckling, weeping or flushing with fever, all in three-second intervals.

What I didn't do well was the inevitable scene work. Why should *I* be interested in *someone else's* words? I was a poet myself, after all. And I was interested in *truth*, not in deception!

That cinched it, and I knew, I didn't want to be Stanley Kowalski, I wanted to be *me*.

John eventually came to focus more and more on the scenes as students became more and more frantic about going out on auditions. Pish posh. And besides that, I would *never* get it together with the man romantically— he had a decided taboo about such relations with students.

Classes became more and more serious, but I did not, at least not about acting. I did attend occasional interviews, did some walk-ons, a Bob Hope special, Pat Boone, and got stepped on by King Kong—fun stuff...

I also played Snoopy in *You're a Good Man, Charlie Brown* at USC, making a bit of a hit, despite forgetting the verses of several solo numbers. I was dating the director. I got a mere two notes short of getting the lead in *Jesus Christ Superstar* (my hair had grown out) getting called back three times—but by the third time I had developed the flu and dropped down to a bass. And I got directly into the head casting office for the film, *Grease*. The casting director, Joel Thurm, was in tears in an effort to get a good reading out of me—he wanted my look—but my reading was abysmal, I gave him all the wrong things, and only later in classes on "cold reading" discovered what a turkey I had made of myself.

It didn't matter, I *really* didn't want to act.

❦ ❦ ❦

Of all the hearts and stars that I courted and collected over these years, there was one that steadily hovered above all the others, inspiring me to forge on when all of my bridges were collapsed.

One evening in the autumn of 1982, in a light rainy mist, I was returning from Sarno's class to my Robertson Boulevard gallery-abode. It was growing dark early for the overcast sky and I was not walking at my normal leisurely pace. As I turned down La Cienega and headed into the parking lot of the local Norm's (the cheapest food in town), I was immediately accosted by a bedraggled clump of calico I dubbed "Puss."

"Well, good afternoon to you too!"

Barely old enough to be out on her own, Puss was getting wet and screaming vitriolic curses into the street. She was pissed and she was hungry. And she had pegged *me*.

I had grown up with a eunuch male named "Tammy," ever referred to as my "baby brother." Through a childhood of loneliness, fear, and boredom, Tammy was the center of my emotional well-being. He lived for twenty-four years, though I was long gone before he died. I was adopted by a gorgeous gray, "Rosie," at Cal Arts (hawks got him), and the summer after by a stunning Persian dude in Seattle that I tearfully left with the chum who took over my Capital Hill garden apartment. I was not ready to be fettered and torn by a feline—I was having enough trouble managing a half-dozen men a day...

I darted into Norm's, ate a greasy meal and returned through the lot. Puss was waiting, her fur matted from the storm and her eyes pointed. As I headed down La Cienega, she loped along, two steps behind me, mewing in the onslaught.

Three blocks later I dove into Aunt Tilly's Health Foods in the Design Center. Puss was waiting impatiently when I came back out wielding two small cans of designer pet food. She diligently followed me the five blocks home, chastening me at every corner. I helped her up the stairs and over the clean carpet into my little back quarters where she happily ate, bathed, and took over the bed.

Now that Craig was finding other pursuits, Vinnie had vanished, and the job of seeing gentlemen was occupying so much of my time, Puss became my one constant. She would pop out on the rooftop and visit neighbors when the action in bed got too unnerving to sleep or reasonably bathe, but she would return when I was finally alone—aloof, loving, ever mindful of her splendid coat.

I cannot emphasize enough the sanity that this tenacious totem provided by insisting on cultivating my world the way she did (as my poetry attests). Through my escalating drug days, my bad trips, my whoring, my bouts with poverty, self-loathing, and ecstasy, Puss alone was the stone in my pocket that kept me from blowing away.

Once again my life revolved around the care and feeding of something other than myself; a consistent pillow for my tears amid irreparably tangled loves, losses and psychic upheavals. A year later we moved together to a dramatic two-bedroom apartment on Hammond Street, just below the Nine-Thousand Building off the Strip with a fabulous view of all of West Hollywood, Beverly Hills, and beyond to the sea. During my stint in San Francisco, she was cared for by a psychotic temporary roommate, Manny, and when I headed east for a brief monastic sojourn, two lover-friends, Steve and Al, took her in and treated her as their own. We ended up in a communal situation in a charming old house on Westbourne, across from the Bodhi Tree Bookstore. Kittens that invaded us gradually pushed Puss further and further from me, until she became ill from neglect, refusing to come into the house to eat for long periods of time. She was the tender age of seven when she simply didn't return to me. I knew she had died.

...And that she would reincarnate... as a splendid little squealer named "Marlene" that I delivered myself.

RAYMOND

*The true poet
never sleeps twice
in the same bed.*

It was the age of disco, and a man's desirability was judged principally by his dance. My own extensive studies definitively indicated that a person who did not boogie well on the disco floor would not boogie well in a bed. This is not to say that because two persons danced well together that they were headed for a lifetime of bliss, but it was at least an indication that a toss in the sack would come up with more than just potatoes. That is, at least as long as the chemical intake were in sync.

Amid all of these divine dervishes, one stood out. There was something about the way he moved, the relentlessness of his belief in the dance, thick black mustache and sad, anywhere-else eyes, his African-esque derriere.

Raymond took some pursuing.

He intimidated me; he was impervious to my predatory glances, in his own private disco world. Maybe the fact that he had no essential need for me kept me sniffin' 'round his door. When I asked him to dance, he always consented, surprised, and we danced. But he would eventually thank me and return to his buddies.

One evening, years into this pursuit, at a smelly little Latin disco known as "The Circus," his buddies never showed. And Craig was not with me.

We danced two dances, maybe three when I asked, "Can we... go home together sometime?"

"Let's leave now," he said simply, no smile in his black puppy-dog eyes. He might've been in shock: he acted as though I had merely asked for directions to the nearest 7-Eleven.

"I didn't drive," I stated. "I'll ride with you."

"Then we'll go to my place. It's a mess."

"Great, I love messes."

We left for his tiny undecorated apartment. It was dingy, dark, with vulgar fake-wood paneling. I asked if we might shower together. "Sure," he said. That was all. He certainly wasn't much for words. Or amenities of any sort. Life was basic for Ray. A job, dancing, the minimal no-fuss package food, sex if it happened.

Sometime later Ray confirmed being surprised at my entree. He said that it never had occurred to him that someone as beautiful as me would be interested in someone that looked like him.

"I've been ogling you for four years now," I told him, "along with everybody else in the discos."

He looked absolutely blank, like he didn't understand the language that I was speaking.

"You never even gave me a second glance."

"Didn't think there was any point," he muttered.

Though he eventually came to say that he loved me, I never had a clue what that might have meant. Granted, we were on drugs almost nonstop for our entire period together, but it was almost as though we needed the drugs to touch base *at all.*

That first night I caressed his gentle sway-back and succulent butt as though it were the Christ Child—it *was* to me. I felt embarrassed to pay so little homage to his face, which I adored as well, and made the effort to lose myself beneath his heavy Italian/Syrian mustache in marathon kisses. Nervously I entered him, until he said *enough,* that he needed to sleep.

In the morning I insisted on sex again, somnolent little curmudgeon that he was, in case I should never again have the chance. "All right already." He kicked me. "Give it a rest, it still hurts from last night!"

He made us a dreadful pile of solidified eggs and singed white bread.

On our second date, he informed me that he was moving to San Francisco. "But why?"

"I don't know. I'm tired of LA." He shrugged. "Need a change. I'll get a job there..."

I was devastated. But within minutes I informed him that I too needed a change. I would move to San Francisco with him, I had friends there, work, we could get a better place *together,* we would be married and very very happy away from Hollywood.

Again he was dumbfounded. But amused. He chuckled his *Yes.*

Rather frequently around this time I was vacationing to San Francisco. I had ascertained that I had already "had" everybody in LA that I had ever wanted to have, so I began cruising SF. Within a few visits, I was having affairs with the three hottest men in the city. This took an inhuman amount of effort to maintain, a lot of flying time, a lot of juggling and lying, a lot of sex.

When Ray became my last great LA conquest, I was ready to go most anywhere with him. This didn't answer what to do about Robert, Jay and Jim—but who can see in such a lust storm? I was sure that a way would be found to maintain my honest affairs with *all of them,* and be completely true to Raymond at the same time. I did, after all, *love them all;* but Ray was, by a long shot, my number one. After Dalton and Vince, he was my "third husband."

Leave it to say that Jo, Peter and Craig took my move north as the final crack-up. But like everything that I did, the family just nodded, cried if they were so inclined, and bid me adieu.

Raymond left the very next week; we didn't even have time for a final date. I was ready the following week and moved into the already-secured basement apartment on world-famous Haight Street, just across from the north entrance to Buena Vista Park where Janis Joplin had sung her guts out so many times back at the turn of the century—1969 and 1970. It was a dreary mildewed hole of a place—though Raymond hated light and noise and volunteered for me the street-side bedroom. The long hall fed into an industrial-sized kitchen, a funky old toilet room, and fed out into one of Frisco's mysterious backyard commons that only the city dwellers ever get to see. I liked it.

Playing house and sleeping with Raymond was thus far the greatest joy of my crash-course life. Though our communication remained perfunctory, we developed an argot that at times appeared almost fluid, even intimate. When *that* failed, there were always more drugs.

Raymond had to be careful with the TT1 (as did most people) or he would simply turn into furniture for twelve to twenty-four hours. I monitored his intake and put up with his occasional use of marijuana, supplied by his best friend Joey, who slept in the living room. When I wanted to be where Raymond was, chemical-wise, I would occasionally indulge myself, hating the high (or lack of one), but craving the congruous allegiance with my spouse.

Sex was ecstatic, even when it was bad. Crying was a joy. I wrote and wrote and wrote, work that would eventually be edited into a book called *Notes From a Marriage*.

But I soon came to discover Ray's ulterior motives for this move. He was bored with the LA disco scene. A massive new disco known as Dreamland was opening down in the industrial part of town. Joey was to be the weekend DJ. And what a dream it was. A "surprise" performance by Sylvester, gorgeous men by the trainloads, Raymond on my arm and dancing all about me in his bubble-butt Levi's and flaming blue spandex tanktop. Pandemic drug use; a waltzing pharmacopeia.

By four in the morning (closing time) we could have blown home in the slightest breeze, and in fact did opt to simply walk—the city was so dreamy at that time, empty but for occasional street people along the long haul up Market, past the anachronistic rows of painted ladies to our cushy little Haight Street burrow. We bathed, simulated fucking, and then crawled out my open window to enjoy the morning, tea in hand, a joint for local passers-by. The dykes next door introduced themselves and joined us with donuts and cereal. Local cats purred by for the leftover milk.

It was *joy*, as totally as physical reality can supply it.

I didn't even think of work. Eventually Raymond got a great yuppie position with Crocker Bank ushering in their new computer banking systems—a job that would've killed me, but one he actually enjoyed—he loved getting up in the morning, assembling his dress-up clothes, flirting with the secretaries who thought him so adorable.

I enjoyed the time alone, seeing the husband off after a quick morning poke, getting to spend days with Bob, Jay, Jim.

Robert, who was out and about as one of the key bachelors in town, simply didn't "get" my instant marriage to this chummy little ethnic person. But we danced at Dreamland, Bob and I—and eventually with Raymond, the three of us together. And soon I began working with Bob, as moving men, the two of us hauling massive Victorian antiques up and down endless third-floor walk-ups. It was a challenging job, great exercise, good under-the-counter money, and, with Robert, endlessly sensual.

Ray thought Bob gorgeous and wondered why I didn't just marry *him* instead. But that was always an issue with Ray, a source of discomfort, that everyone at the disco went gaga for me and (he imagined) wondered what the fuck I was doing with this little twerp.

"I *love* the little twerp" was all I could ever assure him.

"Indeed!" he would say and brush by me with that insipid naked tush, obliging me to pursue him down the hall and drag him back, tickling and biting, to our marriage bed.

He didn't expect me to be faithful; he never asked me to. Jay was never an issue, since he had a lover and a completely workable relationship into which I had been allowed to intrude. He and Ray hit it off great. Jay got mugged and had to have his jaw wired shut; I used to visit for his noon meal, feed him blender drinks through a straw, then fuck him out on their rooftop with his stainless steel grinning in the summer sun.

The third moll, Jim, was a recluse, a kept boy by some mysterious creature that I was never allowed to meet. The most beautiful man that I had ever experienced, I met him in the park one afternoon and followed him straight home. With the excuse that he had had some ass work performed surgically, he was one of the few men that I allowed to conquer me first. I insisted, however, to be arranged near enough a mirror that I could watch his classic bums pumping me from behind. He lived in the shadow of Victorian Frisco, read astrology, the *I Ching*, Tarot cards; he was my special occasion.

Raymond and I developed a tidy way of appeasing my lust, my vanity, and giving his own vicarious thrills with a minimal amount of exertion. We checked into the Club Baths downtown as soon as Ray got off work. I headed straight for the gym and worked out, Ray looking on, until I felt pumped and desirable. Then we secured a room and began cruising around, checking out the locals. By and by I asked Ray if he had spotted anyone in particular that he had a hankering for. He pointed out some wiry young fop monitoring his own action in a hallway mirror and I excused myself to chat the lad up and lead him back to our room. Ray was delighted as I spread our friend open before him and performed my studied gymnastics.

This was a routine that we came to repeat frequently, Ray sometimes participating, but as often as not simply content to watch, touch now and then, or kiss me while I climaxed inside our partner. It was a method that we found to accomplish a number of things: Ray loved to watch me work out, we both enjoyed the waters, the unwinding, the dark and the mystery of the mazes, and I could control my appetite without overwhelming poor Ray (or, at times, work Raymond into enough of a libido to overcome his post-job blahs).

Then we would go home, eat pasta, and he would crash in front of the TV while I listened to music, wrote songs or poems, and awaited the appropriate moment to carry his limp and passive body into my bed, often spending an hour or more gently toying with that protruding belly, his flaccid cock, the corolla of hair under his arms or between the smile of his buttocks. Soon he would grumble, slap me and yank the covers up over his head. I would continue with a new round of poems.

I had another friend, one whom I would always stay with prior to our actual move to the city (three blocks up Haight) named Rosie. Rosie (Charlie Rosenbaum) had been a drag-queen dancer with the irreligious "Le Ballet de Trockadero de Monte Carlo," back before they got slick. I had met him several years before, when Sam had called me from his suite at the Pierre in New York, in bed with the flu. I flew out to keep him company and feed him his broth. Once there, he grew restless with me about and suggested that I go out and have some fun. I did. While wandering down Central Park South I ran into Rosie, leftover dance gear and all. We both passed, turned, and walked back face to face. He offered to take me to the Y to steam and I accepted, then on to his apartment for greasy redheaded sex and brown rice. Though we were rarely again romantic, our alliance as artists and our love of dominating any dance floor instantly created an invincible camaraderie.

Rosie took me to the Anvil, the Toilet, and other establishments wherein the fashionable, the bejeweled, and formally attired mingled with the naked, the tattooed, and the chained, who swung screaming from slings with cocktails up their asses or crouched shivering in bathtubs full of urine. Going to these was a crossing over of the River Styx, a voyage into a world of elegant depravity. We melted into corners and smooched, chewed off morsels of blotter acid and empathized for a time with the catabolic sturm und drang—knowing all along in our hearts that we were but spies from a safer realm.

When Rosie moved out to San Francisco I began regular visits. He, Ray and most of my other friends participated with me in some of the most dangerous drug use imaginable. We would toot up TT1—whatever it was—alongside angel dust-laced dope, barbiturates, amphetamines, and acid downed with a vodka chaser. We were operating, as were the prevailing times, under the axiom "less is more but more is better"; we didn't know different—this illiterate and two-faced society gives few lessons on the applications of "ceremonial" drugs, short of the donnish *just say no*, which is tantamount to telling a fifteen-year-old not to masturbate.

We survived by Divine Grace alone. We spent nights at the various discos in states of awe, rapture, horror and revelation. Consciousness was flying and it was all any of us could do to keep up with it. All belief systems were laid to rest; we were on survival mode.

There were nights spent with friends and strangers creating forms of sexuality that I can now barely recall. I can't imagine being able to live through such times again, but I cherish every moment that we *did* have, and would never condemn another soul to have or to *not have* the experiences that I did. They made me what I am, helped me overcome baggage that I had carried since childhood (and before) and convinced me beyond all preconceptions and societal shibboleths that God was a viable living reality, and that I was a part of that reality that would never falter.

Eventually my TT1 ran out. I returned to LaLa-Land for another round. As our dealer had forewarned, it no longer existed; we had exhausted the supply. All over underground New York, Fire Island, and West Hollywood, we select few were wailing. Something had come to a natural completeness; my life would change.

Now, three months after my arrival in San Francisco, Ray was just a part of the workaday world. It was 1980. Despite the success of Dreamland, disco was on the outs. And I had a career to manage. More important, a God to discover.

I loved Ray, I always would, but I needed to be home. Back to the Center of the Universe. LA. I had had the time of my life. Now it was time for the rest of my life.

Ecstasy is a narrow gate through which all must pass. I had been there with Ray a number of times; I wanted to learn to go there alone.

NED

He who knows God
has no need of faith.

Even as Raymond and I explored the alleys of heaven and hell, during our brief San Francisco sojourn together, my spirit began exploring less transitory realms—before, during, and after Ray—with Neddie, whom I'd met during my year of darkness with Flip. With him as my traveling companion, I would explore my past, even my future, and, more importantly, that ever-present ocean of self that remains unchanged as these ripples of apparent reality ebb and flow.

Ned was Flip's best friend, more due to the misfortune of both hailing from Chelsea than for any true social concentricity. Ned said he couldn't see what a good-looking reasonably literate fellow like me would be doing with a scrawny nervous tic like his friend.

Swiftly we realized we shared more than a frustrating bond with Flip. Ned had secrets to share that sparked my own inner quest. Yes, I believed in reincarnation, yes, I was familiar with Freud, Jung, and Janov, and I had been an avid Bahá'í for two years back in high school and was at least basically familiar with the tenets of Buddhism/Hinduism/Islam, if always from an outsider's perspective. That was good enough for Ned. He had a soul mate.

He gave me a seminal book, *Realms of the Human Unconscious* by Stan Grof. It was a direct hit. In the three years since I'd begun my California journey, I had been vastly impressed by the initial works of Arthur Janov and had come in part to look at Southern California as a location for Child Gavin's psychological salvation. But encounters with Janov's post-primal completees had left me with a very sour taste—all had dissuaded me from pursuing Primal Therapy—and I was wanting for something sweet to fill in the crevasse.

Grof took the basic primal stance that all neurosis is created and locked in in the early stages of a body's development, from ages one to six, and that certain rebirthing techniques were intrinsic to confront and transcend this tangled morass of conscious blocks and defenses in order to bring an individual to full truth, love, and personal power. The technique prescribed was LSD (or psychedelic) therapy, which Grof had been performing with alarming successes for more than a couple of decades, alleviating every symptom from pedophilia to heroin addiction.

But even more astonishing were the accounts of eventual past-life unions/remembrances/awakenings, spiritual transcendence, ego death and the varying stages of ultimate enlightenment. This jibed (in radically different terms) with the premises and texts of Carlos Castenada's *The Teachings of Don Juan* and with *Autobiography of a Yogi* by Swami Yogananda (though the latter had no association with drugs).

I was enthralled. And as with all major decisions in my life, I didn't wait for the invitation. I called Neddie instantly. "Ned, we have to do this!"

"Are you serious?"

"Absolutely. I'm ready when you are. I'll ask my dealer if he can get us some pure acid. I'm sure he can."

"Wowie Zowie!" Ned trumpeted across the wires.

By then Flip was all but out of the picture, and the fundamentals laid bare in the LSD sessions completely eradicated any desire to put up with the bullshit associated with cocaine and its kind. Ned and I were on our own. We were also writing songs together, doing little sets at songwriters' showcases, Ned always singing in his strained but quaint post-Dylan nasal whine. We even won a contract for one song that was professionally demoed and then went nowhere. We were paid $200 for it, which bought a lot of acid.

A very portentous coincidence occurred one weekend in San Francisco, when I flew up to dance with Rosie at a massive all-night disco bash in a vacant downtown warehouse. (This was before I met Raymond.) We did every drug known to modern fagdom and sweated oceans by the time the Sunday sun was getting high and the DJ pooped out. As we were floating out the door in our stupor, I bent down without a question and scooped up a little plastic envelope, which I tucked into my soggy denim. It wasn't until we had made it home that I realized I'd found green sheets containing over two hundred individual hits of acid.

Rosie and I were set, for future parties—though it eventually came to pass that my system was so wide open and emotion-shocked that I could no longer drop LSD in a social setting without ending up on the floor screaming, fetaling, talking in tongues and choking on afterbirth. But, if I had needed a sign—which I didn't—this would've been it. Ned and I were set.

We began the therapy and continued for the longest time at Ned's South Hollywood apartment. His suburban street was quiet, most of his neighbors worked, there was little or no business traffic, and the bedroom that we used was on the second floor and buffered by the upper branches of a row of sycamore trees.

Me being me, and Ned being chicken, I of course went for the first session.

We had both by now all but memorized Grof's drug therapy guides, so we knew what to expect—or so we thought. I had done acid before and had had some rather pleasant and even eye-opening experiences; but this was radical, it *worked*.

Fifteen minutes or so after I'd swallowed my dose, having fasted the day before and thoroughly purged my stomach and intestines, I began to be drawn into a fetal position in the middle of Neddie's bedroom floor.

The time I lay there seemed endless to Ned, who only knew to watch me and wait, his big gray eyes awash with fear, for three hours, not sure whether to slap me or call 911. And endless it was for me, as my brain and spirit swept through an eternal cosm of faces, sounds, smells associated with birth—growing silently in my mother's belly, aware of my presence in and around her, aware of her thoughts and conceits, and the ever-reassuring presence of my father.

I was infuriated at my mother's thoughts about her figure, that she would have no more children after me. I lived her anxiety as we sat waiting in a hallway door for my dad to come striding up the front walk and take us to the hospital.

Eventually I began to move, choking and sputtering on the afterbirth in my throat and nose, coughing out the final taste of blood as the pain of life came flooding into my lungs for the very first time: what ecstasy, what complete awareness I had at that moment!

In this first experience and for quite some time to follow, my hands would come up from the fetal prayer, cover my head, and then push down as they simulated the womb contracting and expanding around me. Rugs, pillows, blankets, all became tools to reenact the pains and the awakenings of the birth experience. With each birth I would experience, a new body part would awaken into remembering—an external layer of skin, the muscles of my cheeks and neck, my eyes as they witnessed daylight for the first time, my nostrils as they opened and inhaled. Part of me by precious part, my consciousness shifted to embrace each new aspect of that ascension from the dark, infernal womb into this phantasmic realm of light, breath, and fire.

As I returned again and again to these experiences, which went on for many months, I could only piece together the unfathomable notion of "birth." And yet that little frail creature, that *me*, knew more at that moment than my parents and the doctor all combined, for I was aware of *what I was*, a swirling dancing and convulsing embryo of God, a cosmography of light and thought, the breath of the universe, the witness to eternity.

There were other experiences. There was the unnecessary attack of the doctor to my derriere, there was the experience of being presented to my mother for the first time, of the breast, of my dad's beloved visitations. I went through another whole round, somewhat different; the same doctor, same mother, but different nurse, different nuances. I eventually discovered I was going through the birth of a baby that was born a year before me. I recalled being thrust a bottle on which to feed—Mom was worried about her breasts—the stench of the nasty rubber nipple, the formula that *was not* my mother's milk. I taught her a lesson; I refused the bottle. I became weak; she was intransigent—it was a battle of wills. On the third day I rolled over onto my face and stopped breathing.

Then I experienced the room in which my parents were to *reconceive* me.

Mother was afraid of having another baby die. I would have reassured her, but she could not hear me. But Dad knew that I was there, that it would be a good birth and that I would live. He had much more spiritual aplomb, I concluded, than I ever gave him credit for.

The second birth was good. Gertrude had learned her lesson; I responded well to her breast and, even though I was a month premature, grew fast and strong.

Not all of these experiences happened that first session. Many did, though the overlapping of experiences was constant as the focus shifted from nervous system to musculature to bones to that networking of synapses that was the brain itself.

The remembrances grew, sometimes larger, encompassing more of the outside world. I relived my animosity toward my brother, a resentful three-year-old who had me wrapped up in a wool blanket, all but asphyxiating, and was slinging me around my parents' bed until Mother returned to the room and rescued me. Having lost the child in between, Mom doted on me, leaving poor Mark out of the picture. I eventually grew to learn that I could blame most any travesty on him and know that he would be the one punished, even for things that were blatantly my fault. He and I have waged a battle that was settled only in our adulthood by almost complete lack of communication for the last twenty years.

And there was the ultimate trauma of my childhood, when I walked into my mother's bedroom and found her in the embrace of a man who was not my father.

I took their act to be violence against my mother. But on another level, I understood what was happening, and understood this to mean that all that I had come into this world to expect—a happy and harmonious loving family —was no longer possible, that my mother *did not* love my father.

I split; my spirit jumped straight through my spine and wasted no time in getting to the gateway to the world on the other side. Beings there, however, let me know that it was not my "time," that I must live this one through, surmount and learn to forgive this recalcitrant woman who would become my nemesis.

I returned into my toddler self, to a body that had damaged its spine (the split occurred at what I later came to recognize as my second chakra, my sexual center; as my body collapsed without my consciousness to hold it up, the left knee struck the floor beneath me, creating a shock that was received directly in the spine behind the sex center, chipping off a fragment of one of the lower lumbar, which still plagues my posture, back, and leg motion to this day). I returned with one thought, that *I will never love a woman, women are treacherous and cannot be trusted.*

This was the beginning of what I came to understand as my homosexuality. I was two.

I would discover spiritual ramifications, choices that I made prior to this life *to become* a homosexual for the experiences of persecution, living through the plague of AIDS, contending with contemporary pseudo-Christian hate/dogma, and above all my own balancing of the scales of the masculine and the feminine in my soul.

I, as a two-year-old who was not physically or emotionally *able* to vie against his mother, became essentially her little confidant. I *knew* her secret! Unable to discern what I could or could not tell my dad, that man that I loved so totally, I simply became shut off from him—I was silent, pensive, eventually afraid. I did what my mother told me, said what I was expected to say. Dad began drinking. And though this affair of Mom's was nipped in the bud, what came to pass was the separation of all members of the family, my mother and I in collusion to create the façade of happiness.

All of this came to me through these sessions. My mother, whom I had always pretended to love, I came to perceive as the villain. For Dad, from whom I was estranged, I began to have greater love, if not respect. We had a good talk about it, he and I, over the phone. He immediately corroborated what I had remembered. "You know I always suspected those two," he said, "but I just never could prove it."

I gave him the strength to move out on his own, where he eventually discovered and married a saint of a woman who was able to love him as much as he loved her. This, also, became the ending of my alliance with my mother.

Then I realized a pattern, a peculiar obsession with hairy Italian gents who all looked frightfully like Mother's paramour: *I was living out her fantasies!*

(I am completely aware these circumstances are only *my* circumstances. I have come to believe that my preference for men has as much to do with a fear and distrust of women as it does an actual *need* or attachment toward a father or other men. In no way do I suppose this to be true of other male-attracted men, much as I am aware of female-loathing and scary, unwholesome relationships between many brethren and their mothers. There are as many thoroughly different stories as there are individuals, and as many reasons for a person's particular sexual variances—if reasons are required—as there are persons. I am also convinced, in hindsight, that I would've created other circumstances to produce a very similar effect in myself had this encounter with my mother and her lover *not occurred*, as I am convinced that my life, at least up until the now moment, was intended to be experienced as a man who is attracted to other men.)

I further went on to the recovery of a lifetime situation in which my mother and I had, in fact, *been* lovers. I was a member of the Roman Guard, and, upon returning one evening from a rugged day on the battlefield, found this same woman (my wife) in the embrace of one of my superiors. I stabbed them both to death.

This "recollection" consequently gave me the understanding that my present-day life is a blessing—now, rather than being in a situation where I resolved conflict by killing it, I am allowed the lifetime and the reflection to go past this anger, and to bring this lack of understanding into awareness.

❦ ❦ ❦

Ned's sessions were more stagnant, slower to get going as his ponderous defense systems fought him tooth and nail. He would become listless, bored, stuck, as it were, his curly brown hair matted about the pillow, his penis shrunken and retreated, lying for hours, muttering, "This is horrible. It's horrible. I can't stand it. Horrible..."

I had my days too, trapped in the entrance to the womb, too late to go back, unable to go forward. *This* was Hell. It went on and on for us, the tripper choking, breathing so sparsely that the "sitter" would panic thinking that the "patient" had died. We screamed, wailed, vomited and pissed ourselves, drawn on only by the glimmering hope of enlightenment, the time in which all this biomorphic trauma and earthly business would be complete.

We moved from Ned's apartment to my brighter and airier modern apartment on Hammond, but as the noise level grew ever more intense, security became more awkward, we moved into the stockroom of the Postal Instant Press on the Strip.

I had begun working at PIP some months before, mainly graphic design, avoiding customers as much as possible and hiding at my desk in the back. My boss was a delightfully overly literate psychotic who wrote daily political quips for Joan Rivers in his spare time. Manny lived in a seedy part of town miles away, didn't drive, and had to schlep to work by bus every morning. I had tapered off the prostitution racket, finding it increasingly difficult to jibe those mixed energies with the constant unraveling that the LSD was presenting to me. So, needing the extra rent, and having a second bedroom no longer filled with Flip's I-*heart*-LA paraphernalia, I offered Manny the room; we were only a half-block from PIP.

It was a comfortable association, with the exception of the nights when Manny would wake up screaming in dreamtime terror. Best of all, he was an avid cat fancier and stayed in the apartment taking dutiful care of Puss during my months in San Francisco with Raymond. When I returned, Manny was freaking out, having been wrangled himself by a hustler or two; he eventually made off with a great deal of cash from PIP as well as an eighteen-hundred-dollar loan from me I never got back.

Be that as it may, Manny thought the world of Ned and me. He was totally intrigued by the idea of the therapy, and agreed to allow us to use the storeroom on Sunset in exchange for doing sessions of his own.

Neither of us could fathom the idea of such an intensely nervous individual acting as "guide," and yet Ned agreed to monitor his sessions. Manny, it turned out, had been born to two neurotic surgeons who had attempted his abortion at about six months, at home, placing the newborn in a bathroom trashcan. Hence Manny's tireless LSD litany "Baby's in the bucket, baby's in the bucket..." When the child refused to die, his semi-repentant parents drove him to the hospital, where he was placed in an incubator and survived. There were other fine moments, such as the time his mother slashed his naked toes with a kitchen knife because he wouldn't stop crying.

Needless to say, poor Ned would come out of those sessions looking more hysterical and soul-raped than he did even from his own. He called me one night in San Francisco and said that he was going straight, no more LSD, no more Manny! I was amazed he lasted as long as he had.

When I returned to LA, the spring of '80, I closed up that expensive Hammond apartment and moved into a lovely old studio on Keith Avenue. It was serene, off the street, and had a private backyard.

"Hey, great place to do acid," Ned avowed with a wry smile.

"You serious?"

"Yeah, I'm dyin' to."

"Ready when you are!"

Here the most traumatic and humorous experience of our sessions occurred. I became certain that I was the Christ reborn, the Second Coming, but that poor Ned was an instrument of the Devil sent to keep me from accomplishing my "mission." While he semi-dozed, as was his wont, I simply slipped out into the garden and around the corner, heading up the street to find my friend Al, who for some reason I was sure would drive me to the mountains where I would blossom into my full Divine Self.

Fortunately Ned came to, realized that I was not in the yard, and came hauling after me.

Ned is a very shy person by nature. Chasing up city streets after a long-haired man clad only in a bathtowel shouting "I have seen the Lord!" at the top of his lungs was not Neddie's idea of a good time. Bless his chubby little heart.

The image that stays with me the strongest is my encounter with a 200-pound black postal lady. I looked her angrily in the eyes as I approached and shouted my greeting, "I have seen the Lord!"

She looked back at me, as casually as only a 200-pound black postal woman can, nodded her head and said, "Umm hmm," without so much as breaking her stride.

Ned told me later he saw some queen out attending to his garden, spying me racing up to him wearing but my towel, about to pinch a loaf with excitement, when I screamed "I have seen the Lord!" Ned said he looked like someone had pulled the string out of his pearls.

How we didn't get arrested on Sunset Strip I'll never know. Ned caught up with me as we marched in tandem through the noonday business crowd of trendy music execs and secretaries on my way to find Al.

Al wasn't home. We sat on his steps until Ned had talked me down. We headed back.

That was the beginning of the end. Not only was Ned completely rattled by the experience, but this "Jesus" stuff was getting into areas that *he* wanted to approach but couldn't. More than that, though, was the realization that we were playing with fire, dealing with explosions of being that were beyond what we could safely unfold in these less-than-clinical circumstances. We were becoming aware of how dangerous and precarious a process this was.

We continued more sporadically, but back at Ned's place.

Not only did the Christ complex return, but the energy that would be released off my head, hands, and arms was so intense that Ned could sit there and trip off the *shakti*. No more birth traumas, every cell of my being was radiant with consciousness, with *God*.

Future sessions revealed greater and greater awareness. My body would die, seemingly, and I would shoot out into the cosmos, understanding the essential balance of nature, the *yin* and the *yang*. I would come back remembering the future; *my* future, even Ned's—I saw myself shot to death while on a stage somewhere, the perfection of that moment, and all the various successes and failures leading up to that time.

At one point my brain simply stopped. No more thoughts. No judgments. No time. Simply the experience of the *Eternal Now*.

But I understood more than my body was able to assimilate. My systems were frying and I was aware of the crackling of brain cells, the schism between my brain and the understanding of my heart.

Soon after that I did some mushrooms and left the body. As I traveled through the "astral" regions, admiring all that *I Was* and seeing Myself *everywhere*, I bumped smack into a gentleman whom I can only describe as the personification of Beauty/Peace/Wisdom/Truth. I fell to the ground.

He smiled at me; *loved* me. Without uttering a word, he let me know that I had seen all that I was meant to see. That I now knew what there *Was*, Who *I Am*, and *What Will Be*. I saw my future, my enlightenment, my death and my transcendence all in a glance. The understanding was that I was to take no more drugs. They had been necessary to show me what there was to learn, but that they had severely damaged my body, my energy systems, and that I would have to clean out, purge, be patient and await the time when I would perceive all that I had recently seen, but via a body that was strong enough to sustain the awareness.

I wept, laughed, and returned to my body as sober as if I had not ingested anything at all.

Ned fixed me a splendid green salad and I explained to him that I would be willing to continue his "therapy" as long as he desired, but that I would myself do no more.

We held each other on his bed and listened to Van Morrison's *Astral Weeks*, one of this creation's finest accomplishments.

BROTHER AILRED

God, unfortunately,
was created in man's image.

Much transpired in that tiny Keith Street apartment. I loved it there and swore that I would never leave, that even after I was rich and famous I would maintain that sanctum as an office and my city pad.

It was a time of basking in the evils of our modern-day panaceas: sex, drugs, religion—the latter, of course, being the most deadly. Still, I *did* survive, and, relatively speaking, evolve.

We were right around the corner from the demiworld of West Hollywood at its prime, 1981 and '82, preceding the furtive onset of the plague by about a year. Gay ghettoes were still relished meccas for the lonely, the outcast, and the sexually prolific. Above all, Puss was happy there. She had her own yard, safe from the street, with very little competition from neighboring pets. She had a marvelous old iron fireplace that we spent many hours curled in front of, reading, writing, preening, and purring. The bed was cozy, tucked into a custom niche in the wall, and the kitchen was sunny and warm with jasmine at every window. Puss and I got lonely, but loneliness has always been the greatest impetus for my writing, and writing is one of the things that I love most—that and gardening.

I wrote and wrote and wrote, a collection which later (all the spiritually oriented pieces edited out) was published under the title *Waiting for the Virgin.* I intended to call it "Fear of Woman." Both publisher and distributor assured me that gay men would not purchase a volume entitled "Fear of Woman" and *How dare I imply that all gays...*

I brought in money through the two or three regular johns/friends that I hung on to simply because I enjoyed their visits. And all that I needed for my dining, athletic and sexual pleasures was within a three-block radius.

I put together an art exhibit at a friend's gallery, Primavera, on Melrose. It was my first solo show since Cal Arts; it was all my *rose* paintings. We had lovely invitations, in each was included a handful of crimson red rose petals. Many of my "star" friends showed: Bear, Bud and Bruce, Greg Gorman, Tony Perkins; and we were written up in all the Hollywood gossip columns.

One day I wandered into the local bookstore, the Unicorn, and chanced upon Felice Picano, autographing his latest book, *Ambidextrous.* I introduced myself; he said that he was a fan from my earlier volumes; I asked if I might bring over my collection of Raymond poems (*Notes From a Marriage*); he said sure. I did and he published them, and later *Waiting for the Virgin,* on his New York-based SeaHorse imprint.

I was seeing Robert (Consolmagno) on occasion, another favorite Probe dancer, a vulpine Italian with an ass always featured in local bar and bathhouse ads. Bobby had done years in jail as a New York street punk for manslaughter and assorted crimes, and once had weighed, he swore, close to 300 pounds. *Now* he was one of the most coveted men in West Hollywood. He was *every-body's* favorite hair-cutter—the *only* person who ever touched mine—and *nobody* fucked with him (figuratively speaking); his former life of violence was written all over his bescarred face.

He would come over to see me frequently, whenever he was getting ignored, stood up, and mistreated by his lover. At first it was just cozy, platonic now, but by and by the sexuality started returning. His butt was beyond compare; his gonads, titanic.

He was one of those people for whom there are very few explanations, given his dramatic about-face in lifestyles, his stringently positive outlook masking an intensely suicidal disposition. He had had by that time about four major motorcycle accidents and his face had been completely rebuilt each time, all the more to his liking. He once lay on my bed and tried to list the bones in his body that had *not* been broken at least once—he came up with about six. Eventually in future years a lover would push him down a stairway. He would suffer two aneurysms, get misdiagnosed by several doctors, and barely survive; he rolled a truck in Mexico and remained unconscious in a hospital there for nine days; he got AIDS, recovered, and then died from unknown causes after the AIDS-related deaths of his two brothers, sister-in-law, and lover all the same year.

Needless to say, *I* was in a very zoned-out state during that time. I mean, when I wanted to "astral project" I simply lay down, closed my eyes and split, wandering around the room or in my dreams at will. One day Robert came over with a little bag of 'shrooms. I knew that it was a mistake, but I am prone to go through with mistakes just to prove to myself that they *are* mistakes.

We started to get off and Bobby started to get sexual. In a rare and cosmic state of aggression, Robert actually switched roles, penetrating me with his grand kielbasa; but the mushrooms had kicked in so intensely that in no time I saw Bobby oscillating between being my rapist to my lover, the Devil to my *mother's* lover. I, in turn, *became* my mother, with all her thoughts and awareness. It was such a complete metamorphosis that Bobby at once bolted upright and exclaimed, "My God, you're a woman!"

Of course *I* was well versed in therapeutic transformations, but poor Robert was beside himself; this was not what he expected from me. I can't recall what happened; I think he left while still tripping. Later I gave him a bit more background for the understanding of what had transpired. But the point made was for myself, that I was in this world to complete a process, and no sightseeing along the way would interfere with that goal.

Bobby continued to show up, always bearing a fresh bouquet from his garden and tears brought on by his mendacious mate.

Steve and Al were lovers of some nine years, both hopelessly from the Midwest. They were Colt Studio's most famous and worshiped male models (*Nick Chase* and *Pat Sutton*, respectively). They were painfully exquisite bastions of homoerotic perfection.

When the two of them walked down a street, all heads turned. I can think of no equivalent; it was unreal, the disparity between these icons and normal men, and certainly *unfair*. I found it both a thrill and a humiliation to appear with them in public.

They just happened to live three doors down in my Hammond Street apartment building. I did everything I could to get to know them. They were unused to such blatant aggression and so were easily seduced. At one point, between apartments, Puss and I even moved in with them for about two weeks.

Steve was dark-haired, mustached, built like a small tank with the clearest aquamarine eyes. When I was on acid he became an absolute god to me, and off acid he was the finest-looking man that I knew of, bar none.

Al was the Nordic counterpart, tall, green-eyed, with a cleft chin and incandescent smile. He and I would pore over the epistles of Da Free John, Krishnamurti, and other bliss-bunnies of the day.

Steve and I related best sexually, and he was the one that kept our relationship alive. We would sneak out of bed in the middle of the night, quietly fuck on the livingroom floor and then crawl back in with Al, me always in the middle. Al simply asked if we'd had fun. I'd curl up around his warm naked ass, my face in the gold of that lush lapin hair, one arm slung over his powerful chest with two fingers resting subtly on the rosy bug of his nipple; Steve would spoon around me, his bristly mustache against my shoulders. There were some eternal moments born for me there.

The two of them eventually separated, which broke the hearts of all our city. Steve married a gentleman named Joe, and Al went off to study bodywork in the Santa Barbara mountains. Steve and I occasionally had dinner dates and would talk about our love for one another and how I would be with him had I not been preempted by Joe, and wasn't so hell-bent on my spiritual quest. Al and I inadvertently ended up camping together at a desert hot springs one year and he made me a splendid surprise stack of campfire pancakes for a birthday cake.

Steve went on to become the mayor of West Hollywood, the first gay-platformed mayor anywhere. Yet it is Al that I continue to dream about and aestheticize as the perfect spouse, now that my patterns and tastes have matured. For Al is versed in unconditional love and has the mind, and the heart, of a spiritual warrior.

❦   ❦   ❦

As the LSD sessions ended, I became more and more aware of the schism between my spirit life and the world of employment, relationships, feeding and basic maintenance.

Sex became awkward and uncomfortable for the most part, so I rarely pursued it. Bear and Sam, the *Dynastic Duo*, and their crowd of patsy patricians seemed a million miles away, doing things that they had done for centuries that I no longer could get it up for. Employment was unfeasible. I was unbalanced—my spiritual consciousness centers were all enlivened, while the lower chakras that dealt with the essential mundanities were severely frazzled, having shorted out as the rash jolts of energy rifled up through them during the course of the psychedelic journeying to my "higher" destinations. I was two nuances away from becoming a bag-man and I knew it. My "Spiritual Father" had been right, and it was time to do some serious reassessing.

I met a man who was entirely symbolic of my own personal rift between church and state, spirit and body. His name was Don. He was a six-four, built-of-iron, blond, blue-eyed, candy-smiled house painter—and a born-again Christian. He was completely engulfed between desire and guilt; I found his plight fascinating. Don didn't have the faintest grasp of anything that I had been through. He was blatantly unencumbered by the stigma of intelligence, and it would have been cruel and pointless to go on and on about my experiences, my theories and/or plans for the future—or to debunk his own. So I observed and enjoyed. The guilt and confusion that ravaged him merely lent an air of innocence that made his emotions all the more fun to exploit.

At first he started inviting me to "gay Christian gatherings," a notion that I have always found quaint, if completely paradoxical. Then he dragged me kicking and cursing to a shopping mall of a church known as the "The Church on the Way," the noble pastor Jack Hayford conducting the indoctrinations. I have to say that, as seedy and scary was the establishment, as well as the patrons, the Reverend Hayford was as brilliant and as astute a theologian as I have heard, comparable to the Reverend Billy Graham, only much better-looking, and nothing like the irreverent and schmaltzy Disneyland histrionics of Jim and Tammy Faye, Jimmy Swaggart, and the other media-crazed showpeople that Don so endlessly paid homage to on his kitchen TV.

We read from our Bibles, sang with the best of 'em, spoke wildly in tongues, flailing our hands in the air and "gettin' the spirit" all over the place. Yahweh's Yahoos. It was like Probe without the beat.

During the sermon, I reached under our opened Bibles and held Don's hand. He squirmed, blushed at such profanation, but welcomed the friendship. Eventually it was no big deal talking my way into this gentle Nephilim's bed. From there, with due abeyance from Don's devils of guilt and self-deprivation, and with oblations made to his gods of loneliness and desire, it was only natural that we should end up with our little Christian soldiers in each other's salivating mouths.

Don became more confused than ever. "I think," he rationalized, "that it must be less of a sin to merely orally copulate than if we had in fact gone all the way and..."

"Done the evil deed itself?" I finished. "Look, Donny, dearest! Fornication is fornication is fornication. Give it up. A fag is a fag is a fag. You think the Goddess doesn't read your innermost tabloids?"

"I think God understands our needs. He wants us to be happy."

"I think *She* could give a shit, myself. Let's just sodomize each other into oblivion!" I sanctimoniously suckled his sacred calf all the way up to its angelic feathers.

He laughed, woodenly, but I was tweaked. This was all more than I could bear. I could no longer live in a world of such flagrant contradictions. So in one fell swoop I gave away all of my paintings and belongings to Don, Bobby, Jo and Peter, Steve and Al, Craig, and the Salvation Army. I was fascinated by Don Juan's concept of eradicating one's past, and I made every effort to strip myself down to the bare essentials and begin this life all over again. *Born again.*

The hardest part, of course, was saying goodbye to Puss. She had so loved the Keith Street dwelling where we had been such good bachelors together, but I bequeathed her with streaming tears and aching throat to the apartment of Steve and Al, where I knew at least she would be scrupulously cared for. Then I left.

My first destination was Asheville, to say goodbye to Dad and Gertrude. Neither one had any notion of what I was going through; they just knew that I was peculiar and would always do what I would do.

Mom, the Christian now, was convinced that I was being moved by God, which was as good an explanation as any that *I* could come up with. Furthermore, as I told her about my two birth experiences, she was convinced that I had had my own eccentric born-again experience, which I couldn't deny either. On top of that I told her that I had seen Jesus—and I *had,* during one of my sessions.

"Hallelujah!" She immediately arranged to have me formally baptized in a freezing mountain pond full of killer guppies which attacked the hair on my naked legs. I went along with it, confused and unsure about when the Lord would strike again, and wanting to cover all my bases, as it were. Nothing happened there. I got wet, cold, and met a bunch of convivially parochial and desperately sincere people heaven-bent on obliging all the world to believe as they did.

There was *more* than this, and I had to find it. Like Moses, like Jesus, like Muhammad, I would go to the mountain and I would speak with God.

I started walking from my mother's place of work at the Visitor's Center up on the Blue Ridge Parkway. It was after the leaves had turned and there was very little traffic left, so I could stick close to the road and not have to have my quixotic insanity interrupted. I sang, cried, screamed, laughed like an idiot, and did a great deal of praying; I was certain that the Lord would lead me into some divinely decorated cave wherein I could sit lotus among the Masters and be handed the keys to eternity.

It began getting dark. I veered from the escarpment into the woods, where caves might be more prevalent. And something occurred to me: I had walked *up* so far that I had gone beyond the water line, there were no more springs or creeks. Well, it was up to God now. I tried striking sticks on stones (just once), but to no avail.

It began getting quite cold. And dark. I didn't bring additional clothing, even a jacket, because I knew that the *Lord* would provide. But it got fucking cold; I had to keep moving.

"God, I'm real thirsty now..."

Then I began to *hear* things as well, scuttling along with me in the woods. "Shit! God...? Goddess...? I hope that's you!"

The ground was fresh with autumn leaves, so there was plenty to rustle. Thirsty as I was, and having walked more than twenty miles, I also figured that the various naturally produced drugs in my brain were kicking in and embellishing the scene. Maybe the stockpiles of chemicals I'd previously ingested were coming back to haunt me as well.

I pulled into a crevice between three large rocks and did the best that I could of covering myself with fistsful of leaves. But this grew uncomfortable fast, and sleep was obviously eluding me, and soon I heard a disquieting barrage of crashes in the leaves nearby. I just lay there.

Then it seemed as though something large were directly above my head, sniffing at my one uncovered ear. I lay frozen; if this was my time to be eaten, it would be a sacrifice to the Divine—and would solve the cold problem nicely. I recalled an account I had read by a gentleman who had been eaten by a lioness: once he had gone into shock, he became aware that the lion was making *love* to him, that she would gnaw off a foot, eat it, purring, then bat him over onto his stomach while nibbling on an arm, purring, making love; eventually the lion departed and what was left of the man survived to recount his tale, and how ultimately erotic it had been.

I prayed to this zoomorphic deity. Not for deliverance of my body, but for the salvation of my soul. I only wanted God's will to be done—as *swiftly* as possible.

The noises passed. The cold did not. I felt myself alone again and I decided that I had to continue moving or I would simply freeze and die.

I needed water and began heading back down the mountain.

Now coming up in the daylight I had traveled through a set of long and dark tunnels, as the scenic Parkway passes through great stone mountains. But of course, with only the moon's light, full though it was, these tunnels became deep black in their long center. I entered each one as a test of faith.

These passages were miraculous. I felt first the consternation of even going into the hole. Then trepidations arose inside me as the glimmering moonlight would vanish behind. Eventually I walked in absolute darkness, the Void; I was given to all kinds of noises, visions, and fears. I panicked and attempted to run, but without a guideline running is dangerous, impossible, and I was not tempted to embrace the cold damp rocks along the side, lest I grab something that squeaked or otherwise was undefinable.

Eons passed. At last a faint glimmer began to appear before me. Now I could run, and run I did, laughing at first, then screaming with exhilaration as I lunged forth into the moonlight that shone like a thousand suns, falling to my knees and wailing with exaltation and gratitude for this splendid and remarkable existence.

Eventually, however, the tunnels ended, the darkness abated, and I came to a crossroad that led to an actual highway. I stood there, looking I'm sure like the Hippie-from-Hell, certain again that the Good Lord would deliver me one more time. She did; a truck stopped, and ride after ride I wended my way two hundred miles, to first-husband Dalton's Tobaccoville farm. Dick too short to fuck with God.

I was unable to walk for several days, having hiked, I figured, close to fifty miles. My feet were swollen and my soul was ice. Dalton nursed me, and we had much catching up to do. I read the entire *Lord of the Rings* saga for the third or fourth time, worked in the garden (it was winter, not much to do), baked bread, and ate ate ate.

And there was Little Frank, Dalton's diminutive boyfriend ever since me. Since he'd met Dalton, Little Frank had been compared to me. He had created his own Gavin cult in his wee country head. He was as sweet as potatoes (when he wasn't drunk), asleep early, up at dawn and out tinkering in junk shops and auctions before Dalton and I even got up. Some mornings he would crawl in with me before he left, rub around a bit in a lagomorphic frenzy, get my legs and sheets all wet and then leave me to fall back asleep. Dalton was patient with him the way one is with a dog that humps everything that wanders by.

But comfortable as the farm was, Little Frank et al, all the good food and wine was getting me nothing but fat. One evening Dalton had a very select dinner party with the hope of amusing and possibly edifying me. Included was sci-fi author, queerbasher and arch-Mormon promulgator, Orson Scott Card; and, in contrast, an elderly "bachelor," Clark Thompson, a professor at Salem College in Winston. The latter conveyed several pertinent articles of information to me, but the one that stuck was that there was a Cistercian monastery in Berryville, Virginia, that welcomed visitors and retreatants, and that in exchange for working a few hours a day in their bakery, I could perhaps stay, make reparations, and meditate on what my heart had to offer.

This sounded splendid, and I called the retreat-master the next day. By the time the weekend came about I was on the road again.

❦ ❦ ❦

Holy Cross Abbey is in a splendid valley in the upper stretches of the Shenandoah River and the Great Smoky Mountains. It is monastery land as far as eyes can see. The buildings are few and, for the Catholic Church, relatively humble: the chapel, the abbey with its fabulous library, offices and study areas, the dorms, the original retreat house, and the bakery that produces the up-to-ten-thousand loaves a day that support the place.

Other than that were old orchards, the fallen apples of which I fed to the pastured nags that the monks allowed villagers to retire on the property. There was a simple and quaint cemetery for the monks deceased, and a lot of free mountain, pasture, and woodland.

It was gorgeous.

After one weekend in the retreat house, I petitioned the abbot to stay on, as a visitor but residing among the monks. They needed the extra help in the bakery, most of the monks being too ancient and decrepit to be anything more than a danger and a nuisance among the conveyor belts and ovens, and the slicing and bagging machinery. I received my own dinky cell, half of which was occupied by a terse wooden cot, the remainder consisting of a two-foot-square desk, a tiny window that looked out onto the frosted meadows, and enough room to turn around and possibly change my clothes without falling on the bed. Meals were simple, and consisted almost in their entirety of the undersized and malformed loaves of bread from the bakery. Fortunately, the monks were vegetarian, and more fortunately, I loved bread, which they whooped up into casseroles, puddings, French toast for breakfast.

The day began with a wake-up call at 3:30 for the four o'clock morning mass. After breakfast we went to our jobs—mine being the bakery—complete with a mid-morning snack of hot and steaming bread, just out of the huge ovens, smeared with honey, molasses, butter—all of which we had as ingredients for the dough—as well as fruit preserves that a sister nunnery somewhere farther north produced and swapped with us for our bread. The majority of the brothers looked rather like loaves of bread themselves.

After lunch there was another mass and then the afternoon time of library study at my own mini desk. Then another mass or two, dinner, bread, a quick before-bed mass and six hours of good sleep before doing it all over again.

I loved it all, actually, except for the insipid masses: dry unfeeling voices droning out ancient Latin texts perfunctorily and by rote, with no meaning and no life but for the occasional farts and belches from the elder bro's, and an occasional swiftly reprimanded whisper or snicker from one of the girlish novices.

The abbot and I quickly got it on to be great pals. He listened with frank fascination through my jumbled tales of visions, experiences, and questings. I was surprised at his world-wisdom and open-minded interest.

Father Edward recognized some of the signposts of my quandary—anorexia, alienation, desperation—as signs of kundalíni activation. I was given a book entitled *Kundalíni, Evolution and Enlightenment*, which contained dozens of similar accounts and experiences by famous Catholic, Buddhist, Native American and Hindu saints, sages and stigmatists. This book proved invaluable to me. From there I was urged to read all the Hindu scriptures, the *Upanishads*, Jung, and the remainder of the writings by Blessed Yoganandaji. Piece by piece I gained a tremendous scope of what had been happening to me, and where I was going. All that I could see as my salvation was that my guru would be sent to me, or I to him/her; that someone with a far greater wisdom and power would begin my healing process and yank me through the golden doors of enlightenment.

Meanwhile, breadbaking was swell. I loved my study time, the afternoon visits with the old horses, the gentle snows and warm cozy smells of the brothers and their lives. I had very little communication with anyone other than Father Edward—except for the terribly sexy, *terribly* virgin, pudgy young foreman of the bread factory.

Brother Ailred was in his early twenties, with a close dark crew cut and glassy blue eyes. He was fat, as we all were, but that being the norm, he still stood out as genetically superior to the other brothers. He had a seductive smile and took a more-than-apparent liking to me; it was nothing overtly sexual, mind you. He was just fascinated by a young new face, one that was not distractingly queeny. He loved my long hair.

Ailred had been in the monastery since he was but a whelp. He was from a "good Catholic" family, the youngest, and only son of a family of eight. The seven sisters were *all* nuns in a nunnery that made chocolates and regularly sent brother care-packages, which partially explained his popularity with the other monks. As guileless as a lamb, he often worked close enough behind me that I could inhale his fusty oven-baked presence like a fix. It gave me lasting satisfaction as I monitored the loaf output for possible undersized or oversized freaks, learning to discern the difference of an ounce by a glance or merely lifting the loaf for an instant.

Ailred and I conversed, during the allowed segment of the afternoon, and occasionally in whispers during "silent hours," tittering like nasty acolytes showing each other their wangers behind the baptismal curtain. He showed me where the Streisand and the Miriam Makeba albums were in the "listening" room; I thrilled him with my tales of Babs, Parton, Nicholson, and other divas and gods of the Hollywood pantheon. We daily liaisoned and listened to Makeba's "Pata Pata" over and over again through adjoining earphones. It was the best sex I had had in months, possibly years. And if we ever touched, I'm certain that only I noticed. But frankly, I was very predisposed to my own obsessions and inner boogies.

Then I began writing songs, excellent songs with a spiritual twist. They would spew out as if from someone else's pen, and I would sing them in my head all through the dreadful masses.

One day I got a phone call from my songwriting friend Bruce Roberts, who had gone to great difficulty to track me down this far, certain I was crazy, not sure how to approach me. It seemed Donna Summer was recording our song, "The Rescue"—Geffen Records, Quincy Jones producing. I would be rich!

"Well that's an interesting thing to hear in my asceticism..." I told Bruce.

That same night, Father Edward came down to my cell at a very late hour (ten or so). I was up praying for deliverance.

"I have been praying to the Virgin Mary about you," the good abbot told me. "And I received this answer: You should pray to her tonight. She will tell you what you need to know; she will direct you to your guru." His eyes flared, he frowned, and then he left—he did not wish to see me leave.

Now, I had been raised a very loose Protestant. I did go through Catholic school, but only because my beloved Georgia father didn't want me around "negras" and my mom didn't want me around girls. *They* said it was for the superior education. Catholic school offered me nothing of religion other than their own peculiar dish and dogma; and our own family Methodism *certainly* had nothing to offer other than fashion consciousness and social position. But I knew one thing: Methodists *don't* pray to the Virgin Mary! "Well okay, I'm a good sport. I've gone this far. And Donna Summer is, after all, waiting..."

I began to pray.

Almost immediately I went into my most powerful hallucination yet. A giant hand—God's?—grabbed me by my collar and yanked me up into the air; I was flying, across a starless nighttime sky. There was a fire, burning on the ground far below, its continuous shaft reaching far up to me and on straight into forever. Down at the base of the shaft, fanning the flames with her scarf, was the *Virgin Mary*. She was black. That was no big deal—I've always loved black women. Any southern boy raised by a maid recognizes black women as the most unconditional love available on this troubled orb.

Without a word spoken, I became aware of two things: one, that I had the *option* of being directed straight over the beam of fire, and two, that if I went for it, not only would my face (my ego, my mask) be burned off, but my life would never again exist in the manner to which I had been accustomed.

It was only a thought, then, that triggered my response to go for the flame. My eyes flooded with light and I was simultaneously back in my body in my bed in my cell, chanting in a sonorous foreign tongue the praises of the Goddess and *All That Is*.

I didn't sleep at all that night. The next day I must've looked thoroughly mad, but both Father Edward and Brother Ailred were extremely attentive, even putting their arms around me in an uncontrolled show of patristic affection. I let them both know that I had received my answer, that I had to return to Sin City, finish out my destiny there and meet my teacher—and Donna Summer.

I was assured of an eternal place at the Holy Cross Abbey, given a letter of recommendation to a Father Bruno at a brother abbey in Big Sur (should I ever need the retreat and desire to learn how to bake fruitcakes) and shed tears with both brothers as Father Edward fitted me with enough army surplus rain gear to get me safely back to Tobaccoville.

VIC

*There is nothing more vain
than affecting humility.*

Having returned to LA, I stayed for the first month with boyfriends named Jeske and Jim. Jeske was a previous pal of mine, a much earlier paramour of Craig's, an adorable little Polack, aspiring artist, habitually played dumber than he really was (I think); Jim was his cute if unregenerate alcoholic hubby of some uncertain years. They both had cereal for breakfast, worked all day, came home, ate pizza, got drunk, and watched TV until they passed out. It was a morosely insensible existence that I could hardly bear to witness, yet they were sweet in their way, gracious to me. And it was a freebie.

Though I had been gone just less than six months, I was disquieted and completely addled by my repatriation to this city and neighborhood that I had been so determined to exorcise myself from. My life consisted of walking to the health-food store each day, the gym, reading or writing a bit, then being polite to the TV-brains all evening.

Again, I prayed for deliverance: to the Virgin Mary, anybody. I got no word.

A couple of weeks into this, however, I visited the tiny health store around the corner on Santa Monica, and as I came out sipping my kefir and gumming down a "conscious" candy bar, I was immediately caught by the knowing eyes of a woman on a flier stapled to a streetpost. I about dropped my cocktail and choked on a mouthful of carob: *This* was the *Virgin Mary*, the woman who had been fanning the flame! This was my *guru!*

I ripped off the flier, ran home and called the number. There was a meeting ("darshan") that very night, and *I* was invited.

I walked the five-or-so miles through West Hollywood, into Hollywood and up into a beautiful canyon, following the directions that a man named Duncan had dispatched over the phone. I was beaming the whole way, nervous to the tits, scrubbed and polished and decked out as Hindu/Buddhist/mystical as I could get with my limited wardrobe.

Terrified and early, I hid in the bushes outside the modest canyon home for some half-hour, wondering if the lady inside *knew* of my presence. Surely she must, this was our awaited hour, the culmination of lifetimes of search and devotion—would she spring forth with a kiss on her lips and exclaim me to be her lover, the Christ, the One they had all been waiting for?

Eventually I knocked; I didn't have a watch, but figured that I was only moderately early at this time, acceptably so.

The door was opened by a wild-eyed, gold-toothed monster named Chuck. "Well hello, big guy! Welcome! Come on in!"

He hugged me and entreated me to tell him who I was, where I had come from, how I had found out about "Big Mama," what my previous spiritual practices had been. He was bubbling over to such an extent that I felt as though I had come home at last, to my *true family*, my Guru and Her Disciples.

Come Duncan, a fat mercurial bag of comedy with bottle-thick John Lennon glasses and as many nervous tics as he had prescriptions to curb them. Duncan was as talkative as Chuck, as friendly, and as vulgar. Less than friendly were the women, Big Mama's *devis*: Sally was a rotund and nervous middle-aged housewife from somewhere out in the Valley. She was covetous of her position, sat as fawningly close to the left of Mama's *chair* as she was allowed to creep, and eschewed me as though I were an incendiary from the Jehovah's Witnesses. She was an ex-Mormon. Kahala was somewhat friendlier, pretty, fat, Hawaiian. She had exquisitely long and wavy black hair, dressed in a muu-muu, and wore no makeup. She too eyed me suspiciously and I discreetly checked my breath and my fly at regular intervals. Jane was a waspy wisp of a woman, and ex-nun, who seemed to rule the roost with an iron ass and a pointed thumb. "Welcome!" she barked, introducing herself in an indelible British accent, official and efficient, then resuming her duties with such a flair and fervor that I decided that this was one broad that *I* needed to be wary of.

One by one we all lined up on our pillows before Big Mama's chair, among an impressive assortment of rugs, blankets, scarfs and other mystical apparatus. It was all too beautiful, too devout, as we silently awaited the presence of *The Goddess*.

She came floating in on a rainbow, her bare feet hardly touching the carpet. It was as though I had blinked and she had simply manifested before me.

And she was beautiful. Spacially gifted, but exquisitely proportioned—as she put it herself, *Built like a Goddess*. *These* were the breasts that could nourish the world, the hips that gave birth to the spheres; yet her face was kind, sweet really, deceptively so.

Her hair was long in what I later discovered to be a weave. "This coffee-colored body is as close as I could get to my previous Indian incarnations," she would claim, "but the nappy black hair just doesn't cut it."

Her throne was artfully lighted, so that the rest of the room went dark and Big Mama all but glowed alone. Another hefty and comely woman, Julia, came in with her as a handmaiden and sat just to Big Mama's right.

To the left, seated behind where Sally wallowed in her afghans, was Ananda, Big Mama's sidekick, straightman and key confidant, a gimpy whiteboy in starched white pajamas with an eternally lost smile on his face.

"Welcome," Big Mama spoke just briefly in a very girlish and subdued voice, "are you ready to meditate?"

The Holy Coterie groaned, nodded and cheered.

"Well then, let's do it!"

She shot me a subtle but direct acknowledgment—was it a wink? I seemed to be the only neophyte there, and I thought: *She knows. She knows who I am, everything about me; She is the One.*

After a thirty-minute period of meditation we came to and croaked out a song of dedication to Big Mama, the Goddess; then she answered questions. She was a marvel, her wisdom was obvious. I asked her if she was my guru. "What does your heart say?"

"But was that really You in the monastery?"

"I am everywhere, my child."

Okay, so she wouldn't spoon-feed me, but I caught the drift: If I wanted a guru, this was it, here She Was, she wasn't going to hit me in the head with a rock. It was my choice and my choice alone. Ananda told me simply, "Don't even think about it, if you feel like coming when we're having a meeting, then come, if you don't, then don't. Day by day, that's all we can ask for. Be spontaneous, that's the Divine Way."

I knew that I was hooked.

Life changed. Jeske and Jim started driving me mad. I wandered into Guru Alan Finger's très chic yoga studio on the corner of Robertson and Melrose, catercorner from where my gallery had once been. The Yogi Roddy was a devastatingly charismatic young bugger with transparent eyes and a broad smile that reminded me of my brother. The class was full of gorgeous Bev-Hills aspirants. I somehow persuaded him to let me move into the one-room studio, store my fistful of belongings under the yogi's dais, and tuck away my bedroll every morning before the first session. I could attend all the classes that I chose in exchange for a daily vacuum and polish, for keeping the incense smoldering. It couldn't have been easier or more perfect, a modern anchorite's dream amidst the very jaws of corruption from which I had been plucked. And it allowed for my regular thrice-weekly attendance at *darshans*.

I even looked for work! There wasn't much that I could conceive of functioning in, but I checked out one place called Altered States, which was a couple of slimy apartments in an even slimier apartment building that featured a set of saltwater isolation tanks and assorted nouvelle meditation aids—everything but William Hurt. The owners were queer. They hired me for five dollars an hour to answer phones, check people in and out, do basic tank maintenance; I could use the tanks all that I desired, even arrange for all-nighters. I could now afford to buy Big Mama presents and splurge for the once-a-month "intensives."

My prayers had been answered; I was a monk-in-the-world.

I met a lovely man through Altered States, a contemporary by the name of Vic.

"Vic Leoni," he beamed.

"Sounds pretty Italian to me."

"Purebred," he assured me.

"Well, you'll have to show me your papers sometime!"

"I keep 'em hidden at home. You'll have to come over."

"I get off at five..."

Vic was the sort of man that is infinitely more handsome in retrospect, and yet had a charming enough façade, a gorgeously gallant smile, bedroom eyes, and an obviously hirsute chest.

Upon entering Vic's humble garden apartment bordering Griffith Park, I immediately addressed a photograph of a stunningly sexy half-clad man on the hallway wall. "That's me!" Vic laughed in his bright and jocund voice.

It was! And just a year before! A puzzle began piecing together: Vic had had a lover, also depicted in the photo; they had separated, and Vic had developed a classic case of anorexia. This gorgeous man in the photograph had sunk into his perfectly proportioned frame, his classic Roman facial features had declined into caricature as the flesh had withdrawn, and the poor thing, as I was to soon discover, had no butt whatsoever. And yet, he was radiant; if I could just find some way to *inflate* him to his natural splendor!

Nevertheless, he was fascinating to a Luddite like myself. His limited space was abuzz with computers (before *anybody* had computers) and an entire fleet of actual miniature flying saucers.

"Each craft," he explained, "functions with only one or two facets of what a complete ship would. The main problem being that, being miniatures, I can't get inside them to control them; and an out-of-control flying saucer is a very dangerous thing."

"Well I can imagine!" I jested.

"These ships are virtually indestructible. They would randomly explode against anything that they hit. Perfectly safe, of course, when you're inside..."

"But of course."

He went on to explain the concept of fuelless motors, the dome shapes, ionic production, power and steering mechanisms, including a collection of patents, full diagrams and instructions lifted from such sources as the US and British patent offices, British Motors, NASA, Tesla and assorted extraterrestrial file cabinets. My eyes (and antennae) were spinning.

"The technology has always been around. Many of our presidents have been in touch with space commanders—Kennedy was the only one who listened—and the government, pawn of the major oil corporations, has tracking stations to prevent public access to non-fuel engines. If I were to build a full-scale model, or even leave any of these guys running too long, they would swoop in and that would be the end of me and all my work. That's what happened to Tesla—happens all the time. Besides," he winked, "even these models will fuck up TV, phone, and radio reception for blocks. I can only play with 'em late at night."

"Well, I'll just have to stay..."

As the evening progressed, Vic began demonstrating each model. I was reeling from the spectacle as the petite talismans performed miniature orbits within the room, chucked out lightning, glowed colors, whirred, and caused my hair to stand on end from the opposite end of the hall. This was one wild genius and I was enthralled.

I was also attracted to Vic, but somehow romance seemed more alien and improbable than his technologies. Oh, I had had a sort of sex with Little Frank in Carolina, and my eating patterns were at least more together than were Vic's; but there was a dark hole there—perhaps it was where my heart should have been. No, this meeting was just a meeting of the minds—and souls. Or so I kept telling myself...

"I'll give you a massage." Vic smiled without question, his hands on either side of my neck. "You're tense. The human body is very much like the space-craft, a glowing ball of light. Through subtle manipulation of the energy between points you can cure anything."

"I always associate massages with seductions," I interrupted as he was unbuttoning the front of my flannel shirt.

"Well consider this a cosmic seduction," he laughed.

"But cosmic only, I don't want to have sex."

"But every breath we take is sex. How can you not have sex?" He skinned off my khakis and helped me balance myself while he pulled these and my shorts from under my feet.

"I mean sex sex. You know."

He pulled me symmetrically across his waterbed. Face down.

"You mean you don't want to have an orgasm."

"Uh... yeah."

"Well that's too bad. They're very balancing. But okay. Why don't you just relax and enjoy the energy..."

I could think of nothing else to say while I listened to him remove his own clothes from behind me. The bed rocked with internal waves as I felt the fur of his bottom seat itself upon my own; his testicles lolled about my lower back as he began running his strong bony fingers along the sinews and skeleton of my spine.

The effect was mesmerizing, with me finally face up and his hands coming at last to pry and needle at the cartilage of my undeniably turgid penis.

"You know," Vic said, "most massage leaves off before it gets to the genitals, and yet men in our society have more tension build-up in the genitals than anywhere else on their body."

I couldn't disagree, but stopped him when I felt his hot breath surrounding the glans. I opened my eyes to see this svelte satyr looking lovingly down at me, one hand on my cock, the other cupped firmly around my balls, his own stately flag waving over this near-conquered land.

"It's late, Vic, I think I need to get back to the studio."

He took me home with only mild disappointment, hanging out and chatting further until I informed him at what hour the morning class would resume.

Subsequent dates we wandered out in the desert, the park; Vic got into a pattern of giving me regular and extensive massages—something I have always had trouble saying *no* to. And we would always end up at the same crossroads. I was convinced that an ejaculation would be *wrong, inappropriate*—why?

"Do you think your guru will mind?" he asked me.

These were fighting words, but I had no intention of losing the only physical contact that I was at that time receiving. "No—I don't know, maybe—let's just not. Yet."

"Okay."

Vic put up with me and my mawkish flirtations and rejections; he had no other close pals either. He took me on an overnight expedition to Joshua Tree National Monument to witness some *real* flying saucers. We lay on our adjoining sleeping bags in a natural "tub" carved in the top of an immense mountain-of-a-rock. Sure enough, just as he had said, at a certain hour— between about 2:00AM to 4:00—there was a steady stream of distant lights going both directions along a particular meridian of sky, fast and slow, often changing paces midstream or even stopping altogether, then resuming. He said it was an energy vortex through which intergalactic ships would "bounce" and become catapulted to great speeds or even other dimensions. Fascinating.

We hardly slept for the rumblings of Indian voices and primordial music that streamed forth out of the rock. Just before dawn the moon arose and a chorus of coyote yelps went up so loud it sounded as though we were riding on their backs.

As the sun was coming up Vic was telling me about a time that a certain group of aliens on Earth and friends of aliens were escorted to a landing site not far from where we were; Vic had been allowed to come along and witness the landing of the ship, the tall long-dark-haired gentlemen who came forth and met with certain people present, ushering a few of them back into the craft and lifting silently off into the stars. Again my hair was on end.

Vic was also in touch with a certain someone from some corporation up San Francisco way that he believed might subsidize a project. "I'll get to construct an actual working full-dimension ship out in the wilds of Australia far from any tracking stations. Then we'll wait until an important outdoor gathering is taking place—say, a major football playoff—fire the saucer up and fly it directly into the arena such that the governments will not have time to smash our enterprise prior to full media coverage taking place."

Sounded good.

He and I began having more difficulties. In part due to his growing impatience that I would not allow a consummation to take place, as well as his distaste that I was seeing a guru—he not only was unsusceptible to my subtle proselytizing, but he held the staunch belief himself that, as God, we all hold the key to our own enlightenment and need never give our "powers" over to another.

"When you no longer see yourself as separate from God," he mused one day from a promontory up in Griffith Park, "you will no longer fear the act of sex, which is the act of creation itself."

I looked at him sitting above me, his chest naked and deliciously pelted, his smile broad and eloquent. Why did he seem so happy at this moment, when I did not?

"I have a heap of healing to do, now. I believe that Big Mama can help. I love you, Vic."

We stopped seeing each other, and when I tried again he was gone, with no trace, no phone, no forwarding orders. Son of a bitch. I loved the man. I still think of what he would've looked like with a little more meat on his bones. And what sex with an alien is like.

KAHALA

There is no such thing
as safe sex.

Through my associations with Sam and Bear, I had studied the inner-workings of the world of mortal power. In true iconoclastic fashion, I had pushed and prodded and tested each and every boundary. Despite the external pomp and majesty, I had come to perceive that power as feeble and sorely limited. My interest now lay in the mechanics of a different kind of power, an everlasting power—a Divine Power.

I became a regular member of Big Mama's clutch—or "Mamarama," as Duncan coined us.

Besides my love affair with Duncan and Chuck (who turned out to be Big Mama's earthly husband), and a growing crush on the intractable Howard (a chiropractor/bicyclist who had a penchant for indiscriminately flirting with anyone or thing that gave him half an eye) I also fell madly in love with Julia, Big Mama's handmaiden.

Julia was a tough ol' gal from Tucson, an ex-alcoholic, with the mouth of a sailor—a lady well versed in wranglin' hogs and bringin' home the cattle. She had profound psychic abilities and gave me occasional bits of advice based on a this or a that going on in my "aura." "When I first come to see Big Mama," she drawled, "I 'bout spit out my teeth when I saw the rainbows of light pouring out from the crack under the front door." She was one of Mama's first devotees, and had, they said, helped Mama do her thing in numerous incarnations.

Julia lived in the house with Big Mama and her principal adherents, Ananda, Duncan, Howard, Chuck, Jane, and Julia's wild little monster, Freddie. Freddie was a charmer and a terror, having the curse and the blessing of six and sometimes more parents. He learned to play one against the other to ultimately get what he wanted, and occasionally would discover himself getting punished by the entire house all at once. Eventually his antics grew wilder and even quite dangerous. Being always the gardener, I was the one that got assigned the duty of replanting the next-door neighbors' front hedge after Little Freddie maliciously set it ablaze. By the time he was nine he was setting the dresses of the girls at school on fire, and eventually he burned the classroom itself. He was incarcerated at a mental institution for grade-school children. Julia didn't talk about it much; Big Mama just chalked it up to the child's karma.

Jane and I got to be semi-buddies, but one was always held aloof from Jane, especially if one were a man. One evening I was called into the kitchen for a rare and frightening parley with Big Mama and some of the house members.

While Mama sat plundering a bag of potato chips like a starved dog, I was informed that if I *really* was serious about hanging around and staying with Big Mama, they just happened to need an American husband for fair Jane, who was in danger of being exported at any moment. Being the resident gay boy, I was the least likely to run up against future conflicts. In a year or two Jane would apply for her citizenship, we could divorce, and that would be that.

"Will it get me enlightened?" I asked.

"It won't hurt," Mama shot back without cracking a smile.

I was flattered, said *yes*, and the marriage plans were announced, to the amusement of all.

Big Mama's meetings got quite intense, with energy flowing off the Lady and sending us all into paroxysms of laughter, tears, and spontaneous "tics" or *movements* known in the business as *kryas*. During "intensives," Mama would really zang out the megavolts and throw us all into states of altered consciousness that would have us bouncing around uncontrollably on our butts, flying across the room in somersaults, screaming and guffawing in languages that would put to shame the mild-mannered "charismatic" Christian meetings that I had recently attended with my mom. Each intensive was topped with a killer mid-afternoon traditional Indian vegetarian feast that Big Mama and the ladies would whoop up the night before. Big Mama had her hands in every batch, loading the chow up with so much energy (*shakti*) that the food itself became a psychedelic experience. And the food was so damn spicy, starchy, and greasy that the entire room would go comatose for the final meditation and darshan.

"This," Big Mama said, "is the time of least resistance, when I can work on you guys the hardest, really digging in and *eating* up your karma like the Goddess *Kali*!" She roared out the name of the Goddess of Destruction, then began a series of snake-like hisses and ululations, writhing about the carpet and snatching karma from us with her nails and teeth. It was a trip.

I also began getting closer to the ever-wary Kahala.

Kahala was in her early thirties, and a virgin. As a revered traditional Hawaiian, she should've been toting around a half-dozen or more grand-children by then, and she was more than feeling her biological clock ticking away. But she was a schlump, fat, dowdy, refusing makeup and modern feminine trappings; she had spent most of her life out of her body.

Her granddad was the most famous of all the Hawaiian *kahunas*, or holy-people. He was the one, in fact, for whom *huna* was re-legalized. Lala explained, "The Christian governor at that time had a young son who fell in a vat of boiling sugar stock. He was hailed as a goner after the doctors had tried every trick available to them. Eventually someone suggested Daddy Bray, so they dragged him from out of the prison in which he had been rotting for twenty years, and they allowed Granddaddy to lock himself in with the kid. Three days later the boy emerged from the room without a scar on his flesh. Daddy Bray was freed along with all the other huna leaders, and Huna was allowed as a religion from that point on."

Kahala had attended the school for native Hawaiian children, mastered Hawaiian song and dance, the language, and had grown up in a house where the astral reality was as pronounced as the physical. From the time that Daddy Bray had given up *his* body—Kahala was five—Kahala continued to speak with and be taught *by* the master.

There was a point in our meditations with Big Mama where both Swami Yoganandaji and *his* swami, *Babaji*, would wander between Kahala and myself, kicking us both and/or falling on the floor laughing hysterically. Only Big Mama and Julia could see these antics as well, and the rest of the gang were in a bit of awe, except for Howard, who remained completely oblivious to anything that was not edible, fuckable or could produce an easy income.

Kahala and I discovered that we could "talk" together—on a number of levels. So, with young Roger, and priapic Howard, who had been coerced by Big Mama into dating Kahala, we found a charming two-bedroom-plus-guest Spanish cottage just across Westbourne from the now-famous Bodhi Tree Bookstore—*cosmic*.

"Off Center," then, was the sweet home that I occupied for the next four years. An accountant, Kahala began doing the books for a huge floor-covering firm, and so we were able to wall-to-wall the entire house in a lovely jade green carpet. Of course I inundated the yard with wild and exotic flora, stealing sprouts and cuttings of bamboos and banana trees of every sort, shape and color. Eventually our view of the neighbors all but vanished and the house took on the feel of an absolute oasis in the middle of bustling West Hollywood.

On the psychic level, Kahala and I became aware of a variety of spooks that came to hang out in our sacred little Garden of Allah, simply because of our association with Big Mama. We would occasionally see some gentleman wandering through the garden that would turn out to be either Yoganandaji, some other Indic saint, a living New York-based saint named Sri Chinmoy that neither of us had ever heard of before, or any one of a variety of other dudes and deities. Our favorite was always Ananda Mayi Ma, the most splendid devi I have ever had the grace to encounter.

One day, sitting on the kitchen backstep looking out into our urban farmyard, Kahala looked at me and started to say "You know what...?"

"Yeah," I knew what. "You and me."

"That's right. It's so obvious."

I agreed. "Fuck Howard." (We both *were* at that time.) "You and me're the ticket. It's already like we're brother and sister, like we're one."

"I know," she said. "I was suspicious of you when you first showed up at Big Mama's. I was afraid of your long hair, thought you looked like one of the *haole* drug lords back home. But I knew that there was something else. It was just my brain that pretended not. In my heart, I knew."

"I was always drawn to you," I acceded. "I didn't know why. I'm tired of men. I need a woman."

We kissed. It was that simple—if *that's* simple. Howard was out; we both said *bye-bye*. I was convinced somehow that being with a woman would be more balanced for me and more in line with where I wanted to go, which was Godhead (or Goddesshead). I was also certain that Big Mama would be happy with the situation and possibly think more favorably of me as well.

Kahala really was pretty if she would just pay attention to herself, if she would realize that it's 90-percent attitude that creates one's appearance. I was not turned on by her body, but I was so totally lost to the netherworlds in her arms and deep lambent eyes that the physical simply did not matter—I thought. When we made love it was an image of the voluptuous Goddess Pele that I penetrated. We spoke together in an ancient Polynesian tongue and did snake-like dances and *mudras* in and around my palette bed.

Kahala started going to the gym two blocks away, ceaselessly wearing the workout fashions that were only just beginning to come out for women, sweating, and dieting. She cooked the simple and luscious vegetables that I was growing in our backyard garden. One evening Big Mama and the other girls cornered Kahala while she was at the Center house. Big Mama held her with her thumb on her forehead while the devis painted poor Lala's face with pancake, eye shadow, mascara, and lipstick. When she came to she was sitting in front of a mirror and, like Cinderella on her first night out, exclaimed, "That's me? I'm beautiful!"

Pretty soon Kahala took on the name of "Maw"; I became "Paw"; Little Roger was simply referred to as "Junior," and as Howard faded away whence he came, we adopted a peculiar new elderly disciple known as "Uncle Doug." I even ran over to visit hunks Steve and Al and reclaimed my treasured Puss.

It was all rather storybook-like. And I must say that the marriage part suited me quite well: the group meals, the house-cleaning and wash all staying current; having a wife was better than having a mother had ever been.

Then we went on a vacation. "Maw" was making good bucks, so she paid.

We started out on the island of Kauai, Kahala's home, where we checked out all the local *heiaus* (ancient stone temples), the wet and dry caves, and all the favored and most sacred beaches. We were forever speaking in our private tongue, falling out of our bodies and dancing in the winds and rains.

Kahala's dad was a crotchety and churlish old *hapa-haole* (half white/half Hawaiian) who hated white people. He didn't like me and made no bones about it. I wasn't supposed to touch any of the sacred objects in the house, but of course I did after the family had all gone to sleep.

Kahala showed me the one main family treasure, a stone globe about the size and weight of a bowling ball. It had what seemed to be a glaze over the top that could almost be said to resemble the continents spread out over the oceans of the Earth, perhaps as they had once been, or perhaps as they would someday become. Kahala called it the "male stone"; it had fallen to Earth centuries before along with a "female" stone. This particular stone had rested in the state museum in Honolulu for many years for safekeeping until her dad decided that it should come back home where it belonged. You could see a tiny place where the state geological survey had done scratchings to remove particles of the thing to analyze it; it was unlike anything else that exists on this planet (except, we presume, the *female stone*).

The stone had been allegedly possessed by Jesus at a certain point. There was some story which I have forgotten about how it came to Hawaii, and some tie-in with the stone, Daddy Bray, and the noble Mahatma Gandhi.

"When I was a kid," Kahala told, "I used to hear scufflings in the livingroom and would run out to see spirits trying to steal the stone. It would be wavering out in midair in the center of the room, heading for the open window. Then there would be a tug-of-war and the kahuna spirits would put the stone back in its glass case and lock the cabinet door."

I further learned that Big Mama had abated Lala's suspicions about her and piqued her interest when, without having even met Kahala, she had Julia relay the message: *Tell her I have the female stone.* The myth continued that when the male stone and the female stone came back together, the world (as we now experience it) would come to an end. *Hallelujah.*

From Kauai we island-hopped to the Big Island, where we toured the volcano and all its old flows. Kahala explained to me, "No true Hawaiian fears Pele, they know that a lava flow can wipe out every Christian house on the mountainside, but it will flow right around and not even burn the house of the true believer."

"Once," she said, "when I was a girl, we stopped on the way to the beach and picked up an old lady. My momma knew that it was *Tutu*, Pele's old-lady form, the Grandmother. She got in the backseat of the car and had the red hibiscus flower in her hair that Pele always wears. She didn't talk much but we asked her where she was going and she said to the volcano. When we turned around again to see her she was gone. That night the volcano erupted.

"Always, when the volcano is gonna erupt, Pele takes the form of a white dog and runs down into the crater. That's how the rangers know when it's gonna erupt, they watch for that white dog—that's Pele—and they clear everybody out right away."

We walked around the crater and Kahala showed me which berries Pele liked and you could throw into the crater for her, and which would piss her off and make her blow.

"But mostly," she smiled, "Pele likes her gin; when the volcano erupts, everyone comes up with a bottle of gin. The woods over there are completely littered with little bottles of gin."

Maui was our most intense night. We were staying with an uncle—she had one on every island. This uncle had done a strange thing and built his house right on top of the local trail of the "night walkers." *Night walkers* are ghosts of huna braves that keep up a vigil every night to guard the islands and their descendants from evil and evil spirits—though some of the night walkers seemed a little iffy themselves, and I never fully understood the distinction. That night, Kahala and I both were dragged out of our bodies forcibly by the band of chanting kahunas that traveled straight through our bedroom. We were carried kicking and screaming down through the woods to the ancient stone heiau that even Kahala never visited because she said it was one that was used for blood sacrifices.

Well, that night *we* were dinner; we were thrown atop the stones and trounced mercilessly from head to toe with large wooden knives and mallets. One big hairy dude who seemed to be the leader kept stabbing me in the heart with his stone spear. In the morning, while I was comparing notes with Lala, she said that he was trying to cleave open our heart chakras so that we could better love. My ribs felt as though they had been crushed beneath the wheels of a semi. *Hmmm*, I'd rather stick to Big Mama's gentle touch any day.

We started taking regular trips to Hawaii with Mama.

Those trips were extremely different, although the visits to the local "power spots" became even more intense in the wake of Big Mama's energy. Big Mama used to call Pele her "Little Sister" and explained that Pele was to the "devi kingdom" (the world of earth spirits, angels and sprites) what *she* was to the human kingdom.

Kahala and I were often at the forefront of these encounters with Big Mama. I recall an especially beautiful day on which I had been offered the rare privilege of escorting Big Mama by the hand up the narrow and rock-strewn trail that led from the end of the road at Ke'e Beach on Kauai's incomparable North Shore to the crest of a hill where an old heiau had once stood. It became immediately obvious to me that this spot was one that had played a great part in my earlier lives.

I fell deeply into a state of profound reverence, chanting the most exquisite ancient dialect hymns as I steadied Big Mama—she had the stigmata at that time and the ruddy square nails in her tiny brown feet were creating pain and swelling.

As Big Mama began to chant, the wind picked up and a delicate spray of mist from the mountains behind us showered over its blessing. Then, as if answering to the siren's call, a host of tens of huge black whales began making themselves apparent just off the coast from us, echoing almost verbatim the syllables that the Devi and I chanted out to them.

Later, in a state park that was actually the ruins of an old Hawaiian fisher's village, I fell on my knees and began weeping, for I had been the gardener there, some eight hundred years ago, and the herb-master for the entire community.

But it had changed, and that's what had made me so sad; when we had lived there we had bountiful herbs and flowers growing on all the surrounding hills and along every path in the tiny village. *This* was a desert!

Big Mama explained that the twelve of us that she had with her at that moment had all lived together in that incarnation in this spot. She was not performing the role of guru, as such, but was the fat old Tutu (grandmother) that everyone brought their babies to to be named and blessed; she performed the marriages, funeral services and the like; she was the village elder. We were known, she said, throughout the islands for our magic. And even though there were murderous and warlike tribes all over Hawaii at that time, they feared us as the Huna tribe and left us alone lest their crops fail or the fish refuse to bite.

Maybe it was that magic to which the winds responded by bringing in the clouds that kept our community snug and verdant. Once we had died out or been carried off, the winds changed and the area fell into its current sorry state. But possibly because of the energy that had been created there, the state had ended up preserving this ground as sacred so that we and others could walk again those hallowed dust trails.

At the end of the road, just as everyone was leaving, we came upon "my house," my grape arbor still standing, and I fell again weeping to the points on which my daddy had died beneath the grapes and my beloved wife in her palm-leaf bed inside the single-room cottage.

"Come, baby," Big Mama came back to retrieve me, compassionately, "this is all past; now it is the present."

Kauai was without qualification our favorite island and we came back several times a year for its lushness, its beauty and its healing aura.

There was a strictly enforced etiquette surrounding travels with Big Mama and only seasoned disciples were asked on such trips. It was explained to us that Big Mama didn't need our white asses, and that she would certainly be able to have a much more equable and carefree vacation without us. Therefore, since we were "allowed" to come along and be in her "grace" on these occasions, it was up to us to follow without question what Big Mama wanted to do.

Much of the protocol was traditional Indian guru stuff; having been whipped into shape by the inclement nuns at a Catholic school, I found all the standard courtesies much more natural to me than they were to many of the crew. In Yoganandaji's accounts I had read and certainly understood the behaviors and treatment toward the gurus and holy people.

And this was a trip modeled very much like that of the Hindu yogi, although Big Mama had been raised a Protestant child, with a proclivity for touching dead bugs and pets and laughing while they sprang back to life in her preschool days in an LA black ghetto neighborhood. She had been given the Sunday School classes to teach all through childhood as the teachers discovered that this precocious babe knew more about the Bible than they did.

Though now, even though she had many of the effects of the Christian stigmata, Mama had the strongest affinity for the Hindu tradition, for the love of Lord Shiva, Goddess Durga/Kali and the other Hindu deities.

Unlike a Zen master, who would certainly castigate us for responding to "the energy" with such fervent movement and tongues, Big Mama absolutely encouraged us to "go for it" however our own minds and bodies might require. It was like complimenting a woman on her great cooking, and Mama laughed heartily to see us entranced and flailing about like bedeviled holy rollers.

One particular Kauaiian escapade, our "hottest" ever, was a stay at some upper-classy condos in Princeville Estates on the North Shore. It was the occasion of three great events, which we planned and celebrated to the max: Kali Puja (the feast-day of the Goddess Kali), Halloween, and a talent show to amuse "The Goddess."

The puja was unlike any experience that I had encountered with Big Mama, and unlike anything that I have experienced since. Everything was teeming with energy, ecstasy, and light. It was as though the goddess had swallowed the sun and was beaming it out through her hands to us, the moons, in our orbs about her. Everyone was chanting in one language or another, bouncing about like the Tibetan Olympics. I felt as though I were exploding, as if every particulate of my atomic structure were enlivening to its own individual consciousness, and I was God the witness, allowing and loving each fragment.

Big Mama ended up sliding to the floor and slithering about hissing and biting people's legs as the Goddess Kali took possession of our evening. Even Howard the Inert seemed moved. Back in our bodies, we amused the Great One with the talent show that we had been preparing for several days. I put on a mini chorus line with a new disciple, James, and two of the ladies of an amalgamated Broadway number that had been altered to honor Kali/Mama, beginning with a rousing chorus of "*Hello, Kali!*" and ending with the self-parodic South Pacific refrain "*Kali Ma will call you, any night, any day, she will rip your ego from you, whether straight, whether gay...*"

I cannot say that I have ever experienced a more humbling and more energized evening than that one. It was simply Divine.

JAMES

There are no victims,
only accomplices.

Kahala had one essential passion—to have a baby. We spoke about it often and it was a pleasing notion for myself as well. We even had picked out the first three names. Kahala and I both agreed that a young-un should be delivered at home, by the father, raised on the tit, fed homemade organic blender creations (none of this jar shit), and always kept within reach of one of its two parents, both when possible.

It was obvious stuff—obvious to me, after all the ghastly rebirthing traumas and my studies and recognitions about childhood and the forming of neurosis; it was obvious to Kahala as well.

Averse to chemicals and thus to the pill, Kahala was a strict purveyor of the rhythm method. Not only did I trust her implicitly, but I presumed her one of the most psychically intuitive people I had ever met; rhythm method sounded fine. AIDS hadn't been popularized yet and *I* had never even *used* a balloon (except as a rare object of kink).

Kahala conceived, as far as we could tell, the very first time we did it.

Some weeks passed. Kahala was prone to active periods; when the moment struck I would invariably find her in the kitchen leaning heavily into the chopping counter and groaning like an intoxicated yenta. I got used to that, but this time there was much more nausea and stomach upset. Lala didn't explain to me until some time after. It was morning sickness.

And then she lost the kid.

Well, he persisted, as did Kahala's estrogen—or whatever was producing the yen. Thanks to the arrival of a man named James, I soon grew out of the picture as her companion and bedmate, and when I did Kahala confessed the miscarriage, explaining that Big Mama had seen our separation coming and had "pulled" the child from her.

Kahala stopped coming to meetings for a month or two, and returned one day with a gentleman named John, whom she promptly married, one month pregnant.

The baby was born a preemie, watched in his tank by some dozen hysterical aunties and uncles. It was "our" child, Kahala explained to me once the hurt of our break-up began to heal. But it was better off consigned to John, a good Midwestern farmboy who worships the ground his wife walks on, as his doting daddy. Young Gavin still had his own diapers to wash.

❦   ❦   ❦

Shortly after moving into the Westbourne house I bluffed my way into the position of pastry chef at a nearby New York-style deli. Forthwith I had the whole town on its knees, making daily pilgrimages for their particular fix: chocolate-chip cookies, triple-chocolate cookies, lemon shortbread squares, mocha cheesecake... We were quite the sensation.

That job transformed when Jerry the owner died a mysteriously debilitating death from an unknown cause.

Then another friend died of synonymous symptoms. I began to squirm when I realized that these two dead friends were both ex-hard-core TT1 users. I began replaying my own scenario and fretting about the way that *I* had been feeling lately (living off of coffee, cookie dough and the lickins from cheesecake spatulas...).

When Jerry's lover sold the deli, not only was I retained as pastry chef, but almost immediately upgraded to manager as well, causing me near-terminal grief and anguish. I began working twenty-hour days, managing from the ten-o'clock opening through the afternoon, evening, then doing all my baking at night to the accompaniment of mainlined espresso and blaring rock 'n' roll. Sugar balanced off the coffee, and I only took the evenings off that we had Big Mama meditations, which had dropped to two nights a week. I became transparent, my nerves like glass, and started doing things like losing my way home (six blocks), not being able to sleep the four hours allotted for sleep, and falling apart and crying at the sight of every lost dog or bag lady.

I split. I moved on to LA's first video bar, Revolver. For almost a year I was the bouncer, too sensitive to cigarette smoke and crowds of frantic poofs to work inside, sitting out on the street every night trying to look unfriendly and callous, which sometimes worked.

Everyone went by me nightly, so that if there were anybody in West Hollywood that I didn't already know, I soon did. I even fell in love a few times: with a Teutonic redheaded bartender named Steven Buker, with a dark-browed and brilliant-smiled Iranian bar-man, Rick Eshoo, and again with an outrageously sexy Australian chap named (you ready?) Tony Italiano —hell, I would've married him for the name alone! The job was often almost pleasant, except for the occasional row. Then one night I ended up having to crack some gorgeous young child's head into the sidewalk to get him to let go of his girlfriend's arm, which in a drugged-out stupor he had chomped down on. I had affected pacifism up until that point, and this all became a bit too low-vibe for where I thought my "spiritual" life was taking me. So I quit.

"Don't leave us!" James squealed in mock terror. "How will we get on without you?"

James was a bartender and video jock. He had of genius IQ, spiritually inclined, a master's in engineering, a large, protruding forehead, and occasional nicely Pointexter glasses. Although masculine by nature, he could put on a marvelous campy queen act that would always crack me up.

"Then run away with me, doll," I whispered in my best Humphrey Bogart-Kate Hepburn voice.

"But where to, my love?" (I think this scene had been brewing for several months, but never felt sanctioned as long as we knew we had to work together in such an incestuous domain.)

"Uh... how 'bout to the Safeway for a couple a pints of yogurt?"

"Oh *darling*, sounds *fabulous!*" he shrilled. "But I have to work! What're you doing at two-thirty?"

"I'll be here. Carrying a book and a pink rose."

James smiled. He realized I was serious.

"Pizza's on me." He grinned.

"Extra garlic?"

"My dear, of *course!*"

He was moderately attractive, though many of my friends couldn't see it, somewhere between hunky and chunky. Best of all, he jumped at the invitation to come and meet Big Mama. I took this as a sign that we were to be wed.

He stayed, falling into the whole guru game as deeply as the rest of us, having already read every book available on the subject, growing more and more enamored of metaphysics in general, becoming enamored of me...

I moved to a position as blender-tender for a juice and health-drink concession in what James lovingly called the "Sports Infection" just down the street. The Sports Connection was the gym that I had been going to for over ten years, since its much more elegant incarnation as the Beverly Hills Health Club. That job went on for close to four years. It was a much cleaner environment than the bar, and basically all the same boys, sans makeup and earrings.

James and I began sleeping together regularly and I fell easily into the cushy pattern of having a man's ass, as it were, to taste nightly. There were certainly more attractive men on the block, many of whom kept a-callin' and a-houndin' me at the gym, on the street. But we were not encouraged to date outside of the ashram group, since any bad vibes would ultimately just get brought back for Big Mama to contend with.

I explained the whole mess to Kahala, best I could, that the baby and marriage were just a spirited dream, but that, after all, I *was still a fag*.

She hated me.

James moved in, Kahala moved out; it was one of the group's numerous scandals, which often seemed to be the major motivational force behind many of our social come-togethers.

James was a puppy at heart, at least when the cur of his monstrous intellect gave him reprieve. When he needed me most he would affect a nap, wearing nothing but a pair of clean white skivvies, flopped face down on his floor mattress; he knew I couldn't resist. I would come in, kneel beside him and slide my hand up the inside of his thighs, the other hand working the knots along his spine; his ass would curl up to meet my gesture, begging me to slip off the briefs and sink my teeth into the awaiting apple.

Married life with James certainly was not the same as it had been with Kahala. He was a clean bloke and a splendid cook, and he soon learned to be completely receptive to my proctological bravado. But we competed intellectually, competed artistically, competed for Big Mama's attention. It was as though we had grown up brothers and had a million mutual references from which to pull. We were certainly not strangers, even when we met, and there was an obvious karma that had yet to be worked out. Everyone sat tight.

Pretty soon the bickering began. Then we were both covertly bitching to other friends in the group about each other, undermining each other's position with mutual pals and with Big Mama. We were brutal with each other, nasty, sarcastic, requiting.

The sex continued, however, insuring that the relationship was still valid. It reminded me of the times when I was a youth when I would be punished by my dad, swearing as I cried that I would never *ever* be friends with him again—hours later, as I sat laughing on his lap, I would wonder where that promise had gone.

Thanks to the low counter, standing all day, and slinging about cases of juice, my job at the juice bar, coupled with my daily after-work workouts, began inflaming an already sensitive back. Now, believing myself to be psychically impervious to calamity, physically indestructible and *always protected by Big Mama*, I ignored all these pains and warning signals until one day I had to have James come and help me to walk the two blocks home. That was the end of the job. I couldn't move after that, couldn't sit, stand or lie down; all that I could do was to maintain the fetal position, on one side or the other, with pillows carefully tucked in the cracks for support. I had herniated two disks.

This hellish condition persisted through myriad treatments: chiropractic, acupuncture (which cured it the first time—the second, the old Chinaman shook his head and said forget it, go see an MD.), Hellerwork (with Nordic Al), Aston Patterning, Rolfing, Feldenkrais, Reiki, Traeger—all to no avail. Three doctors immediately wanted to cut me up, fuse everything, and gave me a 50-percent chance of recovery—*scum suckers.*

I could no longer work. James began paying all the bills, doing his mega-stress bartending job and getting barely enough satisfaction from me to even warrant tossing me an occasional bowl of soup. I could barely take myself to the bathroom, the pain so intense that I would simply black out, which was the closest thing to sleep that would come my way.

"You're faking it." James announced. "You just can't let yourself feel what you're really feeling. It's karmic, just let it go."

"All I feel is pain, James. I'm sorry if that's not such fun for you."

"I don't have to have *fun*, Gavin," he hissed, "I can have fun by myself. More fun than *you've* been."

"Well what do you want then?"

"To be loved."

"I love you, James."

"*I wuv you Gavin*," he mimicked back. "Say it like you goddamn mean it!"

He attacked me, kicking me furiously full-force in my back while I curled around myself on the floor, screaming. I couldn't offer so much as a *Fuck you!* My mind was empty; I wasn't even sure that I didn't deserve whatever retribution he chose to dole out. All I could think was that I would die like this and that he would be hauled away for my murder. And that meant no more pain.

Whether James actually believed that I was faking this, or whether he thought he could somehow magically cure me through catharsis, or whether he just out-and-out wanted to cripple or kill me, I still don't know. I went into paroxysms of primal screams, seeing all of this life and many others flash before my eyes as colors went to black and back to colors again. It was a Bette Davis/Joan Crawford scene from *What Ever Happened to Baby Jane?*; I was a goner.

Well, after some quarter-hour of this violence, this screaming, there stood a fractured-looking Uncle Doug at the door with a hostile pack of LA's finest flanking his rear.

"Are you all right?" Doug asked me, shaking.

I did my best to nod my head and felt like another ignominious queer caught in the emergency room with a bizarre foreign object stuck up his ass. I mean, James and I *were* lovers. *Weren't we?*

The cops dragged us outside. They did the best they could with me. They checked us both out—our eyes, our arms for evidence of needle marks. Neighbors had amassed in the driveway and on the lawn.

"What's up, guys?" one said as they scrutinized us.

"Just a little tiff," James said curtly.

"Is it over?" they asked him.

"Yeah." He looked at me. "Isn't it?"

"Yeah," I said grimly, "it's over." I was too embarrassed to be frightened. I didn't care about life anyway. The worst part was the realization that I frankly wanted to take James back inside and fuck his brains out—thereby regaining some semblance of control—if only I could move.

"Are you sure you're okay?" they said to me.

"I'm fine."

"Do you need a doctor?"

"No."

"Do you want to press charges?"

"No," I said with only slight deliberation, "we're okay."

All I can say is that I believed there to be a karmic debt here—silly me—even though I had long-before dispelled any belief in karma. Still, I was all wrapped up in my theories and confusion over how I had brought all this on myself—how to accept *responsibility* for it, what *I* was doing wrong, what *I* could do to change it. It was messier than peeing upwind.

James I hated, but I understood hate to be merely the shadow of love, indifference being love's opposite. I hated *myself* as well. And frankly, I felt sorry for James; even though his body appeared sound, I knew he *was in much more pain than I was.* My pain was, at least, working its way out; James had yet to contend with his. But of course I couldn't go on in such jeopardy.

Much of this dilemma had come about due to the fact that neither of us would move out of such a great and affordable house. *I* had been there since the beginning, and so refused the notion; James was outright defiant about it, and feeling in-love-and-jilted-by-me, would rather hang around and plow the toxic soil than strike out on his own.

It was a bitch. But I was saved, ultimately, by one of the most loving individuals I have ever met, Helga, a new adherent to Big Mama, who moved me and all my belongings directly to her one-room garage studio. And that was that.

James was obliged to move out into his own apartment, since no one from our group would consider living with him at that point, witnessing his craziness, and fear, loathing, and animosity at every darshan.

Then James stopped attending meetings—and came down with round one of pneumocystis.

From that point on his disintegration was swift. Few of the devotees would dare to visit him during his prolonged hospital bouts, because of his unrelenting wrath. Big Mama had hardly a word to pass on to him; nor would she make any effort to cure him, as we were initially certain that she would.

It was a painful and grueling sickness for all involved. I went to see him a couple of times, but he was generally so caustic and repellant that I simply stopped, instead making the daily pilgrimages to his apartment to care for his flock of bedraggled kittens. His apartment was trashed, cat shit in and on everything, strewn with empty bags of dried kibble that the cats had had to gnaw their own way through because James was either too weak, too incoherent, or too absent to care for them.

"You'll get sick, too," he cursed me, finally, "and Mama won't help you either."

My own misery seemed wan, now, in comparison.

I was glad when he died; we were all glad when he died.

We did what we could with the cats, his belongings, his bilious mom, and that was that; I had lost my greatest adversary, a brilliant pal, and a great fuck. AIDS now had a name and a regular place in my world.

HELGA

Man creates order;
God, chaos.

When Helga first showed up at our group, from another ashram in the Santa Barbara mountains, I thought, *Wow, this is one zanged-out chick, one spacey lady,* but I fell in love with her immediately. Of course, her attention was all-doting from the start, Helga having a particular appetite for attractive young men. Kahala was terrified of her, seeing her as a "loose woman" come to take away her man. Though once James and I became an item, she and Helga actually got to be best of buddies—as did Helga and James, putting the lady in a most precarious position.

There was also much speculation as to whether or not Helga had originally been a Henry or a Herbert: she was six feet tall, broad in the shoulders, with narrow hips, a big head, and breasts that just didn't sag, bend, or fold. She was drop-dead gorgeous when she was all made up and was a featured model in Helmut Newton's infamous collection, *Big Nudes.* Besides all that, Helga had the sexual rapacity and aggressiveness of a man—a complete lack of interest in permanent romantic relationships—and admitted to having had all her female parts long-since neutered.

Her story, as she told it anyway, was that, back in the medication-crazed early Sixties, she was one of those frail little girls whom everyone worried would break a bone. Some wily hack shot her up with a mega-dose of hormones and Goddess-knows-whatall; she grew into an Amazon and has had body chemistry problems ever since. A bit of silicone magic, and she had gone on to a career as a topless dancer.

Once, at a film at the ashram, a few of the gang were contemplating the breasts of the leading lady. Someone said, "They're not hers." To which Miss Helga immediately replied in full-voice, "If she *paid* for 'em, they're *hers!*" It was that irrefutable Polish farm-girl logic that made Helga such an essential boon to our lives and our community.

Helga was a nurse for the elderly, whom she adored. That, along with a relationship with a gentleman who paid a substantial salary to keep her on call, meet with her once or twice a month, spank her delectable buns—no sex—and send her on her merry way, had always kept Big H in the green.

We shared just the one tiny room, so of course we shared just one tiny bed, for over three months. We never attempted sex, though Helga would occasionally comment on, stroke, or otherwise acknowledge my morning salute. I believe it was understood that our friendship would be much more inclined toward permanence without the complications of romance. Besides that, we were too much alike, both with an essential drive toward the beautiful, the masculine, the transitory.

It was also obvious, at this point in time, that I would be little more (or less) than a slow-moving vibrator in the sack anyway, unable to move my back and barely able to rise. Helga massaged me, when the lumbago would allow me to be touched at all, and provided all other services necessary for the care and keeping of an adult male invalid. She was a rotten cook, on her little hot plate and second-hand toaster oven, but she was dedicated.

At the same time, I should add, Nurse Helga was regularly attending to James, both in and out of the nearby hospital, his cats, *my* cats, as well as her own clientele.

My eventual cure was chalked up to several remedies. First and foremost, I'm sure, was the ridding of James and that inimical entrapment. Second, my chiropractor/acupuncturist finally threw in the chips, prescribing mega-dose Valium and Darvon, which kept me comatose, numb, and immobile for the time it took for my body to rearrange itself internally. Third, Helga took me to a clinic that performed a spinal block, injecting some anesthetizing agent into the muscles surrounding the area from which all the pain was emanating.

But Helga's diligent care, on top of all of these things, was without a doubt the single most important element. She saved my life.

Things at Big Mama's, once I was able again to attend, started hoppin'. At one intensive… Mama seemed to be burning especially hot. We had all spent much of the morning writhing around on the floor doing our kundalíni snake routine, yammering in tongues and flouncing about. All of a sudden Big Mama had Julia down on the carpet and was bearing into her third eye with both her thumbs, screaming, "See it, Julia, see who you are! See the light! See Who You Are! *Jump!*" Again Big Mama shouted, "See it, Julia; don't get lost; Who Am I?"

A flood of light came over Julia's face like an instant sunrise: "Why, you are *me*," she said, "and I am you. Hello me!"

"She's got it." Big Mama exclaimed, "Julia's enlightened. The angels are rejoicing."

Helga began a college yelp that started everybody screaming and cheering until Big Mama quieted us, leading Julia out of the room and in toward the kitchen where lunch preparations were meant to begin.

In no time Big Mama was on the linoleum, as was the rest of the kitchen crew, Julia, Jane and Roger. Voices were babbling, Big Mama was singing a hymn to Kali and Shiva, Julia was giggling and tittering, and we were all in our own states of jumbled bliss as the drift came fluttering through the curtains toward us.

There was another pregnant silence, then the sound of chairs flying across the room, plates scattering, and we could hear Big Mama commanding: "See it, Roger. See Who You Are! See the light, Roger, follow my voice. *Jump!*"

Little Roger, too, caught that most-sought-after glimpse—"Junior," was *enlightened!*

After lunch we went directly into our afternoon meditation (or *shaktipat*), and as Big Mama circled the room "working on" each devotee, a steady stream of disciples became Goddess-realized. Jane got it, Duncan, Kahala; Helga got it, or said she did (but later told me that she didn't, but that she didn't want to be left out and thought that just by saying it she might after all *Be It*).

Big Mama sat on me, literally, for twenty minutes, pressing into my head with both hands, banging on my heart until my chest became raw; she kept saying, "He's so close, he's so close..."

I begged her to continue, I could feel the sun just behind the thinnest cloud. She said, "What do you see?"

"A big eye," I responded—I saw the giant eye of God peering through me. But the *"G"* got caught in my throat and everybody, including Big Mama, heard it as *A Big Guy*, to which Big Mama stated flatly, "It figures." Everybody laughed and Mama moved on.

It was coitus interruptus of the best sex I had ever had. The energy had been like sulfur matches igniting simultaneously in all the cells of my being. But I kept anticipating that it would be like it had been with the LSD, that it would just *happen to me*, and as she screamed, "Jump! Jump into the arms of the Divine!" all my befuddled brain could think was *Where? What arms? Jump where?*

When Big Mama left the room that evening we all congregated at the foot of her stairwell and began chanting our favorite panegyric:

We love you Mama, oh yes we do
We love you Mama, oh yes we do
We love you Mama, it's true
Oh Mama, we love you!

To which Big Mama, sitting out of sight at the head of the stairs, countered:

I love you children, oh yes I do...

The enlightenments continued after dinner—Big Mama even went for me a second time—and I drove home the next day depressed and exhausted with a Goddess-realized Helga. *I should go back to drugs,* I told myself.

Big Mama implied that it was the state of my back, the pain I had been through and my resultant shattered nerves, that it was karmic, and that I would soon be strong enough to "join in the fun." But she was just being matronizing. I would never get enlightened in this lifetime: the drugs had fractured my chakras beyond all hope of repair. And according to all my readings and studies, such events as this were seldom if ever encountered. The most revered gurus go on for their entire worldly stay with thousands of followers, possibly only ever bringing one, two, maybe three to the ultimate spiritual goal. Big Mama had just kicked butt with thirteen people!

But not me! James had just died of AIDS; I would probably just die too, unenlightened, crippled, poppin' my Valiums...

TOM

It is the responsibility of the poet
to be naked at all times.

It is not that I didn't love Helga immensely, but the pad *was* a tiny one, and my back did undergo a semi-miraculous salvation. I inadvertently ended up with the ludicrous job of shipping and receiving clerk at the massively frenetic Rodeo Drive Williams-Sonoma. It was an active job, which made the time spin by, bristling with pretty objects, endless gourmet coffees, chocolates and tea biscuits always available as samples; and the other employees were basically dear, if a trifle stuffy.

So having a salary now, and some regularity to my life, I bid Miss H au revoir and moved into my own apartment in one of the funkier parts of Hollywood. The rent was only three-hundred—decent for Hollywood, for 1984—and the building was actually quite pleasant, with miles and miles of barbed-wire coils encasing the compound against the illicit street trade outside.

One day I received a fan letter from the Olympic rain forest in Washington state. The writing was juvenile, but the content was interesting, literate, and seemingly sincere. I answered back; shortly after that he phoned me. "I'm calling from a pay phone," he yelled, "no phone in the treehouse where I live. I hate phones. Everybody's looking at me funny. The locals—mostly Native Americans—all think I'm weird because they see me walking around naked, usually, even in the rain. It's *our* land—they can do what *they* want on *their* land."

I just let him go on. "I found your books by accident at the West Bank Bookstore in Seattle. *Very* impressive. I just wanted to tell you how impressed I am! I have a degree in comparative literature—also a PhD in oceanography—*very* impressive! *Most* impressive! I want to read more..."

I sent him a couple of missing volumes, and invited him to come by any time to read the stuff in the raw, so to speak. Within weeks he drove down for a visit, claiming to have other errands to run in LA.

Tom was the son of an exceedingly wealthy family in Seattle, though he lived by himself in a tiny hand-hewn cottage on the northwesternmost point of the forest, on land among the thousands of acres that his family owned all over the state. He was a genius, considered himself far less attractive than he really was, largely due to the shape of his face and cranium, which seemed as if it had been redesigned to accommodate an excessive amount of cerebellum.

He fell in love with me, drove down to LA on regular visits, always bringing an enormous pot exploding with some species of exotic orchid or rare hybrid azalea or the like, and he told me tireless stories about the ultra-rich, about his sad and bizarre childhood, being schlepped around the world to talk with and associate with geniuses all over to appease his loneliness and his appetite for thought and information. He had been legally disowned by his family, at his own request, ate only at Denny's, drove a small white Honda, was entirely circumspect in his desire to appear proletarian, and most loved to make regular pilgrimages to San Simeon "to see just how insane the mega-elite can become!"

He also worked a regular nine-to-five "for the discipline" at a nearby army base, rarely seeing anyone socially with the exception of an occasional fresh recruit that he would lure to a local hot spring, get naked with, and lust after. "Yes," Tom admitted, "take a look, I'm probably the only thirty-three year-old virgin on the West Coast!"

For four years he had been a Mormon *demigod*—"one whose calling and election have been made sure"—in Salt Lake, and on the road as a missionary in Argentina. Tom's parents were ultra-liberal intellectual Democrats, and during that period of rebellion in which a teen will seek out most anything that will contrast with the wills and belief systems of his parents, Tom headed to Salt Lake City and signed up. Because of his family status, his éclat, his youth, and the fact that he was "outside blood," which was always considered the strongest within the institution, Tom was rapidly promoted to a rare position of rank within the church hierarchy.

"Eventually," he went on, "I was initiated in an inner sanctum far beneath the mother house, in a room entitled the *Holiest of Holies*, by a being... well, how do I say this—had he an actual mass, he would have weighed, oh, three-to-four hundred pounds. But he wasn't a physical being—they called him an angel—he veritably glowed with a pale orangish light, had tiny pig-like ears, no real nose, and long sticky fingers that scratched out the initiatory cachet on my forehead, something which I soon discerned as the backward Roman numerals for *666*."

It was a malefic tale, full of semen, blood sacrifices, atomic bombs, stolen supersonic jets, Pentagon offices and the like. And while I cannot say that I thoroughly believed his chilling words, the archetypes played in nicely with many of my own inner ghouls, and I *oo*ed and *ah*ed at every delicious conclusion. Tom described the situation in terms of the *Book of Revelation*: politics, finances, angels, and a World War III which he claimed the Mormons (this beast) were actively pursuing, as it would be only *after* that war that *their* time would come for total world dominion.

Eventually, Tom said, he fled the cult, and his family's wealth and power hid him in safety, moving from city to city for over a year until the heat had blown off.

Tom gave plaudits on my writing up until the poems I'd written about encountering Big Mama; then his face changed, and he was silent as he read. Finally, he slapped down his hands on my desk, frothed at the mouth, as he has a natural propensity to do, and shouted, "Gavin, this is *crap! Crap crap crap crap!* You have fallen into the trap of religion; you have sold your soul! This isn't you! I know you think that this is you, but this is merely the ravings of yet another starry-eyed mystic, rehashing old adages about God and love. There is no guts, no truth. You have lost your *truth!* It... it's... *crap!* I'm sorry. I just hate to see you do this to yourself!"

He went on and on about the validity of God, gurus and the like, but more about the nature of the soul, and how it manifests through passions, and not "precious adages." *Pedantic* was the word that he finally came up with, ushering in a new model for me of cardinal sin, the idea of attempting to sell someone on an idea or concept or philosophy, as opposed to creating your own reality and merely allowing another to follow along with, or not. "Descriptive versus *prescriptive*," he recapitulated.

I understood the distinction, but the allegations infuriated me. I set about the task of defending my position with Big Mama. But even my speech, I realized, was pedantic, as I asserted my position and attempted to supplant his, discrediting his chiding as attempts to pull me away from my teacher and become available to him as a lover. And yet I knew that *my experiences* were all that *I* needed to validate my endeavors along the "spiritual path." Why was that not adequate? Why did I need to drag along others for approval, or gainsay *their* chosen route? Isn't that just what every Christian, Mormon, Scientologist, *est*ian and New Ager feels compelled to do?

"Gavin, the way to sway someone is through one's own mistakes and example, allowing each and every other person to make *their* own mistakes and corrections. The world changed as the result of the example set down by Jesus Christ, not because of the theoretical pontifications of the Apostle Paul. You *change* me with your poetry—that's why I'm here!—you *educate* me, the virgin, about life and love and sex. Empirical knowledge is infinitely more valuable than rhetorical. You don't have to be a genius, you simply have to tell the *truth*. Richard Nixon is a genius. But he's a chronic liar. What makes your early work brilliant is that you lay it all down in its absolute nakedness for everyone to see..."

I gave in; I allowed Tom to be right. He was not, after all, telling me to give up my spiritual efforts. What he was doing was pleading for me to *not* give up my own inner reality for the sake of some guru or some *hypothetical* God. To not espouse angels and roses, when what I was truly feeling was cocks and brahmascat. Tom continually championed, through all of these arguments, the noble Allen Ginsberg as our greatest bard, not for his philosophies, or for his poetic style and definitive innovations, but for his mere piss–and–sperm reality, his lack of apology, his purveyance of truth. "This is what, in a society where a Nancy Reagan can become queen, we so desperately need, Gavin, and I know that you are the one that can speak this truth. You have! Why do you think I keep coming down here to do what I can to ensure that your words are made available to the world!"

Tom's constant soapboxing revived my pre-Hollywood ideals and made an editorial distinction for me, within the writing of poems, songs, painting, and most any other aspect of my creative and noetic soul. It was a lesson that was not appropriate around Big Mama, where a flowery façade was always the modus operandi, lest Mama get offended or have her lotus-petal feet muddied by her disciples' flying caca. How much further was that from the mother that I had grown up with, where a smile and a colloquial amenity was the guise for the daily murder or treason? Was not this the charm of the Reagans, after all, the specious parents (the *actors*) who smile and wave as their children burn?

Between my first and my second encounter with Tom, I had become one of the first of the initiate *samnyasin* of Big Mama's order. That is, we had all donned apparel of ochre—the color of renunciation—at least around Center functions. I was retagged *Swami Shankarananda*. No more sex, no drugs, alcohol, meat; we were all given our own personal *puja* ceremonies to perform every morning and each evening before retiring. It was now just me and the cats, by ourselves at our spartan Wilcox apartment.

I quit the Williams-Sonoma, I began baking again, this time for a lovely Arkansas gal named Darlene, at her catering outfit in the ritzy old-money Larchmont district. I won the *LA Times* "Best Brownies in LA" award. The job kept my emotional life rich and passionate, in contrast to my onanistic existence back at the flat.

The Sam Harris album finally came out, and I spent endless hours listening to my first recorded song over and over at full volume. Friends would come and visit, amused and terrified by my monkhood, merely sleeping on the couch in the livingroom and wondering *why*.

Tom moved to LA, to join once again with the beau monde, such as it is, to learn the social graces that he had never had the opportunity to participate in, and to be with me. We became best friends. He lived with me on occasion, between other friends' backrooms and livingroom floors, and sometimes not returning or making contact for weeks at a time. He was having a blast. He loved my cats, my laconic lifestyle, ate nothing but soup, sandwiches and crackers under any circumstance, and began regularly attending Big Mama's darshans, if only to monitor me—and to flirt with the other monks. "The good disciple," he mused, "must be continually tested." Together we edited volumes of my work, collecting the more fiery pieces for eventual publication, as *Pagan Love Songs* and *The Naked Poet*. Tom had a biblical ability to pick me up and set me right back on the track; he was essential to my development as a poet. And I believed him to be all mine, my geek angel, my guardian, my promoteer, my magi.

Then Tom met Rand David, a perky blond super-thing from Lafayette, Indiana. Rand worked selling Macintosh computers, was an aspiring Sam Harris, had the dick of a satyr, and all blond/blue-eyed/Americana. He was a catch by anybody's standards. Tom fell in headfirst.

Gavin, Hollywood, 1977 (John J Krause)

Señoritas—Craig and Gavin, 1976
(Greg Gorman)

1978 (John J Krause)

1978 (John J Krause)

1978 (John J Krause)

With Rio de Python on the set of *Stryker Force*, 1985 (John J Krause)

Reading at Catherine's, 1987   At A Different Light, San Francisco, 1987
(Rink Photo)

Hollywood, 1982 (Michael Lassell)

drawing by Tom of Finland

With Rio, 1987 (Stephen Jerrom)

With Reatta and Debbie Harry
(Elsa Braunstein)

With Leonardo and fangs at Studio LEONARDOGAVINCI (Stephen Jerrom)

Swami Shankarananda, 1987 (Steven Arnold)

Poolside, Hollywood Hills, 1989 (Tom Bianchi)

I lost him, then, for great periods of time, putting up with him only over the phone with his maudlin rantings and self-fulfilling ravings about Rand as the most beautiful man in the universe, the most splendid voice in nature, a genius, and so forth. They got an apartment together in Silverlake and set up shop. "I'm now managing Rand," Tom assured me one day. "We're having that tiny bump on the bridge of his nose fixed."

"But why, he's beautiful as is."

"Well it's his only flaw."

"Then keep it and cherish it! Whatever happened to honesty, piss and sperm...?"

Then they had his name officially changed to "Shawn," which, for some reason, they felt was more masculine. All of this was quite boring to me and only interesting for the effect that it was having on Brother Tom's emotional "coming out." But still Tom was available when there was work to edit, or some other literary coup. Then, as Tom's own story began to unravel, I came upon the facts that Shawn was largely supporting the two of them with a quite active hustling career (Tom as pimp!), and that even virgin *Tom* had on occasion stepped into the action for a gratuitous three-way with a tolerant patron. Vladimir Horowitz was a semi-regular customer; a California State Senator, who would fly down from Sacramento on business "vacations" away from the wife; and there were even a couple of calls from an agent of Jimmy Bakker offering round-trip tickets to Bibleland, South Carolina (which they presumed—until later news breaks—to be prank calls...). Fascinating. Soon Shawn shunted Brother Tom and was off to New York with a rotund and jovial mafioso restaurateur. Tom was beside himself, called the feds on the restaurateur's cheated income tax, and became the target of assorted hate mail, death calls, and even, on one occasion, gunfire.

He moved to a tiny back room behind a beachfront home on a very exclusive private beach (Trancas) just north of Malibu. His neighbors included Goldie Hawn, Spielberg, and eventually the exiled Bakkers, Jim and Tammy Faye, themselves.

When that grew too hot, Master Tom fled to New Jersey with a brand-new airline job that allowed him occasional jaunts to the boy-friendly lands of Holland, Sweden, France, New Zealand, Tahiti. All the while, Tom's confidence coalesced as his sexual desirability as a tall and exotic American became more and more coveted and exploitable.

"You know," Tom remarked one day, "maybe I'm not such a troll after all."

"*Droll*, yes, *troll*, no. It's like I told you, Tom, it's 99 percent attitude."

With Shawn and Mr Mobster finally subdued, Tom moved into a position as vice-president of a major international conglomerate, essentially running their Hawaiian offices. He wasted no time in discovering Honolulu's infamous "Hula's" and "Dirty Mary's," as well as the fertile sensorium of one of the few remaining post-AIDS bathhouses.

Some time later, long after Tom had departed, I had a brief but satisfying consummation with precious Shawn—in town on business, ostensibly, and still attempting to trace the whereabouts of Tom. I gave only sperm, not information. Shawn is currently the singing MC of a Bourbon Street girlie show.

Over the years I would manage to squeak out visits to eccentric Tom, in his one-room, paltry basement within Honolulu's scariest Filipino slum. He dragged me around to the "gay" establishments, while I'd pull *him* off to the heiaus and "power spots." We made regular pilgrimages to the homes of both Ms Doris Duke and the ever-charming Imelda Marcos, with regular tongue-in-cheek homages made to the tiny prefab charnel/cathedral that housed the stiff of Ferdinand. When funds allowed, we always included a late-night rendezvous at the Royal Hawaiian for two of my heroes, the incomparable Cazimero Brothers (not to mention some of the sexiest, and most scantily clad, hula boys the islands have to offer). Tom has since been promoted and moved to his corporation's central offices in Auckland, New Zealand, where he is currently terrorizing an island full of pandemically naive, misplaced European youth—much to their delight, and edification. I have yet to indulge a visit.

Over the years, many of Tom's "truths" have proven to be falsities; he has fessed up to every one. It is ironic, then, that I owe Tom for his indispensable meditations on the marriage of *Truth* and *Art*.

DAVE

It takes a little devil
to make a good angel.

By 1985, I had been a reborn virgin—monastic, clean-vibed, and holy—for over a year and a half, and my hormones were giving me plenty of trouble. Madam Helga decided that I needed a good night on the town, to shake the ennui, "Dance some of it out, have a drink, break some rules..." She, of course, had the wisdom to never accept Big Mama's coercion to be celibate. If celibacy were a prerequisite for spiritual attainment, she would be satisfied merely being a sexually content aspirant for at least as long as her talents and desirability held out. Helga was as famous for seducing her various and sundry Santa Barbara gurus and yogis as I had been in school for making it with my teachers and administrators (something about seeing how all that power worked, and *who* really *held the power*).

A semi-friend of mine, Mark, had initiated one of LA's episodic stream of ill-fated off-night discos at a local lesbian bar. That was perfect, as I didn't see myself being up to one of the crowded, smoky, and cruisy Hollywood establishments. We arrived early, Helga and I, eager for dance floor space, and were met at the gate by a wispy young man decked in a railroader's cap, white lipstick, a plain white T-shirt, silk pajama bottoms and Chinese slippers—*vibes*, I thought, it's gonna be one of *those* nights. "Friends of Mark," we informed him, and slipped right in. Nobody else was in the place except a couple of quiet bull-ettes hangin' around the lady bartender in the back. Mark was ecstatic to see us arrive, and promised us an evening of loud and aggressive dance music, from vintage R&B (Aretha, Gladys, Marvin) to Peter Gabriel, Bowie, Roxy Music, the good stuff that you simply *never* hear in a West Hollywood designer disco. Helga and I were in Heaven, downed a few quick tequila-and-tonics (my first in many moons, breaking the first vows of the evening) and set to work.

Now, Helga and I had long established our own rhythm and rhyme on the dance floor. Helga has no rhythm whatsoever, which gives her the creative license to dance in whatever manner the spirit may strike upon her. We are both extremely athletic, sexual, and indulge in a great many gyrations that would bolster any Christian's argument against dance as a harbinger of carnal sin. Helga also has a tendency to get hot, as I do, and dresses accordingly, as she did this particular night in a one-piece sleeveless black knit miniskirt. Given the nature of our dancing, the booze, and the fact that Helga's pronounced and largely synthetic breasts tend to create exotic rhythms of their own, her skirts invariably end up somewhere between her waistline and her neck. This never seems to become an issue for the dear lady whatsoever, as she haphazardly yanks the thing back down without missing a beat.

Helga never wears underwear.

So given these conditions, my own normal half-clad state, the nature of the music—which really was divine—and the fact that we had no mortal impedance on the floor, Helga and I had one of our grandest evenings of all time; while Mark, so excited by the antics and intensity of Lady H and myself that he seemed not to even notice the fact that he had no other patrons for the evening, played like a son-of-a-bitch.

Now the little doorman, Dave, couldn't help but become seduced by the Dionysian passions of our ritual, and bounced atop an unused bar to begin his own empathetic undulations. We went on that way, crazed, blissed and sweating rivers, as I began having some serious notions about this peculiar young nubbin on the bar. And then, in the middle of a prancing turn, Dave's pajama britches, which he had flopped off the suspenders from, simply dropped to his ankles.

Without the loss of grace, rhythm or motion, he yanked the PJs back into position, attached one suspender over the shoulder, and kept on dancing.

Dave never wears underwear, either.

Let's just say that any vestigial attachment that I had had to the swami order simply trajected out the open front door at that time. That hand-sized white ass bounced in front of my eyes, and in a fraction of a second burned an imprint that I am quite certain I will carry with me into the farthest reaches of eternity.

The dancing continued, all the way up until closing time, Helga and I rarely missing a beat, stopping only for another drink, water, and carrying the glasses with us onto the floor. Dave continued dancing as well. It turned out that he was hardly an employee of the place, but was simply assisting his friend in the opening of what he had hoped would be a good New York-style dance club; consequently he was free to do whatever he pleased, which at this point was *dance*.

Dave was cool, so lost in his own insular world that he could've been completely by himself—he is like that when he dances. As I later confirmed, he also assumed Helga and me to be a couple. As we were leaving, Dave looked surprised when I handed him my card.

"Call me," I said. "We'll go out dancing sometime. Sooner than later."

He didn't smile, but his slate eyes flashed my success.

I lamented not getting a number from him, and in the quiet week in which he did *not* call, I meditated on little besides his arresting cheeks, skinny gams and pearlescent lips.

He called. "It's Dave" was all he said.

"Where you been, dude?"

"Had to fly to New York. Wanna go out with Davie?"

"I don't drive. Can you come over?"

"Be right there."

He arrived by motorcycle. Now he was out of his element, though padded and buffered by his leather jacket and dark glasses. We hopped astride his crotch rocket and sped off into the night. The dancing was abysmal everywhere we tried, however, so we went out for late-night gelati and coffee.

Dave was taken aback by my monasticism and the West-LA ashram house into which I had recently moved with three other swamis. I was not yet ready to invite a man in to spend the night. And I discovered that he lived with another young Canadian named Robbie.

"Did you mind the bike ride?" he asked me as he stood awkwardly at my door that morning.

"No," I said, "not as long as I have you to hold on to."

"Well how'd you like to hold on to Davie up Highway 1 to Santa Barbara this weekend?"

"Yes," I said, "I'd love to."

He smiled and fumbled for his goodnight cigarette before spinning off into the fog.

I have always had a bad relationship with motorcycles, having lost more than one friend to their dangerous allure. I decided straightaway, with Dave, on that hot day, as I wrapped my arms around his thin waist and buried my face inside the back of his sweaty hair, I would just as soon die with him than go on in safety without him.

I left this cavalier Zen master in absolute control, of the trip, of the road, of my heart, as I wandered my hands around the revving rhythms of his belly, his hypersensitive nipples, and the streams of water that poured from his outstretched armpits. I knew I had it bad. He gave me very little back; then again, here I was *with* him, at *his* request...

We arrived at the posh hills of Santa Barbara in the early part of the evening, drove into the cactus gardens of a splendid wooded home, retrieved a key from under a flower pot, and entered. Dave's friends, Gary and Arn, were not present. We went about scrounging some peanut butter, making coffee and a salad, dining, and retired to a splendid sunken tub in the guest room.

"You'll love Gary and Arn," Dave said. "Gary's into gurus and meditation and all that, he's really into it, I forget his guru's name; he was married for nine years to Bonnie Raitt, now he manages a whole bunch of songwriters. He's doing really well, you'll love each other. Arnie's a lawyer."

I did not want to talk about meditation, music, or law. I took him by the hands and kissed him. His lips tasted of cigarette smoke and coffee, neither one of which I liked, but on him it tasted like *love*. Kissing turned to a gentle overall play that continued on into the night.

Somewhere in our minds was the presence of Robbie, Dave's mysterious at-home boyfriend, and my own ridiculous situation. Neither of us knew what to make of this, how far to go. AIDS was new on the scene and Dave, I later discovered, had just found himself to be HIV-positive and was distraught, confused, and angry.

Still our malleable bodies talked, until the wee hours, and we lay there, lips together, parting only for the moments it took for Dave to suck down his regulated fags, while I took the break and the liberty to suck on *his* little fag.

We fell asleep like that, our faces in each other's legs—teethmarks in his ass, cigarette tar in my mouth. We had discussed AIDS and "safe sex" in timorous terms, not wishing to curtail our budding sensuality.

In the morning the play resumed, and we grew more feverish between cups of coffee that Dave had magically procured. Dave had me in his mouth and was pulling on me like a newborn calf, I had the smell of him all over me, his taste in my lungs, and with only a brief thought of AIDS, broken vows, and infidelity, I climaxed in his throat.

Immediately I collapsed beside him. Dave jumped up for a towel and spat into its folds. His eyes flared.

"How dare you! How dare you! You who are so health-conscious and holy. How dare you come in my mouth!"

"I—I, uh..." My mind sped through all the excuses known to carnal man, and the realities of being in some strangers' house, far away in the hills of Santa Barbara, lost, without wheels, reliant on this impetuous prick I didn't even know the basics about. I heard only the sounds of two male voices coming coarsely from the next room, clearing throats, coughing and pouring coffee. I was doomed.

"Dave?" the less masculine of the two voices croaked, "Dave, is that you?"

I fell onto the bed, facedown in psychic immolation. Dave simply grabbed the contaminated towel, wrapped it around his waist and vanished out the door. I heard mumblings, a laugh, the coffeemaker gurgle; looking out the wall of plate glass, I imagined myself to be one of the gray mountain squirrels scurrying up an oak and disappearing into the limbs far above samsaric reality.

Fuck him, I said, *skinny little shit. Fucking noisy bike; fucking Santa Barbara anyway. And he's goddammed married. It's Shiva's wrath—Big Mama's somewhere near, laughing. Fuck Shiva! Fuck Mama! Fuck everybody!*

The door opened. Dave slipped quietly onto the bed beside me, and put his smiling face on my trembling shoulder. "Come," he said, "you gotta meet Gary and Arn."

I slipped on my shorts—which Dave kept yanking off me—and followed him in to meet Mama and Papa Bear, two gruff and formidable *bushido* hitmen in kimono bathrobes, circling around a cauldron of coffee in which I, surely, was to be tossed.

"Gary, Arn," Dave said, "this is Gav. My new lover."

❦   ❦   ❦

The rest of the weekend with Gary and Arn was swell. We had a splendid time discussing art, music, and spirituality, preparing and devouring healthy gourmet meals, Dave and I impiously making out, pulling each other's *dhotis* down, pinching tits and otherwise behaving like love-crazed brats. It was a liberation for me, after a year-and-a-half without this. But more, absolution from the *concept* (karma) that asexuality had anything at all to do with spirituality. As if sex and spirit could somehow even exist without one another—blasphemy! *That* marriage is eternal.

Four or five years earlier, shortly after meeting Big Mama for the first time, I was walking through West Hollywood when a thought appeared to me: *hamburger.* I went inside the local burger joint, secured and devoured my first hamburger in fifteen years, and had the most profound experience of release. It wasn't that I desired to begin a diet of meat again, or that eating meat was spiritually correct or incorrect or anything; it was just that I didn't *have* to be a vegetarian anymore. My concept of vegetarianism was gone, and even though I rarely had any yen for meat whatsoever, the fact that I *could* indulge made all the difference in the world. From that point on, my choices to not eat meat were made *in the moment,* and were choices of the *heart,* and not those of *dogma* or *belief.* This is the way that I felt now, with Dave, that I was again free to choose for myself what was right or was wrong for me in each new moment.

My new "ashram" was in West Los Angeles, a long way from Dave's close-to-downtown industrial studio/apartment; I wasn't driving then, had no car. And after the bliss of Santa Barbara, there was the fact that Dave lived with Robbie, shared an only bed, and that I shared this distant house with three other monks, and, being the first samnyasin to defect, did not have permission to drag home a trick under *any* delusions of love. Nevertheless, I visited him almost daily, taking the bus for hours to reach him, then sitting there, in his studio, copying down his puns, serenading him with poems and observing in awe as he tinkered with his tables of broken and rusty icons, putting them all together into objets d'art, then pulling them apart again, fixing more coffee and changing the record. Robbie worked nights, so on non-meditation nights, I was able to stay until quite late, grabbing the dreaded late-night bus and softly crying all the way back to the beach.

This lasted a couple of weeks. We fought regularly, and divorced a hundred times before we even got married. I would yell and cry that there were "issues" here, that I had many emotions at stake, that there were things we would simply have to "deal with." "No no no!" Dave would scream with blunt moxie. "No *issues* for Davie! We're not gonna *deal with, handle, work out* or *process* anything! If it's not easy, and fun for Davie, then I simply don't have the time!"

That was Davie's genius; it was also his undoing. Dave was four years younger than me; I had never fallen in love (or had sex) with anyone my junior (with the one exception of Little Frank in North Carolina, but that hardly counts).

One evening Dave informed me that he was heading off to do a two-week faux-painting job in New York, then down to Florida to see his family, pick up a car his father had gotten him, and drive back home.

I was depressed, and turned out to be even more distracted with Dave gone than I had been with him present. He sent me several cards, calling me things like his "own private possession," and his "personal little sperm bucket." These were addressed to Rita Manson, Dave's having decided that I looked most like a cross between Rita Hayworth and Charles Manson—I didn't really know who Hayworth was, but I had always maintained a fascination for Mr Manson, so I took the name to be a compliment. He called, and when I wasn't there he would chat familiarly with my monastic house members, propounding all kinds of nasty things about me that they would convey, smiling and blushing. It was quite the scandal; everyone was jealous.

Eventually Dave called en route to Miami: why didn't I fly out there, meet his folks, and drive back with him across the southern route of the United States? I was an easy *yes*. I was also broke. But after some fretting, I came up with the realization that my dad would gladly pay for my plane fare, if I were to inform him that the trip was merely an excuse to visit his poor aging mother in Macon, Georgia. I was right, and in a trice on my way.

In the air, somewhere over the Gulf of Mexico, I felt fresh paranoias about this *love,* whom I hardly knew at all (we hadn't even fucked!). I laughed at myself, my impetuousness, my presumption—I was again doing exactly what my dad, Dalton, Bear, Tom and other friends all loved and looked to me for; I was throwing my heart to the wind and all caution behind me.

But when Dave did not meet me at the gate, I experienced my first real panic. Not knowing what to do, or where to go, I started walking, following everybody else, my eyes scanning every face as if I had perhaps not recognized my tangential Eros.

Then I saw him, halfway down toward the baggage claim, simply leaning against a wall in a large black cowboy hat, his sunburned chest blaring through an opened shirt. I knew again that I was right on track—I had no options but to do what I must do. "I can't believe you're really here," he conceded, finally, when we had reached his car. We were in the basement of a massive concrete parking garage; the air was fluvial with heat and rain. "I can't believe you just flew across the country to see yer Davie."

"I'd fly anywhere to see my Davie!" My heart leapt at him. Our lips touched like flames on a slick of grease. We were attempting to inhale one another down our throats, to quell this unquenchable thirst, to sate this madness.

This was passion. This was *Divine.*

❦   ❦   ❦

Dave's parents were both attractive young bodybuilders. Dad met us at the door in nothing but his jockeys and hugged us both alike; his mom fell in love with me when I took over dinner preparations and finished by doing all the dishes and putting things away. His young brother and his fiancée were two of the sexiest things that I had encountered. It was a house abounding with eroticism; Dave and I were even allowed to share the same bed. But Dave would not function sexually in his parents' house. "I just can't," he squirmed, "not here."

The next day we set out immediately up the central Florida highway, stopping only briefly in an Everglades park to ogle a few gators or crocs. My hands stayed in Davie's and my own shorts the entire, sultry way, wielding our respective reptiles like a Cretan priestess; we kissed whenever traffic would allow. By evening we made it to my granny's house out on her own pond in the woods just north of Macon. This time *I* could not function sexually. Fascinating.

The morning allowed only a brief canoe trip around the family pond before we said our goodbyes, took filial portraits (Dave insisted on putting his arms around Henny, the lifelong family maid, preferring, as did I, the reality of the poor southern blacks to the odious artificiality of the bourgeois white folk) and sped off across Georgia. At a hysterical Chinese restaurant in Mobile we fell for a tiny Chinese waitress with one of the most intense (and incongruous) southern accents that we had ever heard. We made it all the way to New Orleans by midnight, had a few dances and coffee-and-whiskies at the queer bars at the end of Bourbon Street, and went on to the YMCA for a couple hours of blowzy sleep.

In the morning, butt naked on our dingy bed, I seduced the half-asleep Davie for the first time, entering his angelic crescent smile with spit and my first gauche attempt at condom use. He was cranky, messy from the quarts of coffee we'd consumed, unused to the passive role in bed; but he said yes (at least by his allowance) and, nervous though I was, the experience was a bonding between us. Barriers went down after that and we relaxed, spanking each other in the grim Y showers, pinching and teasing as we went out into the devilish Louisiana heat, then down across a southernmost off-route to witness the coastline, the bayou, the swamps.

Storms embraced us and added to the humidity and the sweat that bound us. Despite the tension of the drive (Dave had a deadline for a job back in LA) it was a vibrant and torridly romantic escapade, this stewy and delusional environment, the impelling reek of Davie's body as it effused its caffeines and nicotines; this could have been Hell, or it could have been Heaven, and I would have been just as happy for it to continue forever.

We had one other fated stop to make, and that was the poor, tiny town of Port Arthur, Texas, famous as the birthplace of Janis Joplin, the one saint that we both agreed gave Texas a reason for being. I have always considered

Janis the greatest of all singers, and at that time found it incredibly exhilarating to learn that my paramour felt the same passion.

We arrived at Port Arthur in the middle of a storm in the middle of the night, and parked for the evening in a cheap freeway-side motel. We had a soothing and seductive shower together and Davie took me, this time in a much more relaxed and hygienic state, into the magic yoni of his bowels, his thighs, his embrace.

"You like Davie," he said dreamily as I lay devastated atop him.

"I love Davie," I sighed between three measured breaths.

"Then keep it in 'im," he whispered back, "sleep inside Davie all night..."

With that he faded into sleep.

I barely slept at all, exhausted though I was. I jotted the poems that came rushing to me and gazed up and down this nubile alabaster succubus that lay so innocently atop those polyester sheets. Outside it thundered.

In the morning we crawled to a nearby Wendy's for coffee and food-like substances. To our horror and amazement, our waiter was not even exactly certain of who Janis Joplin was, much less where she had lived.

"Why she was Texas' most famous governor," Davie informed the chap, "'cause she was also a big country-western singer. And she was the first lady governor anywhere, and is known as the 'Singing Governess' to this very day!"

The young man was shocked, impressed by Dave's learning, and pointed us in the direction that he had believed he had seen her name on a *real estate sign*. Sure enough, we eventually came to a small cottage on a residential street, beside which, in a vacant lot, blared the hand-painted sign:

For SaLe Janis JopLin childHood hoMe

If we had had any doubt which of the two homes on either side the sign belonged to, it was made obvious by the panicked woman on the porch of one, who grabbed her broom and slammed herself inside the front door. This *had* to be Janis's mother, the fiend that we both recalled having seen years before on *60 Minutes* apologizing for her fractious daughter and snotting about what a lovely voice she had actually had before she "took to rock and roll." We hated her.

We decided that mom wasn't worth the bother, as we studied the exterior of the home, posed and photographed each other about the sign and the front porch. We lamented not having the money to snatch up this great national treasure and create the museum and shrine that that brief life of passion and unrelinquished bleeding so richly deserved.

From Port Arthur, we sped across the relentless bucolic boredom that is Texas, stopping just before New Mexico at a charming diminutive neon motel, with sex in the shower, and sex in bed, as my druid prince collected our filled condoms and flung them at the far wall, where they stuck, suspended, like big brown slugs on a garden trellis.

"Better bash me gash one more time, mate," Dave warned me in his perfect Paul McCartney accent, "'cause tomorrow night we ain't stoppin' 'til we hit LA."

We both knew what that meant.

The rest of the trip was somber, really, knowing that it would end with our resumed separation. Dave would return to his bed with young Robbie, me to my ashram isolation tank.

To appease my jealousy and pain, Dave did make the valedictory promise that he and I were lovers, that he and Robbie merely shared a bed, but that they would never again share physical love.

But the very next day, over brunch back in LA, Dave informed me that Robbie and he had had sex that morning and that he was sorry. I didn't accept his apology and walked away. He caught up to me, and somehow things got settled until they exploded the next day at the beach, when I walked away again, not even wanting to hear his explanations. I was wrapped up in my ashram reality, Dave had his world, and we simply never should have come together in the first place.

We made up, we fought, we fucked. "Guess what Davie's bought?" he finally told me.

"I hate to think. More condoms for Robbie?"

"No sirree, Davie's bought his own bed, just for you and me. You can come spend the night every night you want a piece of yer Davie."

"I'll be there every night!"

It also became permissible for Dave to sleep over with me. He began coming to darshans, having no idea what to make of them; just there. I even learned to drive, again, and procured a sepulchral $200 float known familiarly as "Birdshit-on-Wheels."

We did junkyards together. *My Beautiful Laundrette* and *Kiss of the Spider Woman* both came out that year and we saw each over and over again. I took Dave to see *Satyricon* and *Meetings with Remarkable Men*, and both his life and sculpture were duly changed. I also took him for his first viewing of *The Boys in the Band*, still conspicuously the *only* film ever made about homosexuals.

We did restaurants continually. The most fun were when we ventured into the "hip" or "homo" parts of town: Dave looked, at that time, an awfully lot like a petite Bruce Springsteen. And the West Hollywood girls, as West Hollywood girls are wont to do, are always looking for a reason to perceive as "gay" *any* industry role models, the more masculine the better. So it was more than frequent that whispers would start up across the room, where one table was discreetly pointing out to another table that there was Bruce Springsteen, *and isn't that Gavin Geoffrey that he's eating with...?*

At that point I would without pause or question simply erect to the occasion, pull Davie's face across the table toward mine and hit him with the biggest and the sloppiest kiss that our chips and salsa would allow.

Our sex was spontaneous and good, until I, as always, began waxing restless. Dave had now completely succumbed to the passive role, which we enjoyed, but which offered no challenge. Sex became rote and without foreplay; I resented and grew bored with having to wait for Davie to achieve his own orgasm. What I most enjoyed was continuing to photograph Dave on our regular junk outings, at the shipyards, scrap-metal grounds, in the desert, San Francisco, all about his studio. He has never ceased to thrill me with his flaunting mythic beauty, his polymorphic sense of style, and his solipsistic grace.

Dave got a job doing Cher's New York condo and went off with her for several months. I knew that he was back at his New York haunts, the seedy and underground New Wave discos where he would smoke dope and be carted off to the beds of strangers. I began having transient affairs myself, or trying to, though I was always very much in love with Dave. I was just furious with the notion that he was at large in the Big Grapple without me.

The fights grew worse, over Big Mama, my eventual move into another ashram situation instead of finding a bigger studio with Dave (we had been fighting at the moment of the decision); my blathering New Age rhetorics began clashing more harshly with Dave's return to his nightlife, and his regular attendance of the notorious all-night black disco, Catch One.

We couldn't live together—much as I still fantasize about it—and I would never trust him without me. Not good grounds for coffee.

We also made the mistake of working together, since Dave needed continual assistance on his escalating trompe l'oeil gigs. He would get jealous when I regularly proved better than he at the techniques that he was teaching me, though we had fun making up by balling in the master suite or in an unlocked electrical room while the brute construction workers clomped about outside. But the fights were nasty, and the competing, the indictments and self-exculpations, the inelastic scars of distrust, all ended us.

Some years after a final separation, Dave came down with an acute case of syphilis of the cerebral fluid, a condition that almost killed him, and which greatly impaired his ability to perform the work that he needed to pay for his treatments. I was employed to help, but by this time I was doing *him* a favor and he was infinitely less cantankerous.

When *I* began regularly attending Catch One, I was living in a studio not three blocks from where Davie had once resided with Robbie (on the bad side of town). Dave and I would again intersect, dance together, concordantly at last. The pain changed simply to the wistfulness of knowing that we could not be together, as lovers, had no ability to be friends without sex, and would never be able to be dispassionate strangers. I watched him as though he were a child of mine, one that I was obliged to push out of the nest for his own flight (as well as my own). Now he too has died. I will always hold sacred and immutable the times that we were together.

EARL

Poets are people who
write about their death
before it happens.

The ashram's move from Santa Monica to an in-town address was an exhilarating one. I was back on the market again, on familiar turf; and after my protracted abstention from carnal reality, I was willing and ready to plunge into the world once again. Dave had blasted open the levee of my soul and I was awash with the seemingly endless possibilities of the concrescence of spirit and flesh.

The house was a large and dramatic twenties Spanish-Deco number, selected for its grand and Gothic beam-ceilinged livingroom in which we could hold meditations. I was left in charge of the rather barren gardens, my acknowledged bailiwick, immediately planting all of my and Big Mama's favorite posies and Hawaiian tropicals.

I began working, doing graphic layouts for Princess Patricia, one of our housemates, who moved her entire design studio into our ample diningroom. Which meant that I didn't even have to leave home for work. That, plus the fabulous and flirtatious all-night gym just up the block on Beverly—I was a hog in Shit-Heaven.

With the move came an ever new fervor over Big Mama. We knew that Big Mama had "the Power," but we didn't know why she didn't have the following. It was suggested that the "West" was simply not ready for a female deity, a black female deity at that; or perhaps that Mama, being the biggest and the baddest of 'em all, was simply too hot for most people to handle.

Nevertheless, Mama was always rapping about increasing production, how she would someday address football-stadium-sized crowds, and so forth. Step by step she and Ananda changed the formats of the meetings to more closely resemble the more successful darshans of Sri Muktananda, Rama, Da Free John, or whatever "lesser" male guru happened to be the vogue that year.

And, given that half the swamis were beginning to follow my lead, getting laid, getting corrupted, getting real—it was marvelous to watch!—it was decided that the swami order would be abandoned altogether. It had all been kind of a joke, really, on Mama's part, to show us the foolishness in such extremes of behavior, or so we were told. "*You* were the guys that thought you wanted to be *holy*," she said, smacking smartly on her barbecued chicken.

It had also served the purpose of frustrating and running off dear Chuck, Big Mama's indecorous husband. Big Mama immediately put the make on baby Roger, the only virgin in the bunch, but only after hitting up Brother Charles (our one gorgeous black bro) who informed Mama that he was *too* gay and she was *too* fat.

Roger it was; we all listened at the door.

We did Hawaii again, a select clutch of us, where Big Mama attempted to impress us all with benign tricks like parting the clouds over the Kalalau Valley, stilling the ocean, and so forth. And it worked, to some extent—or at least gave us something to talk about when we came home—but the magic was foundering. No one was sure why.

Meetings would occasionally blossom with new blood. A cadre of lovely female porn stars showed up—*that* put the men in an altered state. Several movie stars arrived—my favorite, Olivia Hussey, some twenty years after her definitive *Juliet*, still one of the most remarkably attractive white women I have ever seen. The enlightenments had faded, mostly, with one or two exceptions. Several had cracked up, become junkies, even died. Helga returned to her tiny trailer at the bottom of a gulch in a mountain yoga retreat somewhere above Santa Barbara. And some of us who were left began pursuing our answers beneath other teachers' tents.

Big Mama perennially considered me the instigator in these moves away from her, since I was one of the louder and more verbally endowed of all the gang, and it wasn't long before I began *not* attending our torpid house meetings, no longer tithing, and engaging in petty games with the Devi like slamming doors in each other's faces. Funny how the tides change.

Meanwhile, there was life to attend to; the egregious Dave came and went, came and went, and eventually went. "With friends like you," he cursed me, "who needs enemas?" But there were new "friends," lovers, and deities in my life.

Then I began getting sick.

Jimmy Barron was one of the most consistent and long-running friend/boyfriend relationships that I had had; he had the smoothest, whitest and roundest butt that I have ever had the pleasure of devouring.

Jimmy cut my hair—perhaps that was how we met. He also cut hair and did makeup for the song and dance man and one-time Liza husband Peter Allen, with whom he was always traveling. It was through Jimmy, then, that I came to work with Peter, finishing, ultimately, only one song, a theme song for LA entitled "I Gave My Heart to the Angels," which had been commissioned of us from Mayor Tom Bradley's office as an anthem for the LaLa Olympics. Peter became overwhelmed, of a sudden, with the beginning production of his great Broadway flop, *Legs Diamond;* we never demoed the song, Linda Ronstadt never recorded it, and I, again, didn't get rich and famous.

Throughout the eighties, Jimmy was always there, even with the occasional lover, proffering that irresistible derriere and the most seductive smile in West Hollywood.

On the rebound from Dave, still shaken and confused, I managed to cop a visit with Jimmy, this time not planning on an evening—Jimmy was on a whirlwind between gigs with Peter, staying at a girlfriend's house, and I was ill.

"I've had this sort of flu thing for over three months now," I moaned to him, whining about my breakups and hard times with Dave, with Big Mama. "I just feel like shit. And of course my mind assumes the worst." After all, it had been several years since the deaths of James and Little Stephen Buker, and however many other romances and beaus I'd heard tales of or received wake invitations for. And yet, I didn't feel like I had any allegiance to death—I mean, I just wasn't buying this terminal band-wagon that everybody seemed so anxious to jump on. I had seen in the LSD sessions in what manner I would succumb, and it's not from some sinister social disease.

"Believe me," Jimmy said, his hands on my knees, planting a stout kiss right on my mouth, "it's even worse in New York than it is in LA. But I know people that are getting well..."

He began rattling off a story about Peter's agent, who had been in contact with a certain Dr Rice about a substance known as "reticulose" which was reported to arrest the disease. The drug was being pulled up from somewhere in the Caribbean and was being dispensed by said doctor out of a small clinic in some nebulous desert town about an hour east of LA.

In all the underground railroading that I have done since, regarding this chemical as well as others, I have always marveled at the caution, negativity, and purblind conservatism that people have shown regarding a safe alternate treatment to a disease that medical science continues to view as terminal. I lunged in with all the lust and rigor with which I tend to fall in love: *Yes, of course. What is the doctor's name and when can I see him?*

I didn't even know what my diagnosis was at that point, whether I had full-blown AIDS or not. There had been no reason to find out. My energy was gone, I had been nauseated for over three months, obliged to change the sheets nightly in order to dry the bed and reduce the chill that soggy sheets further induce. Glands were swollen and sore in my neck and armpits, with minute buboes spreading from the thicket of my groin up and down my pelvis. My skin was becoming dusty and paperous. Many lady friends around me were coming down with the ephemeral and elusive Epstein-Barr syndrome, which created a flu-like attrition that allegedly would persist indefinitely. Perhaps that was all I had, a lesser plague. Still, having the track record that I had, being in the "high risk" group to which I so religiously belonged, and knowing that I was in fact HIV-positive, I knew that it was time for a check-up. Besides, Jimmy implied that the reticulose might be in limited supply. But more than that, my heart said simply, *Go for it!*

"Tell the doctor you know me." Jimmy kissed me goodbye, sliding a leaf of paper in my back pocket on which he had scribbled the critical information. "And Peter—mention Peter..."

It was one of the few times that Jimmy and I had ever parted without diving voraciously inside each other's clothes, mouths, colons, and I wondered what was to become of us all. And yet, I had never before been so aware of how much I loved this soft-voiced man. "I love you, doll."

"I love you too. Let me know what Rice says."

I called Earl that afternoon and drove out to Wherever-the-bumfuck-it-was the next morning for a ten o'clock rendezvous.

Frankly, I prayed that I *had* the disease. Because I knew that if I did *not* have it yet, that I *surely must* come down with it eventually. The drug was *here now*, and I wanted to get this taken care of while I could. It was an exciting prospect; I felt like Rosa Parks. I wanted to be the first cured.

"Hi," Earl said—there was no secretary. "You must be Gavin. Come on in."

Aside from the fact that he spit on me when he spoke, Earl wasn't scary at all—at least in a professional sense. His office was a dinky, poorly decorated hole in the wall in some white-trash desert mini-mall, much like any other small-town doctor's office.

Earl was in his fifties, with coarse Jewish features and a horrendous rug on his head—I think he had it on backward that day—sitting behind a dungheap of a desk, puffing on a continuum of cigarettes and drinking a mobius mug of cold black coffee. "So, tell me why you think you're sick."

"Well, I haven't felt like having sex in almost ten minutes."

"Not to worry," he volleyed back, "wait till you meet my nurse..."

We hit it off great, I asked a zillion questions and he went on at length about every nuance known about this disease, its spread, and its cure. The statistics, protocols, and taxonomies went straight into my left brain and got lost there as such things tend to do; but the romantic aspects took root, captivating me more and more with each new tale and analogy.

There were no other clients that day, so I sat with Earl, gabbing, taking him out to lunch, gabbing, coming back and gabbing some more.

"First of all, I'm a Ph.D.," Earl explained, "so I *am* a doctor. But not an MD. My specialty has always been the cardiovascular sciences, until my lover died. Roger. He was twenty-four. That was a year ago."

"I'm sorry," I said.

"So were we. Anyway, I started looking into every drug we knew about. Then I got hipped to this stuff called reticulose, a drug that has actually been around since the thirties, predating even penicillin.

"The drug was initially touted as a cure-all for a host of ailments, many of which it did in fact cure, but, like aspirin, was considered a bit of a snake oil. When asked to put up some three-million dollars worth of tests and dead bunnies for *each claim*, this small Florida-based outfit simply said *Kiss our ass* and took the drug elsewhere.

"Reticulose was then used throughout the world to cure viral meningitis and a number of 'incurable' diseases like Lou Gehrig's syndrome. About six months ago we began playing with it and discovered it to be a side-effectless eradicator of the HIV virus. So now they're pulling the stock in from Japan, China, whatever back shelves they can find it on, and stockpiling it in its current home base in the Greater Bahamas.

"But there isn't an endless supply. And though they say they still have the formula, I have reason to believe that they in fact do not. Which has me worried."

"It has me worried too. I want to do it. Now."

"Well let's give you some tests first..."

"Test me, but give me the treatment. I mean, if I don't have an obvious case of AIDS now, surely it's imminent. You know what I'm saying."

"Yes," he laughed. "I do."

The stuff was cheap and relatively harmless to use. And even pleasant, for the mild rush that some patients were apt to experience. What wasn't cheap was the ridiculous mélange of tests that Earl required weekly, so that he could adjust the dosage and see exactly what effect it was having. He was learning about this *as* it happened.

For one reason or another some people did not respond immediately to the drug, especially those in whom bacterial and cancerous infections (over which the reticulose had no jurisdiction) had taken hold. And one, out of dozens of patients—unfortunately, the lover of the editor of the *Advocate*, assigned to guinea-pig the drug before his chivalric spouse did—proved to be allergic to the stuff. Reticulose is derived from milk, to which this patient was severely allergic.

Earl had a recurrent nightmare about being shot while driving his car— martyred for his heroic efforts to save patients' lives. He laughed about it, but I could see his fear.

I insisted on immediate treatment, despite Earl's desire to wait for my test results. I had known about my positive HIV status for over a year, since '84, and had lost at least five lovers to the ailment. Having been sick now for some three months or more, even if I were not diagnosed as blatantly AIDS-ridden, certainly the E-B, or whatever I had, would be responsive to the treatment as well. Earl conceded—reticulose did seem to cure Epstein's—and filled up my first needle.

In California, people with AIDS are permitted to do just about anything in order to treat themselves. Earl, however, could not legally inject me with a non-FDA approved substance. So, he simply filled the syringe, gave me a crash course in sub-Q injection, watched me do it, and caught me when I passed out. I was on the road to becoming an AIDS junkie. I mean, it got to be fun, finding new and less painful places to do the shots, taking care of my needles, keeping a regular schedule, and *feeling* myself getting *well!*

I shot up for a month. My *T-cell* count jumped from the low 100s to the 300s. There was a plateau or two, and then a two-month lag after the last injection for the full effect to take place; T-cells were in the upper 900s, tantamount to maximum health. I became well, and no signs of malaise have ever returned. It's been well over a decade.

Half a year later, in 1986, a test was developed that measured the HIV in the blood by measuring an accompanying protein called *P-24*; my tests showed the blood to be viral-negative.

Earl urged me to not call this "cured," any more than to take it as a license to practice "unsafe" sex.

Of course, I did call myself cured, as well as, once meeting up with my next mate, Leonardo, practicing unsafe sex like mad. I stridently maintained that there was no such thing *as* "safe sex" anyway, having ripped and lost as many condoms inside Dave as not. And once Leonardo had been treated as well, we figured that if either of us ever had problems again, we would simply do the treatment one more time and that would be that. It was an airy theory, and full of holes—so to speak—but it's hard to teach an old hog new dicks. Or was it just my pertinacity that I had already viewed my death by other means?

Leo and I would buy a private stock of the drug and tuck it away. The reticulose that we had used was already fifteen years old, which was the last batch that had been made, but the little glass cruets in which the liquid was hermetically sealed seemed to hold the stuff indefinitely.

Besides, I came to deduce, the cure is in the acceptance of wellness, and has little to do with any specific treatment. If reticulose were not available, something else always would be, for the *willing*.

Earl and I got to be greater buddies as I dragged more and more friends to him for congress and treatment. Many came away with their health restored.

"You be my main man in the street," Earl told me in his best pimp accent.

"I guess that entitles me to free tests from now on, huh?"

"No, you gotta put out for that."

"Only if you got the drugs to make me six-two, blond, and twenty-four again."

"When we develop *that* formula," he laughed, "I'll be the first one cured. Then you'll be makin' deals to sleep with me."

"Damn right."

I frequently bounced down to Earl's Laguna hideaway home, where he lived with a gorgeous and precocious teenager that he had actually seduced away from his own daughter. John was an alcoholic at age nineteen, a latent genius, and enthralled by Earl's mad-scientist lifestyle. John later came up with a variety of successful treatments for AIDS and its infections, many of which friends and I guinea-pigged with profound results, having become myself addicted to the mad-scientist program and agog at the possibilities. My own stats remained—as Earl delicately put it—"disgustingly healthy."

It was always a trip, sending people down to Earl's for treatments—after his desert office was raided and shut down for some trumped-up reasons and Earl had been forbidden to practice again in that county. Acolyte John would come out from under his car, screaming at Earl about this or that theory or infraction, draw blood with his greasy, unwashed hands, and rattle on about medical extrapolations that none of us could begin to follow. If someone wasn't squeamish enough about the casual procedures, then John-and-Earl-at-home would certainly send them weeping back to their doctor to get AZTed to death—that is, except for the ones who decided that they wanted to *get well*.

Earl always gave me something to make the trip worthwhile, as my duty was largely hand-holding the individual that I delivered to his home/office. I had no further use for reticulose, but Earl never could stop me from rooting through his cabinets and shooting up with germanium, B vitamins, or going for the hour-long vitamin-C IV-drip.

"You're just a fucking junkie at heart," he'd tell me, laughing.

"Yeah? Hey... what's this stuff?"

"Put that back, that's for the dogs!"

It was a bit of a joke, but I *was* fascinated by the gestalt of the body, wellness, and *getting*-wellness. Besides, given my propensity for living almost exclusively off chocolate and coffee, Earl figured that I could always use the boost.

But when I mentioned the unsafe fucking that Leonardo and I would continue to pursue, he would get truly peeved. I, on the other hand, was duly amazed at the stupidity and sluggishness of mind with which people I confronted came up with questions like "If it works, why doesn't my doctor know about it?" all the while succumbing to a Janus-faced medical establishment that was shooting them up with a scalpers'-priced synthetic salmon sperm (AZT) with a *zero*-percent success rate.

It was over this issue that I split with ACT UP, an organization I was initially excited about, until I realized that they were screaming to the very beast that had presumably created the disease in the first place, for the "cure," pleading money from the state to give back to the medical thugs for a lethal and humiliating drug that had nil success. And I thought, *Shit, the fey community is committing suicide!* At the very least, it is the most sordid case of our community's particular penchant toward allelomimetic behavior—calves to the slaughter—how few are willing to step out of the herd!

Though I also encountered rare people like Leonardo, who, after a brief word or two about reticulose, simply said, *Great, I want to do it!*

There have been other drugs since reticulose that I became aware of the successes of, some even able to claim "cure," even turning people from HIV-positive to negative. DH-22, a decade-old derivative of reticulose and very successful cancer cure, seems to be even more effective than its predecessor, and in more and more acute cases of the disease. I know of people who have maintained their wellness exclusively through classical homeopathy. Chinese bitter melon, an age-old Asian eradicator of cancerous tumors, is available for a buck-a-bundle at any Filipino or Laotian farmers' market. Selenium, beta-glucans, and many herbs such as uña de gato, St John's wort, and elderberry have now been proven to arrest viral replication, at a minimal cost and, more importantly, without endless and unpredictable side effects. Others as well lead me to the cosmic synopsis that there are as many cures as there are diseases as there are people. And the drug itself no longer is the primary issue. The issue is one of *wellness*, acceptance, and the willingness to buck the majority.

Earl also made me aware that the vast percentage of the doctors and scientists who had created and administered these "alternative" treatments had either mysteriously disappeared, been killed, or were otherwise persecuted for their efforts—the same as has happened to uppity docs who have discovered and utilized cures for cancer over the years. This created both a frenzy to my attempts to get my friends treated and a paranoia about "modern-day" allopathy in a plutocratic society, and the demagogic "good doctors" (and pharmaceutical companies) who were tormenting and killing people right and left and being commended (and rewarded) for it.

I came upon the book *AIDS and the Doctors of Death* by Doctor Alan Cantwell, which backed up my suspicions that the virus had been laboratory-created—for just such a desolating intent as we were seeing: political opportunism, rising conservatism, and religious furor.

It was as if a Hitler had devised a chemical to annihilate dissidents, neatly, discreetly, as though it had been their own fault—testing the theory out some few years before with a feline predecessor virus (leukemia) to see how a man-made disease would affect a select percentage of a population; then with the human version in a segment of an African community, and finally leaking into the "gay" community through the deceptively altruistic guise of freebie hepatitis vaccines—*such a deal!* I mean, just how did bovine leukemia and sheep visna viruses get together and mutate within the blood matrix of a green monkey in the first place, except inside the neo-Josef Mengele cages of torture within the miscreant bowels of the Defense Department (now accepting donations from the pietous liberal community for further tests)?

David Geffen has made the self-inflating statement that it is only money now that will save us from this plague, and he is exactly wrong. It is money that has created AIDS, and it is corporate and political greed and malignity that perpetrates the evil.

I pulled back, both from the dragon that had set up the plot, as well as from this reactionary PoMo victim grid that has become so chic. I realized that all we could do was to continually put it "out there" that there were options, and provide a bit of an underground railroad system for those who wished to opt for them, which we have been doing ever since.

Earl eventually moved to a hospital in Tijuana where he could perform with fewer complications, as well as have access to better medical facilities than were available in a clinic setting. For a time he and John had actually coined a clone of reticulose—since they were worried about the inevitable depletion of the supply, as well as the manipulations and unreliability of his source for the stuff—though the clone seemed to be less effective than the original. Earl was eventually able to play a bit with DH-22, interferon, and some other questionable or relatively successful substances. Through John's studies and experimentation we came into playing with the age-old remedy of urine therapy, something that is enjoying more popularity as one of the surest (and safest) cures for Kaposi's.

"Oh please, Nurse Johnny," I jested, twirling his golden locks, "gimme just a swig..."

"Sorry, dude, it's your own piss that does the trick."

"You can't drink his pee anyway," Earl invaded, "it's 99.9 percent beer, and I don't want you to drink alcohol."

With some effort, I did overcome the social taboos against this well-founded eternal tonic. I continue to drink eight ounces of my first morning pee just on prophylactic principles. I relish the fact that this is a cure-all that is not only accessible to everyone, but one that cannot be scalped, or come under any kind of governmental regulation. I have, though, heard of a doctor in Texas who has isolated some curative factor in urine (he's using equestrian) and is administering pills of same to AIDS patients for some not-insignificant fee. Successful or not, he's missing the whole holistic point. *Thanks anyway, I have my own.*

Then all of a sudden both Earl and John—and the reticulose—were gone. Earl was no longer in practice, the phone was disconnected, the house abandoned, and that was that. I have not been able to track them down. I can only hope that they have not fallen prey to AMA/FDA hitmen, but have no means by which to verify their existence at all.

GERMAIN

A visionary is someone who
sees in the dark.

One evening in 1986 Helga swept me away to my first full-body session: a channeled encounter with the spirit/voice/presence of Mafu, one of the twelve "Ascended Masters" alleged to handle this particular creation, along with Ramtha, Saint Germain, Jesus the Christ, Jehovah, and other more ponderous appellations that I can neither spell nor pronounce. A *full-body* channel is someone who actually dies (gives up the body) for the duration of the channeling process, such that the entity that takes possession of said body has both full use of the body, and doesn't have to worry about their words getting muddied by the interpretation or the patois of the person channeling.

The bubbly blonde who was to be the "channel" was charming, comical, and seemingly innocent. She sat down at the head end of this Hollywood Holiday Inn conference room, pulling her hair back into a ponytail and neatly arranging the blouse of a rather androgynous silk pantsuit. She breathed affectedly, adjusted some muscles in her neck, and then her head fell forward as though she had left her body.

"Here he comes!" Helga squealed, as if Mick Jagger were about to leap on stage.

Almost instantly I could hear the massive inhaling of a very aggressive presence pressing out against the bug of her shirt-mike. Her hands swung up and around, as if awakening from a great and long sleep, her chest thrust out, shoulders back, and she stood up, ever so much more filled, and seemingly a good three inches taller than she had been before. A man's voice ejaculated:

"Greetings to you all!"

The enclave, as if in military training, responded as a whole, "Greetings Mafu!"

And the voice continued, "And how are you this day in your time?"

"Splendid!" "Magnificent!" "Brilliant!"

"Ah hah! Brilliant indeed!," the presence conferred, "if you could but see with my eyes! You are like the stars of the heavens, yet shining in all the multitudinous colors of the rainbow. A veritable garden of de-*light*."

Laughs.

"Laughter aligns the body with the soul," he elucidated. Yet he seemed to me almost melancholy, as though he knew a secret to which he realized we might never be privy.

He rambled on, with general and at times quite passionate dissertations as well as more caring and intimate responses to individuals, as he strutted about the floor, asking his fans of their health and happiness. Mafu's presentation was genius, flawless in its logic and its theodicy regarding the unity of all souls, the God-nature of which we all have been born, the desire and yearning in each and every one of us to return to that Divine Source, and the ability that we all possess to do so.

Then he came to Helga.

Every encounter that I've ever witnessed with any male guru or sage, and especially with disembodied spirits, has begun and ended with a note to the Divine Miss H. Whatever it is that the lady exudes, she has them all within her cosmic web. Mafu all but drooled over Helga's presence. He heaved a great sigh, held her hand, and crooned, "My dearest, I have courted you over lifetimes, chased you through the reaches of the millennia, and you have always just evaded my touch. When will you be mine?"

The entire hall blushed. The temperature seemed to rise ten degrees. Then he/she turned to me, smiled, reached out and touched the small gold cross I had worn around my neck since a paramour had placed it there at Cal Arts, some fifteen years prior.

"Someday I will tell you what this means," he prognosticated.

"I—I would like that," I stammered back.

"This was given to you by a very special lady, was it not?"

"Very special, yes," I rouged, "but he wasn't a lady."

"He *was* a lady," Mafu replied, "when you had first known him. And in this incarnation, he came to you as would have a lady, did he not?"

"Uh, yeah..."

"We will discuss this, too, at another time."

He *loved* me; I could see it in the blackness of his/her eyes.

Well, I was hooked. Helga and I attended a number of such sessions, bouncing from hotel to hotel as the group was regularly evicted for no good reason whatsoever.

By and by we attended a weekend-long seminar over the Christmas holidays. There were numerous meditations, visitations, psychic and energetic experiences, but mostly I remember a prodigious disquisition about the life of Jesus, the undisclosed parts. The tale was grim, almost unlistenable, but it was efficacious, humbling; we all sobbed uncontrollably. Mafu glorified the dude as a noble and unfathomable saint, debunking entirely the dogmatic fascist that the churches have re-created him to be.

And again Mafu wooed Helga, but this time he planted a seed with both of us: "You are with a teacher," he commented.

Yes, we both nodded. Big Mama.

"Why have you a teacher to teach you what you already know?"

"I don't know what I know," one of us said, waveringly.

"My child, you know that you are God. So, *who* then is this teacher, and what does she *teach*?"

We had to admit that she largely emphasized that *she* was God, even though it was understood that we were a part of that *Oneness* as well.

"Why do you kiss this woman's feet?" he asked again. "Why does she not kiss yours?"

We had no response. Mafu changed the subject. But our flesh had been pricked. And subsequently bled, as Big Mama began to make fun of and to excoriate these "lower entities" that several of her disciples were reportedly "courting."

Helga and I also discovered a band of extraterrestrial "walk-ins": a group of galactic yahoos currently residing in a compound in Sedona, Arizona, who allegedly had "taken over"—repossessed—prime bodies that had belonged to souls that were just on their way out through suicide or some other form of premature death.

Their message was not of the oracular quality or the integrity of blessed Mafu's, but they were vested with contagious smiles, appeared sincere, and one of the gentlemen was a drop-dead gorgeous blond mesomorph with demonic tattoos all about his arms and chest—it was he that Helga and I vied for treatments from. Tediously, the stud was not allowed by the "commander" to work on us. *Spaceshit!*

"Treatments" consisted of an encounter with one or two of these beings, often assisted by the channeling of a gaggle of others, who would point out damage and problems within the physical organism that they subsequently would attack with everything from crystal wands to interplanetary mantras. A big focus was their concept of exorcism, the throwing out of assorted hangers-on within one's psyche that were no longer necessary for one's "becoming." This proved to not work with me, as the lady that scanned me was psychically informed that she "would be allowed no jurisdiction over my system" and to get the hell out and leave me alone. I don't think that she had encountered such blatant resistance before, for she seemed to be taken completely aback, even offended, and all but lost her intergalactic cool as she informed me that she could not help me, "good luck, and pay on your way out."

The vulpine Miss Helga, on the other hand, received her new space name of "Alura"—fitting—and naturally (or *un*naturally) was romantically pursued by all male entities available through the current channels. *Sigh...*

We gave up on the space people (who soon were recalled from their respective carapaces, due, ostensibly, to corruption, and replaced with a whole new crew from a different sector) and headed out on our own to cull the spirits from the mountains and the skies.

"Aaaa-oooo! Aaaaa-oooo!"

Out in the desert in the middle of the night, we did what the space people called "toning," the spontaneous emitting of single-note sounds that vibrate a healing frequency throughout the body. We encountered streams of lights bouncing in unison across the faces of unpassable rocky cliffs, flying glowing discs, shadowy gnomes and whirling wind devils who came in response to our cries.

We got the heebies and went back to our cabin.

Through whispers at the erratic Mafu sessions, we came to hear of a young lady known simply as Angel who had recently begun channeling Saint Germain. Now, Saint Germain is a fave rave of all students of the mystic and poetics of time—a great and noble French alchemist who appeared sporadically over a 400-year period in Europe's herstory, ever unchanging in his stately countenance, with lengthy red hair and beard. He was most noted for ending the French Revolution by appearing simultaneously at all seven doors to Paris and uttering some words or other that the war was over.

We wasted no time in locating Angel and getting ourselves politely invited to her home in the Camarillo Hills. This time we went with several other of Big Mama's more restless souls.

"Welcome! Welcome!" we were each caressed and kissed by her huggable husband, Ramanda. "So glad you all found us! This is all very new. We're still trying to figure what to make of it. Won't you come in? My wife is in the back meditating, she'll be out before long."

Angel was a remarkably shy creature, with vivid aquamarine eyes unlike any that I have ever seen. Her hair was cut and rolled into a style of some two decades past, and when she pulled it back and slipped into her pantsuit rig, she vaguely resembled a busty Russ Meyer version of the other female channel that we had witnessed: pointedly pastel, attemptedly androgynous, and au courantly New Age. But this one I loved immediately. A Texan, ex-stripper and country singer, who had tragically lost all four of her previous children. My aura flew toward her. And hers responded in kind.

I sat right up front on the floor before the sofa on which the lady would sit. The room was uncrowded and we were thus promised an even more immediate connection with this great and magisterial deity. Our hearts pounded as Angel seated herself and tittered as Ramanda bumbled with the tiny microphone boutonniere.

"I have no real practice with this sort of thing," she began her disclaimers. "I went to a Ramtha weekend once—where Ramanda and I met and he proposed. I had just recently learned to meditate, a meditation in which the consciousness is pulled up the spiral of the energy canal and out through the crown chakra, into space.

"However, one day about five months ago..."

"Six," Ramanda demurred.

"It was five. Okay it was six. Six months ago, or five, while I was still *very* pregnant with our baby..."

"She simply collapsed on her way to the kitchen!" Ramanda was impatient to get all this out. "Go on, honey."

"No you tell them..."

"She just collapsed. Pregnant, mind you. So of course I rushed to her. Then she opened her eyes and a man's voice boomed at me, that of *Jeshua ben Joseph*—Jesus Christ. He explained briefly that Angel had chosen, and been chosen, to channel thusly, for various and sundry spiritual reasons that didn't make a hell of a lot of sense to me at the time, and that she would initially be channeling the voice of Saint Germain, though, since neither of us had heard of Saint Germain, he—Jesus—had popped in to do the introductions!

"Well, of course Angel, when she came to, didn't believe a word of any of this..."

"So Ramanda set me up by a tape recorder and I simply spiraled up and out of my body the way that I believed I had accidentally done earlier while going to the kitchen for a Pepsi!"

"The voice that was then recorded," her husband went on, "was that of Saint Germain, who explained the nature of the whole trip, gave me an extensive reading on myself, and essentially set the whole trip up, which he said would proceed at a greater speed once the baby had been delivered."

Angel further explained that she "misses all the fun"; unlike the other channels, who tend to hang out in the room and listen from a light fixture somewhere, Angel sped off to another world, a world in which Saint Germain spends much of his playtime, and when she returns, she knows nothing of what has transpired. This evoked no sympathy whatsoever.

Her "balancing" act was not unlike that of the other channels we had seen. Conscious breath was a key factor; her form eventually went completely limp, and then bounded forth with a force and a power very unlike that of the original Angel. Her hands swept around in great circles, touching in front of her, and then pulling back against her bosom as if bringing all the room into her/his/*itself*.

"Greetings to you all! Wondrous lights! Precious jewels upon the tapestry of eternity!"

Saint Germain spoke in a grandiloquent and archaic English, very akin to Mafu and Ramtha, which he explained is simply a language with which they are all rather comfortable, and one which distinguishes them from the everyday contemporary. He had a peculiar habit of stroking his/her chin, which he explained he perceives as having a long red beard. He floored me with his wisdom, his grace, style, flourish, whimsical double-entendres and his absolute seductive charm—the herstorical Saint Germain was always noted for that.

Furthermore, Germain responded to *me* as he did to Helga, with ever so much love and attention, amused by my frankness, my sexuality, my impudent questioning which horrified all the other toadying New-Agers and spiritual wannabes. My heart was stricken by this... *god*.

Brother Germain, as we came to call him, described Jesus as a composite soul whom all the sisters and brothers of the *White Light* had "allowed" into being for the "bringing forth of the Christ spirit in the beginning of the Piscean Age."

Most intriguing, however, was his descriptions of Jehovah, which jibed with those of Mafu and Ramtha. "Jehovah is one of the twelve of the *Brotherhood* who chose to divide himself into the masculine and feminine dichotomies back in the beginning of what some of you call time..."

Well, he "chose" to do this apparently to amuse himself with the nature of loneliness and separation. However, having "lost" his feminine counterpart (we all glanced at Helga), he resultantly became the covetous, war-mongering wraith of Old Testament fame. According to Mafu, Jehovah had long ago become jealous of the peace and serenity of a planet known as Maladek in the Pleiades formation, and essentially nuked the whole works. Having been warned of the attack, however, Mafu, head honcho of that solar system, grabbed his population, threw them into space shuttles, and settled Egypt, building the pyramids and related works. Mafu subsequently fell in love with Isis, fell into mortality, and bantered around through lifetimes attempting to regain his awareness until ending up as a crippled leper in the town of Pompei, at which point the volcano blew, his body dissolved, and his spirit catapulted into the "Unknown" and back again with a vengeance—his "ascension" and return.

Germain, too, had fallen into the "play," and had regained his Divine Beingness while watching a twinkling light one stellar night on a hillock in medieval France. Some members of the Brotherhood/Sisterhood had done similar jaunts through the millennia, and others had not, always watching over those who were enjoying their worldly illusions. Others split into many "fragments," all of which will eventually come together again in the form of that one great oversoul of the original twelve.

I was cited as one of these fragments, along with Helga, who have so been drawn to that energy which is the Brotherhood in these various forms, names and voice—all of which Germain dismissed, incidentally, as insignificant, and only utilized for identification, being, of course, themselves nothing but components of the multipartite *Nameless Self* of which we were *all* invariably born.

Life went on, with regular excursions to Camarillo. Germain, unlike *some* saints I've known, never said anything disparaging about anybody—even Jehovah. (He simply said that Jehovah's ignorance is a Divine state, and that he will eventually awaken, through *Love*, like the rest of us, to the truth of All Totality.)

He also provided more clues to the Big Mama issue, though diplomatic often to the point of evasion. Still, we gradually pieced together the concept of energy transference and manipulation. Sort of spiritual vampirism; it was the idea that Big Mama had gradually come to lose her powers, for whatever reasons or infractions—pride, power-lust, perhaps just the belief that these powers were coming *from* her person, and not *through* her from Divine Sources (I am making an arbitrary distinction between the two here, for the intent of an illustration). As her powers subsided, the Devi, being a master of energy juggling, came to rely on and cull the energy from her disciples, only occasionally shooting a wad back to us that might give us a glimpse of enlightenment. That one glimpse, however, in the entr'acte, would keep the disciples pouring in their energies (and stipends) for years on end, in the hope of another "glimpse," another peak experience.

A little test was suggested: we had already noted that the intensity of Mama's powers was directly proportional to the size of the group of believers or disciples about her. A gang of us simply stopped sending her our energy during meetings. The result appeared to be the stasis of *her* energies. She even got out-and-out pissed and threatened, among other invectives, that Lord Shiva would recall her and we would be left to handle our karma all by ourselves.

It sounded like any minister preaching sin and redemption; we didn't buy it. By and by, a sizable lump of us strayed for good from Big Mama's camp, and many of us made Germain and company our regular concourse. It was good to have the people that I loved and cherished from the years with Mama now sitting with me under the splendorous wings of *Daddy*.

Angel and I got to be closer and closer. Helga and I regularly waited until the bulk of the visitors were departed, Angel was changed, and the babies were put to sleep, then took Angel and Ramanda out to the local all-night Denny's for milkshakes and fries. Angel would always insist on sitting beside me and we would giggle and patter about anything that was brought up. She called me her "little brother" and I called her "my little sister."

Eventually she began confiding in me that Ramanda was a drunk and would frequently beat her. Feelings changed, and Ramanda was oft excluded from intimate social encounters, being pussy-whipped into staying home and babysitting the kids, with the eternal *We'll talk about this later!* on both their lips.

Trouble reached Paradise. Saint Germain, though, remained the constant, through several weekend intensives, and eventually regular weekly meetings held in LA, for which I worked the door. "Hurry Hurry Hurry! Step right up, ascend now, be the first on your block...!"

At a marvelous retreat entitled "Father Time," Germain illustrated his cosmic sleight of hand. Utilizing the music of Michael Stearns (*Chronos*—a piece which Germain said was "given" to Mr Stearns *by* the god Chronos), he had us all look at our watches before the forty-five-minute meditation. When the meditation was over, it was forty-five minutes *earlier* than it had been *before we had begun the meditation.*

But the finest moments spent with Germain were those in which we two were alone. These were called "personals," and the Master offered me these for free, given the special nature of our acquaintanceship. I was frightened at first, but Germain immediately took my hands and openly stated his love: "Greetings! *Namaste!* It is wondrous as usual, to be here with such a light!"

"I love you," I mumbled.

"And *I* love *You!*" He held my hands and breathed in and out with me, centering me.

"My heart is so drawn to you, so filled *by* you. I love being in your presence!"

"Mm," he breathed, "do not forget that I am your mirror!"

"What I want to know," I went on, "is just how I am to get enlightened!"

"You already know that here," he said, touching my heart with his finger. "You have not understood it here," he pointed to my head. "That which is your understanding and vibrational frequency, it is given the understanding of *name*, eh? That name which you *have* has what you would call *roots* in the name which was also that of the nephew during King Arthur's time."

"Gawain. Are you saying that was an incarnation of mine?"

"No, but it was a vibrational frequency that is very similar to yours. It was a very brilliant light, very much unfolded. He was serious at times, he was, but indeed a grand source of enlightenment, as you are, and you shall continue to be in your unfoldment."

"I became aware last night at a Mafu gathering how I love Mafu, yet I don't *resonate* with him the same way I do with you, and, as much as I've grown attached to my teacher, Big Mama, I'm not sure that I feel that same connection with *her* anymore."

"Do you understand why?"

"No."

"Because *you* are becoming more unlimited, therefore you resonate to that which is more unlimited."

"Are *you* more unlimited than Big Mama?"

"Mm, in that which is called the bringing forward of the understanding of Divine Nature expressed in physicality, indeed. However, that which is presented is not to be judged, for it is serving a grand purpose, it is very *loved*. It is very much a part of what you would call the heralding of the Aquarian Age. However, there is that which is more unlimited, is less restrictive, less *dogmatic*, ritualistic; it is also more in total fullness of the totality of soul, rather than expressing outwardly through another entity..."

"Something struck me last night that I am concerned about," I interrupted. "Mafu's people are doing what I saw people at *est* do. They are parroting a *rhetoric*, and rather than an understanding that I would hope would come with that rhetoric, he asks them certain questions, and they respond back in the way that they know that he would *have* them respond. And, within *me*, I am trying to find a difference between the rhetoric—or, as you say, the up *here* understanding—and the true *down here* understanding, which is *Being that Truth*."

"There are certain entities that are desirous of what you call rhetoric or ritual," he responded, "regardless of who may be presenting it unto them, or how unlimited they may be. It is nothing to concern yourself about. For as you know the True Beingness of yourself and that which is within you, you will not partake of this, for it does not resonate to your own truth."

"I have an ongoing question about my homosexuality and my fear of women."

"That which is *natural* within you is merely that which your soul essence urges you onward to explore. It is not judged by any of the essences that are of the Light. It is merely allowing you to unfold as you so see fit within your total soul essence self.

"That which you call the nature of your preference at this point in your time is really the understanding of the essence of the love energy which is exemplified within woman: the unconditional love, that which is very like, through the eons of time, the understanding of submittal. It has become, through that which is called the Aquarian Age, in equality. It is aligning itself more and more with that which is true equal nature of the genders, and this is the ultimate in desire. For that which is considered to be *master* upon this your plane is neither male nor female—for they are both. And your contemplation of that which is your gender, and your preference for a particular gender, is a soul essence battle, it is not that which is sexual in nature. It emanates not from that which is third density, it emanates from the contemplation within this your life for the demonstration of both, the male counterpart of you and the female counterpart of you. And it is your desire in this embodiment to bring forward the merging, or alignment of the two, in total balance and harmony.

"And that which is the fear of womankind is the fear of submission, it is the fear of giving that which you consider to be your self unto another entity in submission. You need not do this. That which you call the power essence which is within you as the male part of you, that which is *sovereignty*, it will issue forth as you understand the Divinity *of* You, your nature as God Manifestor, your capacity as that which is the Reflector of the Light and Grand Mirror. Therefore that which is the disparity between you and your understanding of the genders will dissipate. It will align, and that which is *balance* will come unto you, as a natural progression of unfoldment. That which you consider to be this particular nature or preference will dissipate from you. It is only *natural*."

"I have another fear that's brought about now due to exposure to AIDS, having lost two lovers. Not only does it concern me somewhat physically, but emotionally it affects me, the fear of losing that which I am attached to. Anybody I meet now has the potential of just dying, which I suppose was always an option, but it presents itself as a burden on my heart now."

"Indeed, this what-you-call dis*ease*ment *is* an aid, for it brings forward contemplation of superficial partaking of physicality in nature.

"That which you call the *fear* issued forward in your heart, it is bringing forward that which you so fear. You are resonating to that which you fear, and it is magnetically attracting it unto you. So do not fear it, I urge you. That which you consider as consternation for this particular manifestation occurring within your life experience, merely know as God that you may realign your embodiment so that you may not have any deficiency of immunity system or anything else—you understand? That as the *light*, you are in perfect function and harmony; and the knowingness of this—not the *knowledge* of this, but the true *knowingness* of this—will bring forth that which is the turning away of anything you would *not* desire. It will not resonate unto you to come unto you in the first place.

"So, do not contemplate that which you *do not desire*—at all. Walk in sovereignty, in the dominion of your life expression and experience. Walk in knowing that you will experience as you choose, as you desire. You are God and you draw unto you that which you desire, you will manifest for you that which you require. *All will always be peace and harmony eternally with you:* say this unto yourself, over and over. Continue until it is an internal knowingness. Then there is no need to fear.

"If you *do* bring forward this within your experience, part of it will be the resonance of the fear that is partaking of you, and part of it will be the experience of that which you call alignment with that which is third density, for the understanding, so that you may bring forward healing within yourself. And you may do this also while you have that which is called AIDS. You may heal yourself, and therefore prove unto yourself even further that you truly are God, Manifestor, expression of the Divine Creative Source. Is this helpful to you?"

"Very much so. I am aware of my attraction to the concept of dying, of splitting and getting out of this embodiment. But I don't see it as my best option at this time. There are too many wonderful things going on."

"Mmm. And you do understand that that which is called the *human free will* reigns supreme. You may change your mind at any moment, and it is Divine." He smiled. "Whatever you do, my brother, know that you are truly loved, regardless, for you are light that is truly appreciated. And that which is your experience on this third density plane of expression, your three-dimensional stage of drama, it is merely that which is one facet of you. That which is *all* of you is grand and splendorous in nature."

"I feel as though I have experienced enlightenment before."

"Indeed."

"Then it should not be that difficult to pull myself out of this darkness."

"This is so, unless you *decide* for it to be. Not *darkness*, for darkness would indicate that which is negative, but it is not totally of the light. For you see, I wish not to have separation—*lightness* and *darkness*. That is only further separation."

"Given my current rate of understanding, with you and me working together, and the other masters that I'm associated with, may I repair this damage to my auric field in a relatively short time?"

"Indeed. It only takes a *moment* to heal. It is really *less* than a moment, it is instantaneous."

MERLIN

Don't worry when the world will end:
assume it has, then start again.

Once again my mentor Germain took my hands. I looked deep into Angel's obsidian retinas. What was it that I saw there? Was it this powerful male god with whom I spoke, or simply the sagely soul of this timid and delicate young woman?

"If I am of The Brotherhood," I asked, "why am I participating in this drama at all? Why am I looking for my ascension?"

"To experience, so that you may *teach* through experience. How else better to know that which you will be illuminating in your future?"

"But lifetime after lifetime?"

"It has not been lifetime after lifetime."

"I have had enlightened lifetimes?"

"Indeed, but that which is lifetime in third density you have not. When you came forward during that which you call the life experience of Jeshua, you were fifth density, and not third."

"Oh, I see, so I'm functioning on other levels at the same time."

"Of course!"

"Well, in *this* lifetime, the ongoing process seems to be a battle between the side of me that just wants to have fun and make art and express myself and communicate, and the practical side that deals with support and finances and jobs and things like that. And I don't seem to do so well with that. I don't know *what* I'm doing; I don't know what *to do*. I know I want to sing, to act, to write, to communicate; I do all those things..."

"That is the essence of you that is the feminine part of you."

"Well, why is the support not there?"

"For the same reason that you have the struggle within your sexuality. It is exemplifying the same thing. The harmonious union of your maleness and your femaleness, mmm?"

"You see, that which is the sovereign essence of you is powerful and you fear it. You have had many sovereign existences before when you have brought much harm—as you would *perceive* harm—to other entities. Therefore you have within you a seed of fear of it. And you shun it. And when you do participate, you have expectations, and that which is brought forward as the reality as experienced does not conform to your expectations, because you have limited it *through* your expectations, and not partaken of that which is the wisdom and joy within how it *did* occur unto you. And as long as you do this, it will continue not to align itself to what *is* harmonious for you, for it will allow you mirror after mirror after mirror for you to partake of joy in *un*expected results, and what you might perceive and judge to be disharmonious results."

"How can you put into words what my next step is to integrate the masculine and the feminine?"

"Know that there is *nothing* to fear of sovereignty, of power, of your maleness, for you will not bring harm upon anyone, you will not enslave anyone, you will always be tender and loving; *that* will not be dispensed with. You will always have the intuitive *artful* creative part of you, neither will *that* be dispensed with. Do not fear it so, you are in such terror of it."

"I am!" I began weeping; he had struck a serious chord.

"I know, my brother." Again he took my hands into his/hers.

"I remember myself as a murderer, as a rapist, as a controller of people, I— I have judgments about that."

"Of course you do..."

"And even now I'm experiencing degrees of aggression that I haven't experienced before, and I guess I've come to associate that with a lack of spirituality."

"But *everything* is spiritual. Everything!"

"And, I trust my own Divine Essence to not murder somebody again, or does it not matter?"

"If you have that which is the experience of this as the desire of your heart, it will occur. But if you do not, it will *not*. So there is *nothing* to fear."

"Other than the lack of knowingness."

"If it does occur, the entity that will be participating with you has mutual agreement with this. You will not be doing it *to* them, you will be doing it *with* them."

"And the police that throw me in jail will be doing it *with* me!"

"This is so!"

"I see!"

We both laughed. Germain stroked his invisible beard in contemplation.

"But your police will not be here for long. So fear is not necessary. That which you call your next step, that which is the progression of unfoldment, is to *love* the fear, to participate with it as *part* of you, but know that it is not the controlling essence *of* you. *You* are the controller, *you* are the sovereign, *you* are the God, not it. The *male* aspect of you is a *part* of you, if you lost it you would be imbalanced; if you severed it from you, you would not be harmonious, you would not be happy."

"I have not been happy! I have always felt incomplete."

"Of course! This is of which I speak, my brother."

"And weak and powerless..."

"But truly you are wondrous and beautiful, even if you do not allow yourself to know this."

"I feel it sometimes."

"You may know this *all* the time. And not have your frustrations and your moments of unempowerment and confusion."

"Is it possible to not have frustrations within the middle of a city, on this planet? Everything seems so..."

"It is possible, but you *allow* it to be difficult. When you get yourself into that which you call nature, you automatically align, because nature is very healing, of its own essence. But you may participate with nature in the cities—you do not understand *how* completely, yet, but you *may*."

"I know that my comfort comes from tinkering in my yard, and with my cats, and that..."

"But you are still afeared of the going forth into that which is the communion of other entities that are your brothers."

"Yeah. The world scares me."

"But it need not. Be patient with yourself. Love your *Self*. Do not look for love here," he pointed again to my head, "it is not there." He touched my heart, "it is here. And when it is *here*, it will be here," he patted my head again. "But you are placing the cart before the horse. And you know what that gives you?"

"Trouble."

"...Going in the opposite direction. It is only *trouble* if you desire it to be."

"Well, I keep tripping all over myself trying to get somewhere."

"That is because you are not standing solid on your own two feet. The alter-ego and the Divine-Ego, the male and the female, the two aspects, the two polarities of hu*man*ness. And when you stumble and limp, they are not in balance with one another. I desire an embrace!" he barked.

We stood and embraced one another and he continued. "I also desire for you, my brother, to know that regardless of how you judge yourself, or how you bring forth the passionate disallowance of the god that you are, you are always loved and beloved of that which is The Brotherhood, and you will indeed be bringing forth a light in that which you call illustrious future. Take heart in this, and warmth, and allow it to comfort you."

"It does, tremendously."

"And that which you call the *Fellowship of the Light*," (he was referring to the rock group that I was attempting to form of that same name), "you bring your own light to it and it will flourish."

"You see this as an excellent avenue for me?"

"One. Do not limit yourself, however, and that which is the heart of you will allow you the access to many other avenues that you do not even perceive now. You will be a grand traveller and sojourner across this your Earth plane, and you will not have your foot in Los Angeles very long."

"Yay!"

"So be it! I will bid you farewell for now. I do heartily love you!"

"I love you immensely. I keep wanting you to just tell me what to do, but I know that that's not the gig. But every confrontation with you gives me so much... gives me the strength to go on, I guess."

"It allows you the reflection of your own strength."

"That's great, because I'm in a world that's a reflection of my own *weaknesses*."

He squeezed my hands a final time and beamed his answer. "Farewell for now, my brother, and go forth with all the light that you are. Enjoy, *here*," he patted my heart once again. "Remember the joy in your breast! Farewell!"

The Germain saga culminated with the gathering at Mount Shasta during the Harmonic Convergence. It was a seven-day escapade with my closest friends and loved ones, during which there were many splendid occurrences. Among them, the discovery that one of our companions, Pristia, was a channel as well.

She tuned in one afternoon during which we had all flocked to see "the TV angel," a magnificent winged creature who had appeared on the television screen of a local family, who consequently opened their home up to a parade of thousands of pilgrims come to speculate and meditate on the radiant and colorful image. Police, firepeople, as well as TV repair people made every effort to explain, discredit, or even remove the phantom from the set, but nothing short of turning the set off or unplugging it would alter the pulsing form. It was on every channel, cable or otherwise, day and night.

Pristia, upon entering the room, began to channel the passionate, shrill voice of Archangel Michael, who kept avowing that an "angel is love" (shades of *Barbarella*) in a crisp and staccato whine that obviously hurt Pristia's throat. The energy, however, was awesome, and all but overwhelming as the TV vibrated and throbbed with the rainbowed aura of this apparition.

Back in the hotel that night, we discovered that Pristia could "call forth" a variety of entities, including, and most notably, that of Merlin, an aspect (or incarnation) of Germain. Even Germain appeared briefly, though he explained that Pristia's energies were much more aligned (comfortable with) his essence as Merlin, and that was Divine, for Merlin was a loving and creative soul, the "Master of Wit."

Other entities included a gruff and stentorian macho force that was the space-commander/fifth-dimensional lover of one of the lustier ladies present, and a jesteral "Inner Earth" creature whose greatest ambition was to incarnate for just a day as a mortal so that he could drive around in an automobile (he made allegro *varooom!* noises that both sent us into hysterics and stripped poor Pristia's throat to the extent of having to "come back" for water).

But the greatest joy was the Divine presence of Merlin, in such an intimate context. He held my hand and cried and laughed over what great buddies we were and had been. He gushed that I had been a key disciple of his, his master pupil, and that I was a noted "rascal" with the ladies (and fellas) of Camelot. But that the village folk were all very patient with me because they knew that I was Merlin's favorite and chosen heir. I, however—and he wept at this point—came to deny his love because he was so hard with me, *because* of his love. I ended up splitting from Camelot to wander about on my own. My crippled younger brother, Kevin, then became his heir and I died somewhere on the road amid brawls, prostitutes and thieves. (Sounds feasible.)

"But I have been with you," he went on, "through all your lifetimes and in between. And I am here now, as always, to pull you home."

"May *I* channel deities as well," I inveigled at an opportune moment, "that I might have you with me whenever I so choose?"

"My brother," he giggled, "you *already do and always have had* me with you!"

But, he said, I could easily channel, indeed. And he made a note for Pristia to go with me to a pre-sanctioned bower up on the side of the mountain.

We had a marvelous encounter then, in a lovely alpine meadow with our companions, in which Pristia channeled a host of entities, always coming back to our beloved Merlin.

It was here that I spotted a peculiarly comely, yet unusually lost-seeming being some numerous yards up the meadow from where we all sat in a great circle, and asked Merlin if he were desirous of joining us. Merlin explained that "he was from the area of Orion. Oh, he would be much too shy and uncomfortable to join in with us. But I do wager he would enjoy a hug and a welcome!"

So I approached the barely clad, Nordic-looking fellow, stopping with caution just before him. I smiled; when he saw that I had come to greet him, he secured his arms about me in the most dramatic of space hugs and began wailing uncontrollably upon my shoulder. He had a very pronounced smell about him that I could not place, and seemed to want desperately to communicate, but merely made sparse and passionate little cries.

The embrace done, he unfolded himself and wandered off beaming into the woods as I returned back to Merlin et al. Then Pristia and I bade farewell, for the moment, to the group and headed off into the woods ourselves. She left her body and the presence of Germain came through, followed by Merlin.

Merlin had me lie flat at Pristia's knees, and focus on a wondrous and magical image of Camelot which he illumined for me. When I was finally centered, to his satisfaction, he explained that there was a deity who wished to come forth through me—one that I had always held the dearest of the female aspects of God. I merely opened my mouth and the Goddess *Quan Yin* began to speak. She purred eloquent wisdom about my soul and the nature of reality, and then bowed out as the entity of *Mother Earth* (Gaia) began coming through and chatting with the "back again" Pristia.

Soon we ambled down the hill and met up with the rest of the clutch, who were dying to find out how it had gone. Pristia and I then got into what I later came to describe as "dueling channels," in which we were both simultaneously mediating Merlin, Ma Earth, Quan Yin, Germain, Michael, my Hawaiian kahuna essence, Pele, and several other spooks that never even stopped to identify themselves. They were coming through and reconstellating so rapidly that the gang around us were engaged merely in the charades of trying to figure out who was in whom when, as the deities cried and lauded adulations upon one another.

The channeling continued throughout the week. I found myself sneaking off simply to commune with these luminous beings on my own without the questioning of others, and discovered myself surrounded by strangers come to seek the "truth" and the answers to their prayers.

Even a photographer for *People* approached me, who thought this just the miracle he had been looking to depict. He shot me sitting bare-chested and cross-legged on the pinnacle of a great rock, chanting away in ancient Polynesian, which picture subsequently appeared as a two-page spread illustrating the Harmonic Convergence (*People, August 31, 1987*).

The meetings with Germain, among throngs of seekers in the upper parking lot of the mountain, were mind-shattering as well. His virtuoso messages were extraordinarily to the point. We attended those, saw Angel and Ramanda when we could, and hiked endlessly over the mountains to the various tent communities of naked hippie children, dudes, and earth mamas that abounded everywhere.

Once within the lackluster confines of Los Angeles, I became too shy to bring forth these entities for anyone but the closest of friends, and eventually stopped channeling altogether. I did continue to ask guidance, in my heart, from my bodiless pals whenever the need or the spirit struck. I have had repartee with both Jeshua, the Christ, as well as with the unbidden Jehovah; but more than that have I come into the understanding that the Wisdom and the mirth of these sylphs is with me, in me, *as me*, at all times, and that I need only rely on my heart, and not the voices from beyond, to know in every moment what I must do.

So when I bring forth a voice now, it is merely the voice of an old friend, carrying a greeting and a kiss of the soul for a god of equal standing.

When last I spoke with Ramanda (Angel having disappeared for some time with a band of Australian promoters—she has since had her breasts, neck and eyes all tightened and has changed her name to *Azena*), he was left alone with the baby, endless credit card bills, and a broken heart.

He described that the last voice that he encountered through his wife had "most certainly not been the voice of Germain"—although it had attested that it was—that he had been sent on a wild-goose chase to Australia and had come back to find everything in the house gone, except the bills and a starving and terrified baby.

Channeling is a powerful and useful tool that has been used throughout herstory to bring forth indispensable information that has guided, enlivened and enlightened the souls of all on this planet. But it has come to my knowingness that the ultimate joy is in the bringing forth of one's own grand Soul Essence, the *God I Am!*

KEVIN

Things never really change,
they just attain new meaninglessness.

Out of samnyasinhood, and out of Big Mama's ranks altogether, I began thrusting myself back into the world of Hollywood fames, fortunes, and longings that I had copped out on some years prior, this time with the fervent understanding that all actions were Divine and that there was nothing to fear from either my successes or my failures. I no longer asked for or needed the approval of Mommy (in either guise, spiritual or carnal), and was released back into the lifestyle from which I had (apparently) been prematurely plucked.

With Tom's help, and with the financial assistance of Bessie, Dad's beloved new wife, Bhakti Books was created with the slow and painful birthing of *Pagan Love Songs*, my fifth collection of verse, and the first over which I had almost total control. A seductive portrait by Don Bachardy was used for the cover, and reviews were unanimously affirmative.

While the book was in the wings, I was asked by a dear Eeyore-of-a-friend—an ex-boyfriend of mine and a favorite photographer, John Krause—to help construct the sets and props for a major gay porn film, *Stryker Force*. The film starred someone very well-known in the "industry," Jeff Stryker—*I* had never heard of him, but then, he had never heard of *me*. It was a jungle/action/adventure film, narratively nil, but resplendent with flora, fauna, and weather.

Jack, the director, was an insufferable dunderhead who never made up his mind about anything, but merely whined and complained as those around him argued and kvetched. The more grueling rows sprang up between John and an obese and flagitious lighting engineer/pederast. I ended up caught in the crossfire more than once as halogen bulbs came flying through the air and shattered like Molotov cocktails in the middle of our sets. It added a certain *je ne sais quoi* to the fourteen-hour days.

The most sensibility-rending of my activities, as assistant to John, was the task of removing the allegedly superfluous pubic fur from within and around the extremities of the talent. The actors seemed to enjoy the dangerous attention of the sweaty techie's hands around their peaches and plums, but I—having always maintained that if women were hairy, I'd be straight—cringed with each slice of the razor, to see those gorgeous pelted bums turn into mere shiny naugahyde replicas of male anatomy. But then, that was the *one* thing upon which the director most certainly had his mind set.

Another grimy task was the insertion of the alleged AIDS-protectant/lubrication. ("Bend over. Spread your cheeks. Say *Aah...* Oh, *there's* my watch!") This I came truly to resent as I acknowledged the almost complete lack of concern for safety that the director had for the secondary stars. *Non oxynol-9*, or whateverthefuck they were using, was no substitute for condoms, and everyone knew that—even the talent.

Filming was tedious and disastrous. Both for the normal porn-flick maladies (endlessly flaccid penes, mistimed cum shots, a spot of feces in an otherwise perfect close-up) as well as the mechanical horrors. The greatest of these calamities came with the destruction of our magnificent jungle-hut motif, replete with bamboo-thatched shack, swamps, myriad plants, shitloads of sphagnum and Spanish moss about the grounds and hanging from Tarzan vines in the rafters, all in a cramped and ill-equipped sound stage. For when the rain sprayers were turned on, our jerry-rig swamps began flooding, some fifteen hours into the shooting. "We *have* to finish the shoot," the director screeched, "these actors are only budgeted for *one* day!"

"Not to mention that the set is fucked," John added.

"I wish the *actors* were," I hissed under my breath.

Getting the actors fucked took five to six hours as we stood ankle-deep in swamp water, amid tendrils of twisted and knotted electrical wires, plugs, and even the lightning generator, all the while screaming for the dumb blond bimbo on the dais to either get it up, or *get over it* and let the other dolt do the porking. How the copulation was ever completed, I'll never know—I was only glad that it was no longer me in the same bad dream. But the real mystery is why the entire bunch of us weren't fried like a kettle of green tomatoes. It took John and me the next three days to shoo and siphon the water and tons of soppy mosses out into the gutters on the street.

Eventually the entire operation moved to a verdant garden in the back hills behind San Diego where two retired biology teachers had for some fifty years been rain-jetting their tropical forests. Once getting my forty-foot omnibus down there in one piece (I had never driven a truck, or a stick shift before), I was in arboreal Gavin-Heaven amid the walls of bamboos, heliconias, and moss-enshrouded sycamores.

By and by we got through the shooting. John and I had carted down and shored up our entire forest and hut amidst the real stuff, fabricated sawdust quicksand in a dammed-up creek, and otherwise worked jungle magic all about us. It could have been fun if not for the hysteria of a dozen testy queens on a budget.

And then I noticed a curious phenomenon: it was that my position, as techie (running around naked like everybody else, and yet technically not available like everybody else) created interest among the talent, our hosts, and a few other attractive young visitors to the location. It wasn't long before I began to find myself entertaining notions of indulgence with some of these strangers.

But the first of these tête-à-têtes was with a stunning blond love-bump who was in the flick, Kevin.

Having been out of the kindred sex game for some time, between the LSD, monastic, Kahala and samnyasin years, and then back again only semi-steadily with Dave, I was experiencing some trepidations regarding my age and this fresh attraction to babes younger than myself. That, cuddled with my horror that these sucklings did *not* concern themselves with "safe sex" practices, together with the overall ennui and asexuality that porno filming tends to induce in even the most hormone-crazed character, made me feel at once high-horsed and spinsterish about the desire to interact with *anyone*.

This bumptious baby blond bunny-thing was coming on to me. He was the pride of the film, by any outsiders' points of view. And well, I was some months overdue at that point. So off we trekked with sleeping bag and Fritos to spend the night in a distant army camp that John and I had created the day before (which was never used). And a strange phenomenon occurred. Kevin was adorable—blatantly sexual, blatantly young. And, from my leading questions, he had no problem with the concept of getting AIDS and dying for his art, as long as he had fun in the process. If AIDS, as I suspected, was to be the 'Nam of the Nineties, this spritely twit wasn't going to just wait for his number to be called. "I don't want to grow old and ugly, any-way," he assured me.

The romantic overtures went something like this:

"Come on, hurry, get it up, stick it in me." All the while he held his golden cheeks apart and pressed them hawkingly into my face.

Hell, I was still pondering the notions of condom versus no-condom when the brat began getting restless and contemplating moving on to the next camp.

Now, as I've said (and as the movie itself attests), getting it up on command has never been my forte outside of comfortable amorous (or professional) situations, which this was *not*. Leave it to say that sex with Kevin was a bust—my dick was un-cooperative, the condoms kept tearing (or Kevin pulled them off). When I did get inside the imp his grandiose flagellations knocked me out again. I believe we both climaxed, as it was, from one tech-nique or another, but I found myself longing for a dozen billy-sticks or one greasy blunderbuss with which to satisfy this pugnacious pixie beneath me.

I felt feckless, old, and weary, if not gelded altogether.

Nevertheless, the knowledge that the two of us had been together that night merely piqued interest among cast and crew that this aloof and hairy monk was, in fact, attainable. I took advantage of that rumor two or three times more with more evenly measured fauns. But what eventually happened is that the director began offering me greater and greater sums for the reversal of my insistence that I would not participate in the film. As the pressure mounted (so to speak) and the coinage increased—I *did* need a new vehicle. I came up with an offer, which was immediately accepted. The day that all the cast and crew departed, I simply meandered around with the cameraman, taking assorted establishing shots of me, in nothing but Woolworth's jungle paint and beads, within this botanical Eden. I ended up in a thorny oak tree, eating kumquats (appropriately) with one hand and masturbating with the other. It was fun up until that point, but I was enfeebled from relentless "fluffing" and had no mustard for achieving an orgasm. "The sun's going fast, Gav," the cameraman insisted. "We've only got about ten minutes left. Gotta get this shot; movin' out tonight..."

God I hate sex. "Um, perhaps I can help you," said the gentle lace-curtain queen who owned the place and had been following me around all week.

Well now's the time... "Sure," I consented, and he did indeed assist in the achieving of a quasi engorgement; I ran up the tree and jerked off all over the cameraman on the ground below me, and that was that; they interspliced our scenes throughout the movie, I didn't have to touch any of the other actors, restitution was prompt, and I got the Jeep Wagoneer that I'd always wanted.

Curiously enough (or not) reviewers commented heartily on the jungle boy segments as the only spontaneous and, consequently, interesting parts of the film. And as *Pagan Love Songs* came about, the notion that I was just appearing in a porn flick made news of the fact that, "Oh yeah, he writes poetry too..."

PHILIP

*You can't chase a rabbit
that's not running.*

As Bhakti Books was created and *Pagan Love Songs* began making the rounds, I became more aware than ever of the rudiments of PR and hype, the mythical foundation upon which The City of Angles is built. I began to search the memory vaults for authors and creators of note that I could posture an association with in order to... well, sell books.

My dancing buddy, Rosie, from Frisco, from New York, had long had a masseur/client relationship with the noble Jerry Lawrence, famed playwright, co-author of *Mame, The Night Thoreau Spent in Jail, Inherit the Wind,* and dozens of other now classic American dramas. I had Rosie send the libidinous Uncle Jere a copy of *PLS* for a response. The response was more than favorable, and I was soon set for an encounter at Jerry's sprawling cliffhanger of a Malibu estate.

I was most impressed, upon entry, by the towering walls of Chagalls, Dalís, Picassos, and the pièce de résistance that outshone them all: the one simple black-and-white Matisse. What's more, the vast percentage of these masterworks bore, along with the signature, the message "To Jerry with Love..." I was nonplussed.

But Jerry was gracious, hardly the wicked Broadway erlking. In fact he was perhaps as nervous as I. He went on and on about how wonderful my poetry was. He explained that *he* has had the lifelong hobby of photographing writers and artists, and that he would like to photograph *me* for *his* collection.

"Why, uh, sure," I coughed, caught entirely off guard.

"Oh splendid! I'm *so* happy," the author avowed. "I am *so* impressed by your poetry. I just take snapshots, really, I'm *not* a photographer, it's just a hobby, really, just a hobby. Perhaps we should have lunch first, or should we get the photos out of the way? Would you care for a drink, perhaps I can give you the official tour?"

After the show of the rooms full of play posters (in every language imaginable), archives and libraries full of rare and personally inscribed first editions, Jere held me in thrall with his volumes of snapshots of prominent authors, each shot signed by the study, and placed neatly on a page with two or three others, all labeled with the date and the place of the encounter. And we're talking about *authors* here, from Ginsberg and Isherwood, Vidal and O'Neill, all the way back to Gertrude Stein, Henry

Miller, Jean Genet, *DH Lawrence!* Jerry asked me if I would mind being added to this entourage. (Who would mind?) "Gee I don't know, Mr Lawrence, let me phone my agent."

"Perhaps," he laughed along, "you would care to ring him from the hot tub?"

"I *always* do!"

We popped into the Jacuzzi, and then the pool in which Jerry swims his daily fifty laps. Amid gentle massages and casual physical contact, he amused me with a medley of accounts of bygone stars and faded decadence.

"Gosh"—I struggled desperately to compete with his seventy-three years of illuminati—"I *did* have a date with Ethel Merman once. Just after she finished her *Disco Ethel* album, bless her heart. Went to Roy's and dodged the clouds of cocaine. Everyone stared, even Diana Ross, from across the aisle. It was rather eventless, really, I was friends with her manager."

"Ah yes, Ethel..." Jerry almost sighed and returned to his ricocheting from one end of the pool to the other, counting as he went, after which we moved on to a brief sauna, shower, and the lunch that he had already prepared.

During the course of a number of social encounters, Jerry came to rave more and more about the work that I showed him, wrote a delicious blurb for the back of my next book, and had me up to meet a contingent of his cronies, students, and pretties. Highest among the hierarchy of current guests was the visiting John Patrick, Pulitzer-Prize-winning author of *Teahouse of the August Moon* and some fifty other plays. John was a ruttish old lush, and, accompanied by a gaggle of agents, lawyers and "masseurs," dragged me out for several West Hollywood and "theatrical" dining experiences. He was in town for the formulation of his latest play—possibly his swan song—a play about an AIDS hospice entitled *The Green Monkey*. The play was charming, really, if a mite trite, maudlin, and already passé by about two years, and was slated to star Perry King, a lust of mine since *Slaughterhouse Five*.

Without audition or even list of credentials, I was chosen to play the role of the Italian heavy, Tony (of course), a bisexual New York street punk on his way out.

It was a splendid and moving role—Jerry confirmed that "Pat" was absolutely sincere about my casting. I presented the best arguments that I could conjure that the Tony character should, at least once a night, be obliged to kiss the Perry King character. They didn't buy it.

By and by investors got disgusted with the ever-sauced author for his pompous refusals to make essential concessions regarding the story; egos raged, the entire project was dumped and Mr Patrick and company went back to St Thomas to drink themselves into the grave.

Again, no stardom for Gavie. And worse, no Perry King.

As my noteworthy consolation prize, I was set up with a blind date with another member of the Malibu clan, and friend of the production, Philip, a parlously sexy, overly literate actor who bore a frighteningly seducing resemblance (especially in speech pattern) to number-one Mr-Daddy-Fantasy-Thing, William Hurt.

Philip had created and starred in the role of *The Elephant Man* on Broadway, relinquishing it some two years later to David Bowie. I never saw the actual play, but found no way (at first) to conjure a monster out of the creature that taunted my heart that evening.

"Gavin, hi," he greeted me at the door, "I hear you're quite a poet. Love poetry. Come in. What a lovely shirt."

I couldn't help but notice the Calders and Matisses in the foyer, and commented on same. "Yes, I collect art." He took my hand. He was six-two or three, strong, chestnut hair, unshaved—just like I like 'em. "Dinner won't be long. Let's have some wine."

I could've made feast of that imperious yet sullen voice. I was lost to his arrogant charm, his cold driftwood eyes, his open Hawaiian shirt. And he did ramble on, dulcetly, all through the delicious stir-fry that he had prepared us in his beach-front duplex. "I confess I'm a bit overwhelmed just now. I just got back from filming and discovered that I had to have my dog put to sleep." He showed me pictures of some huge gray thing that looked more like a horse. His voice was bursting with elegiac passion, even when he talked about the most insignificant things.

"It's okay, Philip. I'm sorry. Just relax. We have no agenda," I lied, since my agenda was to devour the man, to have him break into tears in my arms, to ravish me in turn.

Our conversations went well, despite my concupiscence, and the fact that Philip continually baited me to assert his intellectual superiority. I was happy to be dominated in such manner, if only to be allowed to assert my own powers of youth and sexual prowess.

Then the physical Philip put me to the test, as all of a sudden he burst out onto the back terrace, doffed his slippers, shirt and slacks into the sand, and sped into the black February midnight sea.

"Come into my ocean" was all I heard him say. I got only a glimpse of his dancing orbs as they plunged capriciously from out of my sight.

There was no time for trepidation. I too shucked my clothes and followed him into the ravishing surf. "Shit. Mother fucker. Shit. Goddamn..." Philip pressed up against me, hot like liquid wax in the biting waves, splashed me, then dove away again, coming up some distance beyond. "We've been having a lot of sharks this winter," he remarked.

I shuddered. But by damn, if I was to die, I was dying in his embrace; I lunged toward my naked Neptune. But he sped away. I followed.

It became a race down the coast, in water so black and so cold I thought that if I ever did catch up with him my balls would never be of any use. We swam past twenty, thirty houses, never seeing a soul on the beach. I looked for the omen of oncoming dorsals. Then I caught him, just briefly for a cop of physical warmth before he lured me back the way we had come. When I finally reached his shore, he was awaiting me at the back steps, towel open and ready.

I was mortified to emerge. My genitals had retreated to some pre-natal condition. *His* pendulous monstrance dangled freely and without guilt. I shivered, but ran into his arms; it was the first affection he had shown me.

We showered together and toweled each other off. Rather than prolong the dance, he led me straight into his unmade bed. He competed in sex too, and I fought back instinctively, despite my desires to the contrary. I wanted to give in to this tyrant, but I could not. We ejaculated, perfunctorily, toweled again and pulled apart. He did not invite me to stay, nor did I invite myself.

I left him with but a book and a kiss, and that was that—cold Malibu surf—one of the sexiest men that I have had the pleasure of encountering. A voice like the changing of the tides.

Jerry later confirmed that my poetry was my undoing, that once Philip had figured out that I write about all my loves, his homophobias got the heart of him and froze it to a cube.

"Philip doesn't like to think of himself as gay," Jerry chastened.

"Perfectly understandable, neither do I."

Well, perhaps it was my indiscretions about the Bear or other industry conquests. Though these had certainly not squelched the evening's essential venery.

This could've been one of those perfect fantasy dates—like being stranded on a tropical isle with just Gilligan, the Professor, and Ginger's wardrobe.

I shivered, to think of that frigid mer noir through which I had been lured. "I'll call you," he said flaccidly through the rift in the closing door.

And I headed home along the lightless coast, constructing poems about him in my head...

CRAIGELE

*Today's Hitlers are tomorrow's Jews
(and vice versa).*

As I mentioned, I had the privilege of taking the last photos ever shot of Christopher Isherwood. This was part of a half-assed ruse to introduce myself to writers, painters, and photographers of note. I didn't get very far with this ploy, however, lacking ambition, chutzpah, gumption, and time. Christopher was a major coup, though I was already connected and had been openly invited to Christopher and Don's home. Setting up a photo session was a formality that gave me a certain professional or legitimate presence.

The other few dignitaries included the effulgent and spritely Quentin Crisp, Greg Gorman, Bud Cort, and Andre Miripolsky. And eventually, shortly before *his* passing in late 1991, I shot Tom of Finland, the "Father of Gay Art"—intimidated by the camera but reveling in the attention. As I had hoped, he insisted on photographing me that same day, subsequently immortalizing me in one of his drawings.

Of them all, I must say that Chris was the most natural and comfortable with the camera as well as with my role as image maker. Although shy by nature, he seemed to have no notion of how he *must* or *should* appear— undoubtedly the result of four decades of subjugation to Don's ceaseless pencils and paper.

In the spring of '88, I decided to foist myself upon LA's hottest socialite and master of the surreal, Steven Arnold.

I wanted to be photographed for *his* books. Requesting to photograph him seemed a more colorful and sure way to approach the matter, disarming him, and lending myself an air of credibility.

Steven was delighted by the offer and invited me over immediately. He would not pose in the nude—I asked, but didn't push the point—and also, like Mr Gorman, Paul Jasmin, Bud, Miripolsky and other visualists, had such an alarmingly limited concept of how he must appear that I felt as though I might just as well have been photographing a photograph, or a statue. "Are you nervous?" I asked him.

"I'm not terribly comfortable having my photo taken," he pouted. "I'm used to being on the other side of the lens."

He kept wanting to put on more makeup; I kept saying that I wanted him as natural as possible. Then I got a flash. "May I take *my* clothes off?" I asked.

"Darling, of course," he purred.

I did, and the effect was immediate. Steven was completely warmed and willing to be pushed around and molded into tableaus that we both began brainstorming; it was as though I had given him a drug. I got the photos that I wanted—among the only ones ever taken of him without the same tired stance, the stagnant Napoleonic hand, grim face, epaulets, and necrophilic makeup.

Steven wasted no time in deciding that he wanted to photograph me as well, which he did the very next night. In those sessions we got so hot and in tune with one another that the images we created scared even us. Steven would scream "Bravo!" as I smeared on my neo-aboriginal lines and masks, later shrieking from behind the camera: "That's right, baby, give me God, *give me GOD!*"

Steven's Twelvetrees volume, *Epiphanies*, was soon released, including just one hardly flattering upside-down shot. (The next volume contained a number more.) For the book's release, there was a huge disco party thrown downtown at the massive old LA Stock Exchange, complete with original Arnold decorations, painted models, the whole quasi-surreal trip. I was asked to be an almost naked go-go dancer, along with an occasional boyfriend, Buck (West Hollywood's most requested phone repairman). We were iconically displayed in gilded cages, wearing nothing but gold lamé cups that Steven had designed, held on simply by the shape of the gonads and a short bend of coat hanger that wrapped under the balls and wedged, hopefully, between the cheeks in the back. That, plus a pair of strap-on plastic wings ornamenting the shoulders. Buck and I contoured our bodies, with gold-painted lips and mascara, and used pounds of golden powder and sparkles in our hair (top and bottom). Sequestered in our shimmering prisons, we taunted the impressionable Valley girls who tried so discreetly to avoid our noticing them notice, as well as the feys and artsy ladies who blatantly reached through the bars to touch a leg or a flagellating lamé.

It was toward the end of the evening; the makeup was transmuting, the glitter was in my contacts, and my body had shifted into autopilot to accommodate for my exhaustion.

All of a sudden there appeared before me: *Shiva*—a little Shiva—a Hindu god.

His face was blue, red lips, and he had seven eyes, two on each cheek and three across the forehead, the one in the middle facing sideways, like the traditional Buddhist depiction of the third eye. On this Mahesvara's head was a red Tibetan hat, covered with bells, stars, and broken pieces of mirror that captured the ichorous lights of the room and cast them back up to me on my tiny dais.

I was in love. It was bad. It was even more abrupt than my first sighting of precious Davie. The broad and irradiant smile that shone upon me was the grandest light I had seen since the better of the Big Mama days.

And he just stood there, gently swaying, almost dancing to the music, but almost standing still, right below me, with that murderous grin mirroring all of my dreams and my desires.

I tried desperately to remember what I had imbibed that might possibly have induced such a chimera—but it was no use, I hadn't been stoned in years. This hallucination was as solid as steel, stabbing at a point between my ribs.

I motioned for my blue *gandharva* to move up to the cage, which he did. Without abating my dance, I swooped down on him and embraced his lips with my own, sucking what breath I could from this Nirvanic smile.

I continued dancing, and he remained transfixed before me. Occasionally he would dance off, only to return again and turn back on me that incandescence I have not seen in a man since. I motioned to him again and handed him a matchbook from the bar just behind me that I had managed to scratch my number on. He accepted the number, looking completely surprised and off balance for the first time since I had noticed him.

When the evening was winding down and I had been paroled from my station, I jettisoned out immediately to find the daemon, and found him, with another attractive youth of much more traditional pretty-boy features and costuming.

"At the risk of committing a gross social indiscretion," I explained as subtly as I could, "I am fervently in love with you and would greatly appreciate the opportunity to see you at your earliest possible convenience."

"Sure," the Shivaic smile stated, "I'll call you. Thank you."

"Thank you!"

Craig called the very next day, came over, and took me to a perfectly hideous old Spanish art film. Afterward, we sat in his car on the street across from my house, kissed lavishly, if sporadically, and discussed my romantic delirium. "I just don't understand," he said, "how you can fall in love with someone just like that."

"Don't you believe that love is fated?"

"Well, sure. It's a cool thought, at least."

"Then love that exists between two people," I hypothesized, running my forefinger along the indecent line of feathery black hair that rimmed the crew collar of his plain white T-shirt, "*pre*-exists. So all we need do is tune in to that existing love. Why must that take more than an instant?"

"I guess I've just never experienced it that way."

"Well, doll, I've been around a bit longer than you. Perhaps I've just learned to waste less time." (Goddess, did *that* sound like a jaded queen!)

Craig was a cool intellectual, not prone to falling in love or in *anything*. He was also a mere twenty-four, just finishing up a stint at Otis Design Institute; *yes, we guessed it, he makes art and sculptures out of found objects*. He was as sexy out of the folkloric makeup as he had been in, and almost as much of a fantasy. He had that distinctly Jewish-American rabbinical parlance of one that has been raised by parents who care both about his education, as well as his creative output. He had a pronounced knob above either ear—one of few choice flaws—close-cropped hair, that subtle fringe of curls emanating from his chest region, piercing gray eyes, a pronounced beak that I simply could not keep out of my mouth.

"My friend Randy," he warned me, "has been my almost-lover—exclusive male friend—for over six years. Our sexuality could virtually be labeled adolescent experimentation, though Randy has had fairly regular encounters with others. I've been true to him. Perhaps I'm a bit limited in my scope of male-to-male relationships."

"Let's say that you're *practically* a virgin," I said, trying to help.

"Practically. Yes. Maybe. If I *ever* was. I mean, there were problems in my family as well..."

"Sexual abuse."

"Yeah..."

As the psychoherstory unraveled, I began also to see dietary symptoms of down-home teenage anorexia, as well as the sexual and emotional ones. I took heart, sighed as he forestalled my advances, said goodnight, and drove away. (Whatever happened to good old-fashioned date rape?—if only he had left his T-shirt for the cover of my pillow!)

The next day I found his place on the way back from my job of yacht-rigging at the Marina del Rey. Craig lived in the second bedroom of a small middle-class home with his addlepated grandmama. It was the symbiotic solution to both getting away from his parents, and of looking out for the eldest and most solitary member of their clan. Rent was free, and Craig had converted the unused garage into an elegant and substantial studio, where, once we got past Grammy and two horny male shar-peis, we settled into for an introduction to Craigele's art and a few brief late-night rituals.

Craig's work was frightfully akin to Dave's; as my visit to his studio was frightfully reminiscent of sitting awkwardly in Davie's world while he puttered and tinkered about the inviolable flotsam and jetsam, uttering profundities that only loving ears would acknowledge as significant. Craig's brain was noticeably more in charge than was Dave's, though his social manipulations were considerably more awkward and naive. Nevertheless, I felt practically at home there—or, at least like I *wanted* to be at home there. I kept smooching Craig on the vinyl car-seat couch; he didn't refuse, but kept thrusting photobooks of his burgeoning portfolio into my lap and between us.

"Show me everything," I coaxed, my free hand on his denim thigh.

His work was charming, if undeveloped. The bulk of the studio was encompassed in a ceiling-high, bony white circle made of long gnarly tree limbs wrapped in plaster-coated medical gauze. This formed a sort of skeletal Stonehenge within which he set up Promethean rituals using candles and primitive bronze icons he had created and cast at school. He burned herbs and wielded a Polaroid camera, with which he took candlelit out-of-focus images of us both. These are the only recorded memories that I have of

Craig, with the exception of one or two "love letters" composed of seemingly meaningless hieroglyphs.

After the photos, what necking I could instigate, and the inevitable attack of two jealous shar-peis, we returned to Craig's room, where he confided other cherished objects, including the poem he had written in response to the two of my books that I had given him, which he had already devoured, underlined, and sketched his way through.

He had a habit of leaving his small TV on with a rolling color test pattern. "Abstract logic," he assured me. "It's all I ever watch."

"Infinitely more intelligent and profound than the normal idiot programming," I agreed. "Do you smoke a lot of dope?"

"Used to. I'm trying to quit."

"Aha..."

"I would ask you to share my bed with me," Craig apologized, "but it takes Gram time to get to know someone. Once she knows you, she wouldn't think it odd at all. Though she gets kinda weird with people she doesn't like. One girlfriend from school visits and Gram always bursts in wielding her can of Lysol, spritzing the air, wrinkling her nose and exclaiming, 'Don't you think it smells in here?' What can you say?"

"Fuck you bitch get out of my room?"

"It's her house!"

"It's your room!"

I wasn't ready to have my lungs polluted or my social status bludgeoned, so I kissed him and meekly slunk my way out. I had enough of Craigele's taste in my mouth and on my fingers to get me through the night.

Sunday evening I lured Craig onto my bed, stripped, with the promise of "just a massage."

I massaged him for four hours, intimately soothing and caressing every hair, follicle, and morsel of flesh that enveloped this mensch. I memorized every smell and its source; I separated and pressed every muscle, gland, and ligament I could locate; I gazed long into the immodest smile of his callipygian rear attributes; and ran my cheeks, my fingers, nostrils, and tongue through his tense and pungent morass of pubic hair, lolling testicles, and his little unfurled putz.

I worshiped this man, this flesh, as the Divine, reveling in all its sights, its smells, tastes, and the calescence which my touch invoked. He was Gomateswara, the ineffably beauteous young naked god adored by Jains. His nipples hovered on a chest of no adult dimension. His arms were thin, like his legs, his waist, his back; yet his manly shoulders, equine neck, head, and saintly derrière were of implicitly flawless proportions. He was perfect to me; I loved him. It would've crushed my heart to see him leave and I told him so. Already exposed and four hours into his stupor, he consented to remaining, and slept by me all night.

In the morning I made pancakes, coffee. We spoke briefly about AIDS,

Dr Rice, and reticulose. Although Craig had "known" only one man, and tenuous as that had been, he was worried about the fact that Randy had done some roving. This was obviously a harsh point with Craig—what limited sex they had shared had not been "safe"—and Craig wanted to be tested, to meet Earl, to *know*.

The test was easy enough. Craig saw me shoot up for the first time—I was just ending my reticulose program. He was plainly nervous. We argued in the car, about relationships, the absurdity of falling instantly in love versus the absurdity of having to "think it through," and of the always-absurd-to-me arbitrary semantic distinction between "making love" and "having sex."

We fought; I lost my head. I was romantically unnerved and afraid that I would lose out to Craig's Randy, or to his ever-more-apparent anorexia. I even said as much, criticized his marijuana usage, and, for the first time (that I have ever applied the insidious notion), told him he was "too young to know what's what." (*Goddess!*)

"Shut off your brain for a second, doll," I urged him. "Listen to your heart." But what I meant was, *Listen to mine!*

We had blandly made up by the time we reached Steven's Beverly Boulevard studio. Steven and I were discussing my moving in with him—this was the meeting that was to decide. Steven's roommate of some four years was just departing—in a huff—and Steven needed an immediate replacement. (My obligation at the 5th-and-Sweetzer ashram house was ending within the month.)

Craig was completely awed, as everyone is—especially artists—by the volume of space, the sets, creations, and dramaturgical hodgepodge trappings of Steven's twelve-year lair. We all sat to tea as Steven and I discussed the options, even that of Craigele potentially moving in with me, initiating a gallery in the front for Craig's sculptures, photos that Steven would do of the two of us, the whole *n*th-degree fantasy. Largely because of my desire to snare Craig, I agreed to move in immediately.

"Darling, I'm *so* excited!" Steven sang.

Craigele and I had just a few encounters during that following week. Craig was finishing his quarter at school, and completely crazed about finding out his HIV results. I stopped by his studio more than once after the marina and found the situation difficult, awkward, and the kisses token and mechanistic. I prayed that Craig would test positive.

He didn't; I drove him out that Friday. On the way back we fought again, with same dialectics, but with a new fire and passion.

"You just want to manipulate me into bed, that's all."

"Get out of your head, Craig. You've narcotized yourself into an intellectual impasse. Wake up. Find your passion. Your heart. Eventually you must."

I didn't carp any more. I didn't want to force him to say that he didn't love me. I hoped that someday he would say he did, once the brain cells had reawakened, the anorexia abated, and perhaps after he, too, found himself infected. But Craig would never sleep with me again, that was clear enough even if he wouldn't say it. I was a leper now; I was von Aschenbach and he was Tadzio. In my defensiveness I insulted him, and he let me know that he was looking forward to the next weekend—I was heading to San Francisco to do a reading and book-promo tour—so that he would have the time to "think" (he had previously considered going with me).

I stayed in SF with porn star Scott "Biggest-Dick-in-San-Francisco" O'Hara, whom I had not met before, but had discovered, through our mutual friend the writer John Preston, was an avid fan of mine. Scott and I had begun corresponding—he is a brilliant writer and conversationalist—and he had invited me to bed with him whilst in SF. I did, and all was lovely —the contrast between Scott's mature and experienced twenty-six years and Craig's naive and troubled twenty-four was extraordinary, bolstering my theorem that maturity begins only from the point of losing one's proverbial cherry.

I called Craig only once and we had a perfectly simple, pleasant, and banal conversation, and that was that.

Had *I* been the one that had proved HIV negative, and *he* the one who was positive, I then could have pontificated on the principle that *true love* does not recognize such earmarkings. But given that the rubber was on the other penis, I fell silent to the Fates (cursing them in my heart).

I had some time ago coined a notion that because of the nature of the spread of HIV (then believed to be the sole cause of AIDS), that anybody that was worth "having" (anybody that knew how to have good, open, active sex) would end up dying, leaving behind a world full of gimpy wimpy white boys who were plainly too milquetoast, inhibited, or inept to have ever contracted the disease in the first place.

Would we never know spontaneous, passionate, celebratory and carefree sex again?

When I returned home Craig was a stranger. I was never able to see him or communicate with him again. I keened for months for the loss, and still cry now.

Of all the AIDS-related losses, the deaths of lovers and friends alike, I consider my forfeiture of Craigele to be by far the most grievous and inexcusable. I am still in love with him. We knew each other for only one week.

ANGIE

The dog's not dead
till the tail stops wagging.

Just prior to my move into the Beverly Boulevard address, Steven Arnold called me up one evening and let me know that he had shown some of his photos of me to Angie Bowie, who was in town putting together a cabaret act.

"Darling, she *flipped* out, she's *desperate* for you to audition for her show."

I showed up at the Actors' Center in North Hollywood with my collection of head shots, fliers, and PR items, an assortment of demo tapes, Sam Harris album, books, even my Colt Studios portfolio. I encountered an apparently coffeed-out woman of, say, forty; short bleached-white hair, red painted lips, svelte, wearing a sleeveless vest/shirt that made her lack of breasts a fashion statement. She reminded me of Sally Bowles in *Cabaret*.

Equipoised in a subdued but attentive stupor by her side was another bleached-blond character: male, English, sleeveless T-shirt, with an assortment of presumably hand-hewn tattoos; most likely he was both friend and lackey, by the way that Ms B flung orders and asked for opinions.

And that was all. I had arrived early, per Steven's instructions, "to avoid the crowds," but there *were* no crowds; I was it. I should've made a connection there and then. Yet Angie was thrilled to meet me, knowing all about me, she claimed, from Mr Arnold, and she wanted to get on with the whole thing before *everybody else* showed up. She was clearly nervous, though excited, desirous of seeing me "do" something, at the same time assuring me that I was just *exactly* what she wanted.

"I have no tracks for the pieces that I want to sing," I explained, "but they are pieces that I wrote, and they do well a cappella."

I had never done such a thing before, but Angie seemed sympathetic and said to go for it.

"I do sing big, when I sing," I warned her, "a veritable Ethel Mer-*man*."

"Make me *cum*," was all she responded.

Angie was either horrified or elated, and Lee, the sidekick, was either delighted or thought me a joke, but they asked me if I would like to do a second song and there beneath the austere Gestapo halogen fallout I obliged. Angie then met me with tears in her eyes and said that I was *just* what she was looking for. She was ecstatic, and so was I.

She then insisted that things would get crazy and they needed to get "everything" in order. So I split; there was clearly nobody else in the wings.

We met the next day at the same locale, this time with all the chosen actors, singers, and other talent present. They were a pretty untoward bunch: drag queens, big scary dykes, a bag-woman comedienne, a middle-aged hipster named Doug, a salacious, buxom and ballsy Jewish chick named Sheri, and an Italian choreographer named Gui with a *major* case of small-person's disease.

We all started dancing. Gui didn't want to see if we were dancers, per se, but just whether or not we had any basic sense of rhythm, and/or were able to take the most bare-root directions. I had a blast; I figured I was in, so I simply dropped the nervousness and rocked out.

The group was eventually honed down to about fifteen postulants. The show was to be called "Krisis Kabaret," and there was no script, no nothin'; it was up to us to provide the show, as rehearsals evolved, and it was suggested that material be vaguely political or otherwise contemporary-chic. We began immediately putting together a few ghastly numbers of Angie's, as well as attempting to alchemize pieces of our own that we thought might be apropos. It was up to the group, then, to decide on the work—but really, it was up to Ange.

I won't get into too many details regarding the show. Let's just say that rehearsals went on, and on, and on. Reminiscent of Fellini's *8 1/2*, in which there was a definitive deadline, but in which the director could never decide what the film was to be about. We were all there, singing, dancing, snacking, and wasting as much time as not while Angie and Lee ran about answering phone calls and making Xerox copies of this song or that. Gui would come when he could and whirl us around. Mostly we did our own thing while Angie paced in the background gesticulating grandly and spouting at the top of her lungs, "Make me *cum! Make me cum!*" Then she'd dart out the door and we'd not see her again for the rest of the afternoon.

Rehearsals were escalated to almost every day, five to six hours each, but we began to impute that a great deal of the problem, the wasted time, was that Ms Bowie was arriving in a less-than-sober state. Had the work been getting done, that would not have been an issue, but fifteen or so actors in search of a script can be a pretty wearisome sight. And so it was.

Eventually things got even stickier as a date was set in which we would audition for the head honchos at the Actors' Center.

I had selected a number of mine that I wrote about being a whore in the world of Hollywood. It was a tearjerker, and I discharged it reasonably well. However, I felt *less* comfortable about the assignment of an Angie Bowie number which proved to be both a painful key, a vague and relatively incomprehensible lyric, and patchy choreography that consisted largely of my getting moved about the stage, wrapped in a bat manteau, hanging upsidedown from a stick on the shoulders of two Nubian queens, a few somersaults, a cartwheel or two, then bolting through the aisles of the theatre screaming in people's faces. Okay, it was a bit of a stretch even for me. The rest of the show, it was decided, I would be wearing both my pair of black businesswoman stilettos and a black jockstrap. Nothing more. Less of a stretch, perhaps, but it had been a while since I had done this sort of drag—and the heels didn't help the dancing any.

I can't say that we didn't have a lot of fun during this whole process, but it got very discouraging when we eventually did what we had of the show for the Actors' Center Theatre constabulary and were told to get the hell out immediately and don't come back.

There were moments of rehearsing at Angie and Lee's Laurel Canyon crash pad/drug den, then eventually a rented theatre in downtown LA, but Angie clearly felt that she had let us down—although she touted fulsome platitudes about "art" and "dedication" and "what will prevail," as well as egging us on with promises of London, Paris, an eventual film, cast album, et cetera.

Several actors dropped out; Doug got in a major row when he suggested that the draconian Ange attend one of his AA meetings. I brought in a wonderful friend named Helen Heaven to replace somebody. Helen had been a two-hundred-pound earth mama when I knew her at Cal Arts. She had gray hair, dressed like an absolute frump, and would spend much of her time cooking massive macrobiotic meals for our dormitory floor. At school she and I worked together on a number of film projects, always starring the (even then) infamous and raffish Paul "Pee Wee Herman" Rubens, always in drag (our films have all since been pilfered from the Cal Arts Library). Now, fifteen years later, Helen ("Heaven"—the last name was a new one) was a slender redheaded fox; a dancer, rock singer and rock-video director. She did fabulously until eventually she, too, suggested Miss Bowie seek professional help.

Potential producers were brought in from time to time, some of whom seemed vaguely amused by our histrionics on stage. There was one gassy and unctuous New York thug, replete with cigar and *spats*, who made even Gui nervous—Angie was all over him, but he didn't come through either (at least not with financing).

Eventually Angie began having an affair with the congenitally dazed drag queen that I was interested in but could make no conversational headway with. The cast was down to half, all impetus sapped, and we simply decided among ourselves that it had been fun, and "good luck, Ange." Similar stories from my performance friends had all proven this gala disaster was an annual event.

Then one night a bunch of us went to see Angie perform with Christopher, the drag-queen lover, flanking her at a Sunset Strip white-trash dive. It was remarkable. *She* is remarkable; the woman has no talent whatsoever, no rhythm, never hits a note. The songs were ghastly and could make any song-writer swear off marijuana for good. Christopher swirled and pranced around her, a sycophantic fairy queen from *Fantasia*. *Nevertheless*, Angie is *compelling* in her ineptitude. More than just an inebriate huckster, she is pathos personified. The woman *is* Sally Bowles.

However, what keeps her going is beyond me. It's amazing the mileage that one can get out of an ex-husband's name.

And all the while I kept hearing Mick Jagger singin' *"Angie, Angie, you can't say we never tried..."*

The show behind me, one evening I got a call from Miss Shari Famous, one of the brighter lights from "Gross Encounters with Angie." Shari was doggedly determined that *something* was to come from all of this torture and thwarted expectation. She had been speaking with hipster Doug about the same thing.

Shari and I got to be bosom buddies (her bosoms, my buddy). Life around the two of us was never serious, and I would call Shari daily for a comedic sparring session: "Yo! Shar!"

"Yo! Gav!"

"Shar, do you think that William Hurt really loves me, or is he just stringing me along 'cause he wants to someday be in my films."

"He told *me, I* was the only one!" She would break out sobbing.

"Why that *bitch!* Aren't men the worst!"

"You're telling *me?* You don't have to tell *me,* 'cause *I know!'*"

"Say, Shar, what's this dish I hear about you and Ange...?"

With that she would break into her loudest and raspiest Angie Bowie interpretation: *"Get off my fucking tits!!!!"*

And I'd counter back *"Make me fucking cum!!!"*

Doug was a fascinating case, an ex-lawyer who had been a *Rajneeshie* for some nine years. At one point he was the official lawyer for Rajneesh, Da Free John, Sri Muktananda, Guru Maharaj Ji, and about six disembodied spirits—my kinda guy.

Then he bottomed out of it all when Rajneesh's Oregon Ranch fell into conflagration. Doug moved to Mill Valley and became an alcoholic, joined AA, moved to LA, and became one of the LA-chic underground's leading poets and showsters.

When *Pagan Love Songs* arrived from the printer, I arranged to throw an epic book-opening party at my friend Tommy Gear's exclusive club on La Brea, the now-infamous Catherine's. With Tommy's help, and Steven's input, the event was a rave success, written up in every social column in LA for the celebs, the performers, and the effect of the whole fray. I put on a show and reading featuring the talents of, among others, Helen Heaven, Shari, Doug, the illustrious Michael Lassell, and several other inmates from Krisis Kabaret.

Catherine, the proprietess, was so elated at the clientele that night, not to mention all the publicity and referrals, that we soon arranged to take over Tommy's gig and turn it into a weekly affair, every Friday night. Shari Famous and Doug Knott and me; we called the club "Famous Knott

Gavin." Andre Miripolsky designed a card for us. Stars and the press began attending regularly, and write-ups in the trendy LA Weekly, as well as the more Republican rags, produced a barrage of visitors to see our eclectic and tastefully tasteless shows. Shari and Doug did most of the MC-ing. I wore skimpy and bizarre outfits each week and stitched through the throngs playing hostess. Besides Catherine's lush and elegant hors d'oeuvres, we had bowls of M&M's, candy corn and other down-home novelties. Checker boards, Parcheesi sets and tic-tac-toe pads adorned every table. The room was a plush and overstuffed masterwork, with Deco windows, fabulous fabrics on the walls and the sofas, poufs and settees. It really was lovely, before it grew unmanageable.

Our favorite act was always John Fleck, the flamboyant and sultry psychopath god of underground performance space, whom we booked as often as we could for his pithy vulgarity and beyond-intimate affronts on our patrons. "I'm gonna shit now, I'm gonna be sick, I'm dying, I love you," he'd wail as he crawled over the laps of aghast matrons, rending his nylons and bras, playing peek-a-boo with lampshades and fornicating with himself against the mirrored side wall. "What verve! What nerve! He terrifies me!" the terribly British Maggie Peach exclaimed to me from the doorway through which she would not entirely enter. "But he *is* awfully funny!"

On rare moments, the three of us would put together some little ditty to offend and amuse. Shari and I had a splendid number that I'd written for the Angie Show, complete with Gui's lewd and copulatory choreography. It was an homage to the AIDS phenomenon, entitled "I Got Those Marry-Me-Don't-Bury-Me-in-Latex Blues," a pulsing, finger-snapping dance which we performed a cappella, never actually touching one another as though we were infected and forbidden to do so:

Latex on my body, latex on my brain
making love is suicide beneath a ball and chain
it's prophylactic city, with prophylactic rules
got condoms on my titties, got condoms on my tool
I got those marry me, don't bury me in latex blues

My life's a vivisection, a bunny in a cage
my sex is an infection I've traded for old age
I'm not afraid of dyin', I don't mind movin' on
but I don't wanna be left behind
when all my friends are gone
I got those marry me, don't bury me in latex blues...

It was always a show stopper.

Shari's best piece, to my tastes, was a skit in which she would don pillows and a muu-muu, flop down on the floor on her butt and elbows, and discuss being obese whilst chowing down a bag or two of potato chips, chewing and talking so feverishly that the chips would veritably drool and spit down her chin and onto her bountiful frock.

"I hate myself!" she would moan, depressed, chewing, "I'm so fat!"

With that she would attempt to rise, flounder on her elbows, and give up, too huge to do anything but eat.

"Why don't you lose weight?" Doug or I would prompt from the wings.

"*Buli-mia*, I would if I could!"

Eventually I consented to do another poetry reading, though they bored me to tears. After much deliberation and consternation, I decided to do the reading in my altogether altogether.

I came out wielding only a book and a gaudy candelabra (borrowed from Steven), which provided the only light. And I discovered something: it was the first time I had ever encountered a room that was absolutely involved in listening to poetry. Instead of giggling and jeering, as I might have feared, the listeners were completely humbled by my vulnerability.

I decided that *naked* is the *only* way to read poetry. Richard Rouilard, then gossip queen for the *Herald Examiner*, planted me with the now cozy moniker "LA's Naked Poet." But the most impressive thing was the audience. Dressy little housewives from the Valley, come out for an evening of Hollywood-hip, came up to me afterward with mascara streaming down their cheeks saying things like "I never knew that a man could feel like that..." Plain and simply, they had *listened*. It was marvelous. Hence the title of my next volume, *The Naked Poet*. I have since done in-the-buffs at cafes and bookstores in both Los Angeles and San Francisco, and have never had more empathetic and affirmative responses.

But Famous Knott Gavin grew way out of proportion. As the crowds increased, the salon atmosphere vanished and we turned into a "club." And with the subjugation of the bustle and the hustle and the smoke and the noise, only loud and rude performances made it through the din at all.

I began dreading Fridays and eventually bid adieu to the entire affair. By the time *TNP* came out, I was able to do my naked reading/book-opening at my new art gallery/salon, "Studio LEONARDOGAVINCI," where the guests and the crowds could be carefully selected and monitored.

The errant Angie has thus far not redescended into my life, but I occasionally hear stories of her crashing out in this apartment or that. And not long ago the news relayed a tale about Angie on *Oprah*, ratting about David and Mick Jagger sleeping together. Give'm hell, Ange!

JEFF

Life is a mirror which riddles the truth:
age is but an excess of youth.

By the dawning of 1988, Steven and I had decided to be roomies and Big Mama and I were on the outs. Oh, we had stopped the slamming of doors, and even gotten to the point of occasional civility, but it was clear that I was gone from her saintly clawing order, most likely never to return (in this incarnation). And it's not that I ever condemned her as having deceived me, or ascertained that she was *not*, in fact, who she professed to be—we *all* are, after all, Durga/Shiva/Goddesshead. How, I ask, is a disciple to judge the attributes of an *avatara*? This is like asking a pre-schooler to decide among college professors: you go with whoever has the prettiest smile and offers the most candy.

The woman gave great goddess. But if the truth be known, there *is* no goddess, any more than there is a god. And I was unwilling to buy her doublespeak any longer, or play by her rules. Big Mama's precious Charles became our most vehement witness. Charles would spend hours with me ranting about how caustic and cruel Big Mama could be, what a bitch she was, telling me all the contemptuous things that she used to say behind my back, about me, about fags in general: that she hoped I would die of AIDS, it would serve me right. I felt somehow vindicated by his rage. Further conversations with right-hand ladies Jane and Julia revealed horror stories about how Mama maintained cages full of Persian "breeder" cats in tiny quarters in her hundred-degree garage, never petting them, letting the shit pile up until one could hardly fight one's way into the room, and so on. My hair curled. We were all, without exception, strapped to the tits with credit card debts and liens against anything that any of us happened to own from the endless vacations and essential pilgrimages that we had taken with Big Mama (always, as a group, paying her way and bestowing upon her the lavish gifts that the Goddess so richly deserved). Filing bankruptcy became a spiritual discipline, our principal *sadhana*.

Part of me wishes to maintain that there was an innocence there, a bon motive, and that, through bitchiness, rivalrous greed and flagrant inconsistencies, we were all simply forced out of the Divine Nest to find our own wings. The way a mother bird will truculently attack and peck at her offspring until they're all but featherless and bleeding. We were.

I tried, as per the many examples of Saint Germain, to give everyone the benefit of the doubt, to perceive the good in all actions, and to realize that whatever occurs, no matter how otiose, seedy and low-vibe it may appear, it is for my ultimate growth and well-being.

Nevertheless, the merits of beating a dead guru are swift to fade. I moved in with Steven.

Steven was my ticket back into the social high life, this time not of the hard-core Beverly Hills/Hollywood set, but of the more trendy and artsy would-be's, wannabe's, almost-weres and had-beens.

Upon my arrival we wasted no time with preparations for my grand "studio warming" soiree, une petite affaire of only a hundred or so of our most intimate friends. Four hundred showed up, people we had never seen before. They came out of the trees, off of the streets, to be seen, heard, and, they hoped, photographed by Steven or any one of the barrage of press-related paparazzis on cue. It was frightening. The social pages were full of us: a shot of me wielding young Raetta (the smaller of two pythons) in Debbie Harry's face, Steven with Timothy Leary, Paul Sands, Helmut Newton, Miripolsky, Dennis Christopher, Michelle Pfeifer, Jamie Herlihy. The place was thrashed; we were out hundreds of dollars' worth of wine and booze. "You can't *buy* PR like this," Steven raved.

"We just did!" I groaned.

I played hostess in a pair of paint-splattered Goodwill overalls, discreetly unbuttoned down the sides, rolled up at the ankles, with my toilworn black spikes. That was enough to send Helmut and his wife into rapture—we *had* to come to an intimate going-away party he was throwing himself, and *I had* to wear those shoes! We did, gladly: a beautifully arranged encounter at a small and dark wine bar/restaurant at the east end of the Strip. This time I wore a tux—a short-waisted military tux—with my heels.

Within the hour Helmut had my heels off me and on himself. Then Barbara Leary had on the heels and Helmut had on Barbara's wig. Timothy took back his wife's wig and tried it on as David Hockney fought desperately to get his size-twelve feet in my size-ten spikes. Helmut grabbed the wig from Hockney and flung it across a table where it landed on Billy Wilder's little bald head. It wasn't long before Vincent Price, who had been amusing Steven and myself with endless fanciful dessert recipes, began to display and explain the operations of his newly installed pacemaker. It was one wild-assed party.

We had another grandiose fete after that—I can't recall on what pretext—before deciding that we were too broke and it was too exhausting to warrant *any* amount of PR. Though eventually we put on a massive art-opening, casually hosted by Ellen Burstyn, to show off our most recent accomplishments. Paintings sold, but again not enough to offset the wine budget.

We focused on smaller, more manageable ados.

I finally got to be pals with author Jamie Herlihy (*Midnight Cowboy*), a tall, elegant and learned gentleman who lived not far from our studio in the quaint hills above Silverlake. A handsome "Sir" with immaculate long white hair, a voice like Talmudic thunder. Jamie had been a "channel" and a guru/sage back in the Fifties when such things were barely explored (publicly).

I was, however, terrified of his rabid disputations and pontifications. But I sought to curry his approval, as I do with the strongster in any given social set. I received such, in the form of magniloquent praises over my poetry and, especially, my naked readings. Only the naked are dressed for Heaven, we agreed.

We spent many hours in his terraced north-sloped garden exchanging plant secrets, cuttings and tubers, and he allowed me to use said locale for the shooting of me for a layout or two for *Advocate Men* and an *Advocate* video magazine.

Jamie completely converted me with a single line of wisdom that I continue to hail as the definitive of all modern/eternal axioms: *"Don't look for a lover. Be one."*

As a result of Steven's continual cortege of naked models, who adorned our jumbled studio like maraschino cherries upon a Waldorf salad, there was the normal onslaught of boyfriends. Few bear deliberate mention. Only one or two, really, could be said to have purloined my heart from my longings for Craigele.

There was one of note who deserves a brief description for the part he chose to portray in a much larger and exceedingly obtuse picture: I was bored/horny/restless and beginning what would become a fairly regular pattern of bouncing down to The Catch for Friday night dance-meditations. The floor was packed, swirling, sweating, copping attitude. I spied this blond youth in your basic contemporary LA-arts-fag Bedlington-terrier hairdo (appropriately moussed), in your basic LA-arts-fag sexy black apparel (à la Dave), Doc Martens et al, doing your basic LA-arts-fag casual swingstep *en solo*. The child was gorgeous and did not object when I moved in close for a few dances.

Then while we danced something occurred to me; I gazed fixedly into those celery-stalk green iridescent bedroom eyes and asked flatly, "Do you make art out of found objects?"

He glanced flatly back at me and smiled his *Yes*.

"Just thought so," I winked.

His name was Jeff.

The next day I connived to hang out briefly at his creatively constipated garage studio and aided him in the assemblage of several large tulle clouds that were to hang in some convention hall somewhere. Where had I seen *this* picture before?

We made it as far as his kitchen, where he indulged me in a lengthy and evocative nicotine-flavored kiss before he explained to me that his deadline was pressing and that he had no time for dates or such pleasantries for the next two or three days.

"But are you interested in pursuing a relationship?" I asked him.

He shone me his killer smile. "Yes, I'd like that."

I was exultant. And horny. I ran home and called up my friend Paul, a catering designer, for a flash swing in the hay to steady my nerves. And son-of-a-bitch if it didn't just casually come my way that our very same Jeff ("Do you know Jeff Bell?" Paul asked) was over tossing the linens with Paul's humpy-but-not-very-astute surfer roommate.

There are only eight million people in LA.

I never called Jeff back.

He never called me.

Is there some sin, I pondered, in creating art from found objects?

One party that Steven did not attend with me proved to be the grandest ever. It was Randy and Dolly's annual Christmas affair at Randy's castle/house in the Hills behind Beverly. The entranceway was a red-carpet walk through fields of impatiens circumscribed by twelve inches of *imported* snow as far into the trees as eyes could behold. The trees themselves were aglow with twinklelights, and a jovial Santa guarded the huge sleigh piled high with gifts for the underprivileged, which were our admission to the gala. Prior to crossing the narrow wooden footbridge that led to the becandled front porch, we were accosted by a vitriolic and vulgar Mr Scrooge screeching profanities and curses against the season. Atop the carriage house across the yard was a choir of some fifty robed angels singing an eternal medley of Christmas tripe. Inside the grand foyer, lining the tall winding staircases that hoisted up in either direction, was another entourage of songsters, some hundred or so.

Dolly and Randy both greeted us at the front door, to the flashing of a bevy of paparazzi there to make us all feel like *stars*. Dolly was radiant, as ever; even Randy looked edible.

I recognized many people, but not so many that I knew or had known. The Pointer Sisters were *not* there, Patti LaBelle was *not* there (both clients of Randy's, both on tour). I was disappointed, but Kenny Loggins swept by on the way to the chow line, Madonna danced along in the arms of Sandra Bernhardt, Bob Dylan remained inert in a corner surrounded by his usual pride of buxom middle-aged "sisters," and I chatted workout with Ryan O'Neal in Randy's massive personal gym (I was awed by how extraordinarily beautiful Farrah truly is). It was the first time I had spoken with Jane Fonda and Tom Hayden since marching behind them in a picket line when Presidents Thieu and Nixon were in town.

Paul Rubens accosted me in an effort to butt into the food line.

"*Gavin*, my old friend! Ha ha! May we just scoot in here? Ha ha!"

I hadn't spoken with him since dragging Bud Cort to the first "Pee Wee Herman Show" at the Groundlings. He had attacked Bud, backstage, seething, "People always accuse me of being like you! I'm *nothing* like you!" Bud had jumped back into my arms, mortified. Yes, it *was* the *Paulene*

Rubenfeld that I so remembered from Cal Arts days.

Wandering from room to room I noticed one very peculiar phenomenon: in every room of the house, be it the one that I was leaving, or the one to which I was arriving, there stood Shirley MacLaine, surrounded by a sincere and adoring clutch of followers, preaching the gospels of reincarnation (in one room), astral projection (in another), crystals (in still another), UFOs (in yet another). *Holograms*, I surmised.

And then, finally, as I had witnessed all the trumpery that I had needed to witness, in the center of the main hall, there he stood, the man to whom kings bow, the Don Corleone of Hollywood; there was Bear.

It was all I could do to channel through the archipelago of clutching partyboys for that sweet smile, stately deportment, and even a seasonal kiss (he was loosening up in his old age). Lovely (as always) to see him again. We (as always) both promised phone calls within the week, to get together, have dinner.

It was a party the likes of which I may possibly never experience again. I don't need to.

Among the more sacred of the profane encounters of that time was my first brief schmooze with Anne Rice. I suppose it all started with a Mick Jagger video that Shari, several other friends, and I all danced in. The taping was done and they were calling out our names for the payroll checks. As they called out the name *Gavin D*, I stood up and collided with an intensely radiant young actor by the name of Gavin Danker.

Gavin, as I spoke with him after, displayed the most remarkable set of canine teeth that I had ever seen, which immediately intrigued me, frightened me, and titillated my fancy.

Upon other social encounters with Gavin (which became eerily frequent), I continued to make note always of this discreet anomaly of his dental façade. Then one evening he introduced me to a gang of his comrades and I almost fainted when I saw their smiles. They all had them!

I pulled him aside. I had to ask—the Rice books were all too current with me, and vampire sensuality was high among my list of desirable (if perilous) traits.

It turned out that Gavin, a Rice fetishist like myself, had been, in fact, taught by his dentist to construct small bridges of authentically colored and personalized canine teeth. These he had created for all of his friends, as well as, I believe, the movie *The Lost Boys*. It was mere moments before I had him in his apartment fabricating a cast of my mouth from which to build a set of these ingenious prostheses.

The teeth were subtle, and, once one learned to talk properly with them, became only marginally discernable by the nighttime public at large. Of course, one *never* wore one's fangs before dark.

Waitresses in all-night restaurants would stare, fiddle nervously with their pads and pencils, but the teeth were really much too subtle for someone to say, "Hey, those are funny vampire teeth you got there!" The most comment that one ever received was the dropping of a bowl of soup or one's change at a checkout counter.

Eventually, through my buddy John Preston, author and best friend to Ms Rice, I was able to meet Anne at an autographing of *Queen of the Damned*, teeth intact (it was daylight, but for Ms Rice we felt we could make an exception). But by this time Anne had already heard tell of the fangs, and described on a morning talk show the gangs of dark and insidious LA fans who professed vampirism and wore these strange cult teeth.

Anne, of course, is the sweetest, most lovely and unassuming genius that one might encounter. I merely passed on the invitation that Gavin would be delighted to create for her her own set of custom fangs.

Once Studio LEONARDOGAVINCI had been initiated, during one of our fests, I was accosted by the beautiful smile of Tom Bianchi, requesting that I look at his portfolio and consider him for our next show. He promised me a splendid pasta dining experience. Since I have trouble, you must see by now, saying no to *any* Italian last name, he did, I did, and we did.

Tom's work was good, certainly more interesting than the nudes of Ritts or Gorman, for Tom (although also hopelessly entrenched in the hackneyed milieu of chunky white males) would often at least have some minor conflict or emotion expressed in each tableau: some child grimacing at the edge of a pool, a shadow dissecting a critical moment, an object falling from a table. Mind you, he was *not* Diane Arbus, but he wasn't bad, he was alive, and when he offered that he would enjoy shooting me, I blushed, guffawed, and acquiesced.

We met up again a few days later and drove to Tom's friend's exquisite Schindler home in the Hollywood Hills, shooting mostly around the pool. A shoot that later surfaced in a boy magazine entitled *Heat* (one that I had edited briefly). Fluffing, of course, became foreplay, and the autoeroticism of being photographed soon encompassed photographer, whose clothes came off, and so forth. "Are we having an affair now?" I asked during our second night together.

"Yes, it seems as though we are," he said.

"Splendid. Just what the doctor ordered! What was your name again?"

"Pedro. Pedro Gonzales."

"I *love* Scandinavians!"

We never quite made it back for photos, though Tom (student of belles-lettres since his youthful amorous discipleship with Edward Albee) became enamored of my poetry and soon started including poems in large charcoal and constructed art pieces. The pasta dinners expanded to include a medley of young honky hunks that Tom collected and updated like revolving bouquets.

The dudes were, for the most part, boring to my tastes—poofed-up little WASP bodyboys, wannabes and would've-beens—and ex-lawyer Tom's own stories, now circling for the fourth and fifth times, became flaccid and even grating. The nights were comforting, if unpassioned in our sexual similitude, and I did enjoy his chipper Abyssinian cat, Dickens. But after two or three weeks I slunk back to my anonymous dervishing at Catch One, and the passionate nights of photography and painting alone with Steven.

One evening in the winter of '89, on the day of the death of a friend, Steven and I were painting and sculpting until midnight, as had become our custom. Tonight, we took time off and headed out to a local leather dive for a quick drink and change of atmosphere.

Sitting across the bar from us, in a stupor over our buddy's death, was dear Philip Littell, my first LA boyfriend, ex-roommate of Steven's, all-around sexy and rare creature, far out of his element—*our* side of town, drinking mournfully.

"Baby, come and join us right this minute," Steven ordered.

"I'm depressed," Philip said. "Can we go someplace a little more happening than this? How about West Hollywood?"

"Oh God," I yelped, "too scary!"

"Let's do it!" Steven insisted, and away we flew. For want of better options (it was a Tuesday) we ended up at some foufie streetside bar/disco, the sort of place that I hadn't been to in years. The decor looked like an airport fast-foods concession. The clientele was *young*.

We danced, Phil and I, and it was (dare I say) like "old times"; with the exception that the homogeneous dudes we were ogling were now younger—considerably—not older than we were. In fact, if there was anybody in the room who was within ten years of our age, they were squashed against the bar, Scotch in hand, and trying to forget.

"As before, Philip, you're *still* the most gorgeous man in the bar. And you're with me!"

"And you're with me!"

We found ourselves dancing all over in an effort to remain behind some poor sprout who had seemingly lost the seat of his trousers, revealing a sumptuous set of bonbons, and the lust in my soul made the fears in my head intensify by the obscene number of years that divided us. I was disgusted. We stopped dancing.

We found our way to the bar, and I confessed my pederastic quandary. Then Philip said something remarkable, one of those truths so simple that we continually look beyond it for something less easy, something more profound. He said: "Just remember, Gavin, that we are *now* those attractive older men that *we once* lusted after."

He floored me. A light came back on that had been dark for years; I was satisfied. I told Steven that I wanted to go back home and resume painting. We did. I was happy.

LEONARDO

If it isn't revolutionary,
it isn't art.

Dwelling at Steven's, slimy part of town that it was (three blocks from where Dave's studio had been), I recalled something that Davie had told me before our separation a year before. He had stumbled upon an establishment that was built upon a bona fide natural hot springs, mere steps from his studio, right on Beverly. It was a bizarre spa, pissy, expensive, mysterious, and often filled with an attractive young clientele—as well as the obese, vulgar, and antiquated mafiosos (Korean) that dominated the lounges, TV and steam rooms, farting, belching, and expectorating on the floor.

Having a new credit card or two, I came to rely on the baths as a daily purge of the grime of carpentry, yacht rigging, house painting, and landscaping that I was enslaved to at the time. I relished the primordial pleasures of the presence of comely (and naked) peers, the hot and cold lightly sulfured waters, the darkness and near-silence of an ancient cave.

One evening, in my normal state of exhaustion, temperature-induced altered state, and instinctual cruise mode, from the cold-cold pool all the way across the spa, through the fog of the vast hot pool and the steam of the shaving area, I beheld the most extraordinary profile of a derriere, protruding from a small but decidedly firm and ample body.

Almost immediately answering my psychic subpoena, this lubricious figure-of-a-dude walked straight toward me and gyred down into the icy pond without so much as a flinch or a grimace, trawled over to me, and breathed, "'ello."

"Greetings," I splashed back.

The face was homely, but the sort of homely that borders on handsome and endears one immediately. The butt, which was now obscured by the blackened waters, was worthy of excusing even the most ogre-esque of countenances.

His name was Leonardo. His accent so thick that in the echo of the spa the last name, a lengthy and peculiar Polish device, was obliterated altogether. I commented, though, that it didn't sound Italian, and through a jumble of "whats," "huhs" and "excuse-me's," eventually came up with the story that this waif was an Italian/Polish Jew from Argentina, an architect by trade.

He was considerably more handsome in the light of the locker room afterward as he gave me his slickly designed business card, and I couldn't help but notice that his appendage was most assuredly *not* of small-person's proportions. I soon came to realize that Leonardo had, much to my envy, a cunning cockatrice that was almost entirely as large when flaccid as it was when erect, giving him an infinitely more secure social demeanor whilst naked than those of us whom a phallocentric ladyfriend once referred to as "growers."

Leonardo was polite, friendly, obviously intelligent, reeking of sexuality, and overtly interested. He suggested, as he handed me his card, that we get together sometime for the euphemistic dinner.

Though beguiled, I was a trifle more reticent. But to not fuck a butt like that would be as unnatural an act as leaving a starving kitten in the rain or putting skim milk in coffee. I told him about my club and suggested that he drop by some Friday night with my compliments.

He did, two nights later—he even paid.

"Hola, dude!"

"Hola," he grinned back.

"Welcome to my—*uh*—nightmare."

"It's lovely."

"Well, that's one word for it. But you! You're lovely! Thank you for coming."

"Thank you for having me."

"I ain't *had* you yet," I camped, brushing my fingers over the extended pleats of his trousers. "But we'll get to that..."

He laughed. But I could never tell with Leonardo whether he was laughing *at* a jest, or merely to appear that he had understood the jest.

Leo seemed small in the wall-to-wall crowd, unacculturated and out of place, which I am certain was simply my unrelaxed party/hysteria/hostess mode in contrast to the relaxed/sensual/dream mode of the springs in which we had met. But he seemed blithely content simply eyeballing the space and the crowd while I fluttered around. Before he departed, he invited me to his Venice apartment the following night for some magic mushrooms— *Good Goddess, where did this man come from?*

I had not done any kind of *real* chemistry in almost a decade, and the concept of participating *with* somebody in a ceremony (that could possibly have sexual overtones) was incredible, frightening and enthralling at the same time. "Certainly," I said.

I was *not* thrilled by Leo's grimy, tiny, and slovenly fiefdom—not what I had expected from the *très chic* architect, and not the most conducive of environments for whatever 'shroom realities might rear their uncontrollable heads. Even Terence McKenna would be aghast.

"Um, make yourself at home," he stammered without apology, flinging piles of sorted laundry from off the bed onto the industrial carpeting.

Leonardo was not a master at this; he neither knew how many of the mushrooms to take, nor how to take them. I suggested a large, but less-than-lethal dosage, pulverized the buggers in his blender, poured boiling water over the top. We waited about fifteen minutes, held our noses and divvied down the mush. Leonardo was not offended by the noxious taste—I later realized this to be a commentary on his macrobiotic cooking. It was all I could do to keep from gagging the stuff back up. But then, I had an extensive precedence already set for the associations of pharmacological ingestion with bodily trauma.

Fifteen minutes later we were in our own autonomous universes. I immediately got that "Oh-no, why-have-I-done-this, Goddess-deliver-me" feeling, pulled away from Leo and stretched myself out on the couch for *The Big One*.

There was a bombardment then of archetypal memories involving strange and foreign places, arcane languages, chanting (I think we were listening to Philip Glass—either Glass or Mahler, it was hard to tell) and I perceived Leonardo's soul to be popping in and out of memory's reach in the guises of assorted lovers, comrades, and adversaries. While I could still focus, I glanced at Leonardo down on the carpet involved in his own inner music video; he was self-absorbed and/or respectful of *my* self-possession, and I was grateful for the social hiatus.

After bouncing through a maze of brightly colored whirlwinds and inner-or-alternate realities, I came upon the presence of God, soaring through me like a giant flaming falcon, roaring through my veins, arteries, skeletal and nervous systems in a momentary all-inclusive awareness. *I Was God*, and It Was Perfect.

And as I lay there in All My Divinity, I made notice from time to time to make sure precious Leo was progressing safely, as well as to ascertain whether or not he had any aperçu of Who I Was. He didn't; he was doing fine, and *that* was perfect.

Then I perceived violence in the neighborhood around us (Leo's back alley was a declivitous smack-dealing-Venice-kinda place) and worried about our integrity within this tiny confine. There was noise in the apartment next door, a dog scratching in the hallway...

My paranoia turned to Leo, whom I suspected of being a possible ally with these ignominious dealers, street people, and psychic demons, inducing me into this state to steal my power and ultimately destroy all that I had worked to accomplish these past few years on the spiritual path since my previous psychedelic ingestions. And *I had been warned against doing this, advised in no uncertain terms to cool it with the vegetable allies and to develop my control through more disciplinary channels. And Leo was the culprit, the Deceiver—of course! he was a foreigner, and Jewish—Leonardo was Satan!* But then my eschatological Center came back to me. I remembered that *I* and only *I* controlled *my reality*. That neither Satan, nor demon, nor even earthly intruder could hinder my universe should I not allow them. And *That Was Perfect*.

Leonardo then became the personification of Satan/Pan, even as I became the amalgam of Buddha/Shiva/Christ, and I realized the yin and yang of all

Creation, how *good* does not exist without *evil*, that the two are fraternal cross-fires in this Whirling Apple of Eternity. And I loved my little Satan/Pan, with whom I had tussled and trundled through all the eons. I went over to Leonardo, now kneeling on his bed with his face in his hands. He sat up to receive my embrace, smiled at me as if in recognition, and *We Were Perfect.*

He was the paradigmatic embodiment of Dionysius: round, voluptuous, his curly hair flying into ringlets from the perspiration of his brow; *the penis that never deflated*; the lusciously lunate smile of a rump with its fragrant plum-skin aperture, designed for the pleasure of the gods; the eternal and ever-pervasive corpus of sexuality, lust, *yes*. His entire body was covered with the most distinguished pelt, wild and vibrant in my heightened acuity. I could almost perceive the tiny tail, petit horns, and those endearing cloven hoofs. His entire form my receptacle, my Divine Counterpart, it was among the most ecstatic conjunctions I've had. He opened up to me with a sigh of passive pleasure, as I manipulated him around my centrality like a submissive and revolving moon.

"My darling. My Pan."

"Mi amore..."

We slept like that, rapt, with me inside him until dawn, his fur wet and shimmering with the coalesced stars of the heavens, his body the supernal bed, the Eternal Yin, *and We Were One.*

Leonardo continued to court and pursue me, between his hysterical daytime schedule and my pertinacious evening obligations. He would come by the club every Friday, complacently alone, or with a friend of his named Patricio, a famous Brazilian drag queen who played several of the characters in the film version of *Kiss of the Spider Woman.* I made an especial note of their promise to come by one week with Sonia Braga (which they never did), but other than that it was difficult paying much attention to Leonardo or anybody else at those frenetic times.

And even though I was aware that I had never fallen *in love* with him, the way that I had with Dave, the way that I was with Craigele, still, *I loved him.* And that was certainly ample. "I know that you don't feel in love for me," he told me one night, "but I would be happy to just hear you say that you are every once and again."

Leo was moving out of his Venice apartment for reasons that were unclear to me—if there *were* reasons—seeking a warehouse or loft-type situation for himself, and... well, he moved right in with Steven and me, making himself as carefree a fixture in my universe as possible. We continued regular pilgrimages to the spa, even though the experience altered dramatically. One day there was a sign at the front desk regarding lewd and lascivious conduct, which we took to mean *us*, even though we were as discreet as passions and playfulness would allow. The already exorbitant club rates actually *doubled*. On another day we witnessed a Korean gentleman buying an annual membership at the old price—when we tried the same, we were refused.

Things began to change even more. The quiet dark waters now had harsh spotlights aimed directly in your eyes; the lounge chairs in which Leonardo would take his routine after-work nap while I continued my repetitions of hot-cold-hot disappeared and were replaced with narrow upright benches. All the pretty little faeries got the picture and began flying elsewhere. When the management was asked about the changes, which Leonardo in his Latin fury certainly did, they claimed health department requirements.

Leonardo had been raised in Argentina during a time in which his friends would simply one day not appear in school, nobody would ever hear from them again, nobody would ask a question. His parents would tell him, *If they hadn't done something wrong they would still be around.* By and by Leonardo had realized his turn would come up soon. He had grabbed a few belongings and escaped to Germany, where he finished his schooling and remained until Argentina cooled down.

Leo was *very* sensitive to the evils of fascism, and he was continually in outrage and dismay, watching it creeping into the United States with all the sure and telling signs that he had witnessed just a decade or so before in his home country. He all but attacked one of the owners of the club one day when the jowly panjandrum refused to comment on the fact that we were now smelling chlorine in the cold pool—the pure and natural waters had been the only reason that we had stayed.

We began going to a tiny Japanese spa on First Street in downtown Little Tokyo called Tawa's, which, although sporting LA's godawful polluted city water, had very sweet attendees, a great deal more charm, more amenable clientele, and far superior shiatzu massages at half the cost. Afterward we could simply wander down the street and have California sushi and Japanese noodles at any of a dozen small family-run operations. *This* was perfect.

Just before he moved in, and shortly after our 'shroom adventure, Leonardo came up with the splendid notion of an excursion to the Yucatan. It was one of those places that both of us had always longed to go to, as we both were fanciers of religions, cultures, and peoples of pre-Christian/pre-industrialized society.

Off we went, Joseph Campbell and Margaret Mead, flying through the bleak and dismal Mexico City airport, then on by cattle plane to Mérida, where we rented a dilapidated Volkswagen. As we drove south, the façades on all the aged, simple plaster and stone hovels consisted of the most splendid and fanciful patinas of decades of chipped and washed color overlays: paints and pigments combined with the greens, grays, and browns of mosses, lichens, and stains from the rain-decomposed palm and grass-thatched roofs. We were stopping and dancing through every little alley, taking slides of each other diving across the face of each of these splendidly haphazard compositions, and the dogs, cats, and amicable and excited children that flocked every garden wall and gate. It was our entrance into the sojourn of photography with each other, an artistic and aesthetic commonality.

When we arrived at our first destination, a Club Med just through some trees from the great Uxmal pyramid, we simultaneously decided to turn and retrace our steps to an older, more elegant grand hotel just passed. Canceling all further reservations, we sought out these rustic and beauteous hotels with hacienda-style rooms and cabañas, all havens of artistic possibilities. We went from reading our beloved texts (Anne Rice's *The Vampire Lestat* and Stein's *Picasso*) to photographing and drawing each other hanging over balconies, swinging from chandeliers, taking shits and spreading moon through mossy windows and broken blinds, eventually pausing long enough to engage in sultry and sticky sex.

"Are we in love yet?" I asked my hornéd honcho.

"Oh, *si*, mon petit! *Y tu?*"

"Won't be long now," I panted, wrestling him to the tile floor. What could I say, here we were in this sensuously sweltering garden, free in our saturnalia. Not to mention *that butt.*

Food was bad everywhere; people were rude and inhospitable. What had existed of a quaint and powerful culture had long been shredded by Catholic priestcraft and capitalist greed. We eventually roamed into tiny off-road communities where even Leonardo's Spanish was to no avail, where Mayan was spoken and the Maya culture still hugged the earth like an old abandoned orchard. Little was left, that we could see, of the grandeur, the mystery, the spirit that had once surely been intrinsic to these people's lives. Nevertheless, there was a charm present, as the tiny brown natives pissed, shat, cavorted, and napped unperturbed around the cathedrals swiftly falling to ruin, leaving the awe and the stultifying strength of the Mayan and Toltec temples to tower over them once again.

There were no attractive men in this impoverished culture. Native corn and beans had long turned to white rice, white bread and Coca-Cola, leaving behind a society where teeth and health are abandoned with one's teens. We took solace in the sanguine youth and the artfully aged for their respective aesthetics, photographing them as they passed or as they sold their wares in the odoriferous and fly-infested public markets. And we cherished the lush, deserted one-lane sand roads that bounced from one small village to the next, passing only an occasional phone-booth-sized hut in which a bevy of Mayan kids reposed and sold colas from an antiquated tin cooler; or the damp stretches along the trails where myriads of yellow, orange and chartreuse *mariposas* (butterflies) congregated and danced as we threw off our clothes and ran naked through them, camera lenses erect in the equatorial sun. "Bend over and smile, my pretty!"

"Cheese!"

Mostly we cavorted in and out of the great stone pyramids, taking photos of a naked butt extruding, a penis dangling out a narrow black doorway. It was off-season, the hot season, everyone was at the beaches, where we decided *not* to go, and we had many of the smaller pyramids all to ourselves, to climb, drape with our bodies, to fuck within and without. It was a flawless playground. We could have played there forever, our fallen sperm crystals adorning the mystic stones like jewels on a temple floor.

When we returned to LA, something miraculous occurred: I did my first painting in over a decade. It was a timely piece, inspired by the Mayan skull and skeleton motifs we had been so enthralled with, and the vampire imagery I was impregnated with from the astonishing Anne Rice mythologies. The piece was on a circular chunk of tin and was a crude rendition of a smiling skull, a broken glass halo emanating from its cranium, a glass and painted snake circling over the halo and gazing straight into the skeleton's face, shrieking the words *!Dios Yo Soy!* ("God I Am!"). It was a simple piece, but immediately successful in my heart's eye, and set about a flurry of painting that has yet to abate.

By and by, Leo hopped on the boat and began using the pure and primary pigments that I was prone to. Steven as well jumped aboard with his first piece in some fifteen years. Our evenings were spent with the three of us painting and sculpting all over the Beverly Studio to candlelight, amidst clouds of incense, and intense, Gothic, and primitive musics, interspliced with the incantations of Sade, Van Morrison, Peter Gabriel and Tracy Chapman, the saving graces of modern music. Again, this was perfect.

Leonardo had moved in on one condition, that he discontinue smoking marijuana. "But of course, my darlink, for you *anysink...*" Leonardo had maintained an inexorable rhythm of smoking to create, to sleep, even to work at his drafting. "I have been looking for an excuse to break the pattern," he said.

So he said. But he eventually resumed using the weed, at which point my initial hesitation recurred. And I noticed that the brilliant clarity that he had achieved with his painting reneged to the dark and muddied confusion of his earlier work once he again began to smoke the shit.

But times were good, despite my frequent lack of work and funds. We visited Saint Germain; Leonardo fell in love with both spook and channel. We attended Catch One on Fridays, Sundays and other off nights—Leonardo had no particular rhythm—perhaps *many* particular rhythms—and whirled in his own fandango trance, leaving me to dance mine. And Leo, more solid in appearance once he stopped smoking, his hair longer, and often sporting a very delicious and Prussian beard, began to take on a whole new sensual dimension.

Then I went to Hawaii to make a series of films about tantric yoga, and further to Bali. Leonardo was naturally jealous of my time, my whereabouts, what I was doing, and whom I might be doing it with. We weathered my trips; I was granted absolution; Leo was thrilled to have me back. We set about the beginning practices of tantra as a way of alleviating and succoring what had become our (*my*) sagging sexuality.

We listened together to the effulgent and infective tapes of fey tantric Joseph Kramer, following his exercises and tantalizations as well as the bits and pieces that I had brought back from my Maui foray. We sat together, Leonardito snuggled onto the besmegmaed pole of my lap, breathed, went into altered states almost immediately, had passionate and wonderful sex until I, of course, got bored with tantra as well, seeing it only as yet *another* distraction, another self-imposed limitation, another mere *facet* of the whole with which one might get preoccupied to avoid *seeing The Whole.*

But more than that, I mourned, "I'm *not in love,* and I *want to be...*"

"I know," Leonardo whispered, "and I am so sorry."

We held each other and cried.

"Perhaps," he suggested, "we should do another trip with ze mushrooms?"

"To get back to that first fabulous night?" I said. "I don't want it that way, Leo. I've done my drugs. That night was sumptuous indeed, but I don't want to make a regular diet of mushroom aphrodisiac."

I kept thinking about Dave, Craigele, and how swiftly my heart could beat when provoked by the Sirens of Passion.

"You need to find someone," I suggested, "that will love you as you love me."

Our grandiose factory had become too small. I was enamored of painting again and desired more and cleaner space to show, as well as to paint larger canvases and more of them. So we leased a large and splendid warehouse just catercorner across Beverly where Leo could live, spread out, and we could both have some privacy, as well as enjoying the added space to create and to display.

This was the birth of Studio LEONARDOGAVINCI.

All along there had been the issue of Leonardo rising to work each morning at eight-ish—Steven and I were predisposed to paint at least until dawn. Which meant that I was crawling into bed just before Leo would be crawling out. At night, of course, he tried to sleep amidst the assault of music, animal racket, and the eternal Folies Bergere of quivering queens, pompous pedants, and pitiable dowagers who made Beverly Boulevard their regular haunt. *I* found the schedule rather conducive to my basic requirements; it was pleasant having the petit homme to dine with, spa with after work, make available a clean and seductive butt, and yet I had all those daylight hours in which to sleep, to paint, to enjoy my relative solitude and the cherished company of Little Bear, Marlene, the four snakes, and Leontyne, the hamster.

Developing the gallery took a lot of work. Leonardo's business, now booming, took more and more of *his* schedule. *My* budget was dwindling pathetically as I sank all my time and energy into the place, leaving me with no real income of my own, out on a fiscal limb, and becoming more and more reticent about asking Leonardo for monies that were not directly write-offable as business necessities. And of course, as the sex begins to wane, little things like money take on a new and greater meaning—without the social framework, that is, of marriage that good Christian wives everywhere use to justify their emotional retirement.

Nevertheless, the business *was* there, and we had made an entrepreneurial commitment to keep up a certain modus operandi with ads, reviews, business cards dropped about town. There *I* was, in what was increasingly becoming "Leo's space," sex occurring for us only intermittently and surreptitiously on the hottest of afternoons, and Leo, I thought, besetting me with the full-out Latin-chauvinist trip—ie: the dwindling sex was bad enough, but the loss of income was irreparable.

Shows were fabulous. We started out with a group show called, simply, "Six LA Artists," which included Steven, Leo, Dave, Andre Miripolsky, Alex Alferov, and me. The group-show idea was a fulcrum to *a)* exploit the slick and cavernous space, and *b)* to legitimize ourselves as artists by association, as well as to fabricate our gallery mailing list from the combined lists of artists whom we respected or at least emulated.

The show's opening was mobbed. Five hundred people crammed in to smudge our freshly painted walls, trash our floor, and to inhale some two-dozen cases of cheap wine from Trader Joe's. "The Party of the Year!" everyone hailed as they tottered out: drag dolls, millionaires, artists, social columnists, movie stars. The party set us back hundreds of dollars; we sold two small pieces, which barely covered the expense of our invitations and postage. But it was *rave!* for everyone except me. Even the diffident Leonardo was drinking, smoking with people in his curtained-off bedroom, hobnobbing all about the joint. And there was jittery me, keeping the coffee flowing like other people's wine, slaving to the needs of the barman, the wench at the door, the sound tracks, trying to be an equable hostess to several hundred friends, most of whose names I simply could not recall.

Opening Two was thematic, destined to get attention; the theme: "UNcensored." We went all out. Just coincidentally, the first mention of Mapplethorpe, and Jesse-the-Tarheel-Tobacco-Queen who made him a household word, showed up in the paper merely a week before our show. Synchronicity was with us.

The press came, even the *LA Times*. They saw: Two long-haired naked bartenders, Buck and Stefán, pubic hair shaved, Buck air-brushed as the God of Fire, Stefán air-brushed with the waves of the ocean; sexual and politically dangerous paintings and sculptures from thirteen LA artists; a chubby little Chinese girl on pedestal, naked beneath a glass and velvet see-through creation; Mesmera, the exotic and erotic snake dancer, complete with her ménage of pythons and boas; David Zasloff in his boxer shorts on jazz sax; a furry roving "Pan" playing authentic reeds; and the wildest assortment of fags, hags, and drags decked to the tits in leather, chains, pearls and sporting naked cabooses.

I showed up as the pope, icon of all God's oppression and hypocrisy, presenting some twenty penis paintings of my own, from tiny collages to massive wall-sized fighting cocks. (The phallus is both the most revered *and* feared symbol in human herstory; it had become my favorite graphic metaphor for the Divine in physical form.)

Timothy Leary was all over the floor; Lance Loud waltzing between bathroom and bar; Steven, Don Bachardy, David Hockney, Tim Burton, Sue-Sue Tyrrell, Tom of Finland, Paul Winfield, Bob Crewe; all the essential party people without whom an LA party is simply *not* a party.

Two sales. A few trickled in afterward; the place was doubly thrashed and bashed. We got mention in the papers, but nothing noteworthy, nothing political, just gratuitous social shit—nothing to write Ms Helms about. It was bar none the wildest party anyone had ever seen—we were disgusted. Mind you, I would've loved to have *attended* such a crush, but I was the host, the *party was on me.*

"Okay, but we're getting noticed. We're making a name," Leo argued.

"Sure, 'Dito, but where to go from here?"

The next show was called "Animal Rites," a benefit for PETA, the Humane Society's anti-fur campaign, and Greenpeace, a benefit that we believed we could get the elusive and most-coveted Rachel Rosenthal to perform for, animal rights being her one certain call-to-judgment. We were right. Rachel barked a miraculous and awesome piece from the top of our bar. A vegan caterer provided us with volumes of "animal free" delectables; PETA sent a duo of representatives; a dozen or so artists from all over the country graced us with paintings and sculptures of animals in both bondage and liberation. I wore Rio and Raetta, the two pythons who had cameoed with me in *"Stryker Force,"* who slithered from shoulder to shoulder working the sizzling wall-to-wall crowd. There were ample celebs, volumes of consumed booze. We sold two pieces: one of Leo's to the representative from PETA, and our friend Samantha's entree to Jamie Herlihy.

We were plucked, gave a piddly three hundred dollars to PETA, and swore off shows altogether. Leo and I were on the outs, he was frantic about money, *I* was frantic about money, and we had learned that LA party people were not the big spenders we had expected. They came to drink, ogle, and be ogled, not to purchase. The occasional daytime stragglers were simply not enough to justify the time that I had to put in to keep our doors open— much as I appreciated the hours to paint and to write.

It was time to regroup, rethink, refinance, reromance.

During the period in which things were still happening with Steven, Leo, and me, we attended a New Year's Eve gathering at Jamie's house. Jamie lived on the lower floor of his modest but extremely well-adorned house in the nearby hills above Silverlake. Wine suffuses Jamie's house—usually too much for my tastes—as the guests wax more and more profound, loud and foggy-eyed. Dope circulates (grass or hash, or the dregs of the spring poppy harvest). I participated in a token puff or two—ostensibly not enough to ruin my evening, but enough to impart the vague proximity of distortion enjoyed by the others. I was nervous about Leonardo. Leo is generally most quiet and reserved in unfamiliar social gatherings, but prone to extreme opinions when inspired or provoked—Jamie is highly opinionated, very outspoken, and often pedantic to the point of religious fervor. They did clash, too, but in such a way that began to endear each to the other.

Painful singing from a would-be Leonard Cohen, and psychotic ramblings from this actor and that artist, Steven's usual stupor, and *my* traditional party ennui and preoccupation with the dessert table, allowed for much banter between Leo and master raconteur Jamie. There was the occasional growling that turned all our heads, then the resolution as Jamie recoiled into his inimitable basso profundo laughter and offered 'Dito another pipeful.

All this to say that Jamie and Leo began hitting it off from the start as *amigas buenas*.

The New Year's instant was spent holding hands in a circle on the floor. "Om!" we chanted thrice, then each recalling an aspect of the previous year for which we were especially grateful. I shifted uneasily, then mumbled something about my cats and garden. And together we sat silently in prayer for the future. I was ill from wine, smoke, and too much food, however splendid; we came home and slept for a day.

"I love Jamie" was all Leo stated.

Following this encounter were a series of regular get-togethers between the architect, the novelist and myself. An occasional other friend or house-guest of Jamie's was present, but they inevitably retreated into silence as Jamie and 'Dito pontificated on the nature of fascism and the ruination of Amerika. "Revolution!" Leonardo would shout, and Jamie and I would raise our glasses high, "To the revolution!"

Leo would horrify us with the tales of his youth. The maps would come out as we pondered all the splendid and exotic and tropical possibilities that this planet has to offer when it comes time to escape the inescapable onslaught of fascist Amerika. Then we would fall back in our discussions into the reality that there is in fact a certain predisposition to comfort that comes by virtue of harboring in the Belly of the Beast. Another round of chocolates, some more wine, and Leo and Jamie would go on ranting as I faded into some volume of Dalí or Picasso erotica.

They were splendid evenings. The catastrophic conundrums of two great intellectuals with such varying perspectives were enough to shake the thin Hollywood walls; Jamie and Leo would enjoy a sloppy kiss or two, some feely-touchy, verbal innuendoes, and we would slide back down the mountain and into our own glamorous lovehole beneath the streets of Beverly.

When I went to Hawaii, Jamie and Leo became regular smoke buddies and confidants, to an extent that Jamie and I (due to the missing essential herbal component) never would. Months later, as Leo and I began falling out, he and Jamie again took up this essential solace in each other. I thought that was swell. But by and by I began to notice a distance between Jamie and myself, which I attributed to Leonardo's expressed Gavin-grievances.

Soon I found that, between Jamie and myself, even the token social gropes and amenities were no longer present. This I let glide for quite some time until just before heading north to Yosemite, when I dropped in on Jamie to cop a cutting of a plant or two I wanted from his garden, and to give him a gorgeous two-toned iris that I had been raising for him.

In the midst of my transactional goodbyes and come-up-and-see-me-sometimes, Jamie's boil burst with "Leonardo told me that you didn't want to see me anymore, so I really don't understand what all this is about!"

"All I said to Leonardo," I assured him, "was that I had made a decision to not spend time around people who were smoking dope, be that you, Steven, or Leonardo himself. That doesn't mean that I don't love you—I *still* love Leonardo—I am going north to be by myself and purge, that's all. I don't want any drugs in my house. It's not meant to be a judgment, simply a choice—but *you* are certainly welcome any time. I would love to see you there. I love you, Jamie."

I forced a hug, indeterminately sincere on both parts, and bade as pleasant a farewell as possible. I never saw Jamie again, he killed himself a few years later and left his home and estate to Leonardo.

Neither did I encounter Leonardo again for quite some time. We have become distant friends, and I have included one of my sexy photos of him in my most recent book, *Between the Cracks*.

And yet now, oddly enough, when the mornings are slow to start, and my mouth and thighs want for fur and flesh, it is to that satyr 'Dito that my thoughts most always turn.

AUNTIE EM

Rules are created by small minds
and followed by smaller minds.

Just after New Year's, 1989, I received a prospectus for a film project being produced by a gentleman named Scott Catamas. *Men in Love* was a syrupy story about a fellow who loses his lover to AIDS, takes his pent-up rage and frustrations to visit a community of New Age tantra-ites on Maui, and, of course, eventually swallows their bromides and gives in to their vastly superior way of life. In the end he bids farewell, despite the offers to remain, and takes this "good news" gospel back to the Bay City to save the rest of humanity (or at least the dying queers). It would rely heavily on a copiousness of attractive naked men to pull it along, without ever achieving the level of political honesty of unalloyed porn. I would not directly be involved in the feature, having arrived on the scene too late. Instead I would participate in several shorts to be filmed alongside the feature, about tantric yoga (which I pretended to know something about). Scott offered me a generous sum for my talents (which figure I was not to disclose to the other actors, many of whom were performing gratis), promised a gourmet vegetarian chef, and a cast of sexy and—did he say *willing?*—available gay men. Not to mention two *paid* weeks on Maui.

With Leo managing the menagerie, which had grown by about five snakes and a dozen or more pet rodents of varying needs and personalities, I packed off early one morning to the airport, arriving hours later at the compound on Maui, at the end of a long unpaved road, rain-pitted and continually swamped in mud. The house and accompanying outbuildings, offices, and dorms, nested atop a tremendous rock cliff that overlooked one of the planet's most verdant tropical valleys. A massive waterfall filled half the crevasse with pools and natural rock slides, then cascaded downward toward a rocky and thunderous beach and out into the vastness of the great gray Pacific. It was Paradise in every inch of the imagination.

After being led to our rooms we eliminated all our clothes, as per orders, and congregated in the cozy hot tub that hung dangerously over the edge of the lush canyon. There I met "Emerald Dolphin-Heart Starr," our host, producer, master of revelries, my soon-to-be partner in the tantric "how-to" films (and the "bad guy" in the feature). He was an eloquent, friendly, soft-spoken and effeminate gentleman of slight build, whose bizarre sewing-machine row of hair plugs all but ruined an otherwise perfectly attractive receding hairline. "Auntie Em," as I was soon to tag him, was married to Lauri, the mistress of the properties. Lauri was queen of this particular sect of New-Age swinging singles, a small and overtly self-protective woman who only breezed through on occasion, laid down laws that had best be followed, and breezed out again, leaving everybody nervous and ready for a smoke.

Included in the Jacuzzi bisque was an attractive yet frightening character named Nick. Within moments of encountering his tense and stubbly legs against mine in the swirling pool, I recognized him as a man I had attempted to date four or five years before, when I was working at Williams-Sonoma and bouncing regularly around Beverly Hills. Nick had cut hair at a ritzy salon nearby, and, after brief flirtations, came to fry a strip of my bangs and give me some exotic and new-wave color that would shock my boss and her tushy clientele. At some point back then I ended up at Nick's flat, his pants pulled down and my face in the cleft between two profoundly noble and befurred cheeks. Then I all-of-a-sudden remembered that I was a sworn renunciant of Big Mama's order. "My, what a lovely aquarium," I bubbled, leaving Nick spread-eagle without explanation. "It's saltwater, right?"

"Uh, yeah..."

"And are those lovebirds in the next room? I *love* lovebirds! Mercy, is it really seven o'clock? I have to get home..."

Things were never quite the same between us. And now here we were, partners in at least one of these PC sex flicks.

Nick had been working out, much to my displeasure—although he would be described by anyone as "quite the hunk," *I* quite preferred the svelte and more supple Italian that I had psychically date-raped some years before. His face was exotic, ethnic, with the most dynamic and pronounced eyebrows I have ever seen. Though he was good-looking by most any standard, a truly observant person would be put off by the unmistakable characteristics of emotional pain and general confusion that radiated out like an invisible cancer from this otherwise elegant specimen. These maladies were only thinly veiled by the blissful façade he and the other transplants obligatorily voiced. "Yes, I live here now," he mooned, "it's paradise, it's magic..."

"Do you cut hair here?"

"Oh, sometimes. Nobody works on Maui. How can you work in all of this? Anyway, I'm trying to focus on my acting career."

"In Hawaii?"

"Well, you just have to have a clear vision..."

We had some catching up to do, so when Emerald was called inside to attend to business and production matters, Nick and I slipped quietly off to my room for an extended metaphoric chat. I was ready for some wild and tropical love. All I can say is that we did everything *but* have sex. "I no longer have ejaculations," Nick told me from our circuit-69.

"Well that's cool," I drooled, "do you fuck?"

"I'm working on my tantric techniques with another actor named Joey. He's a local. He's great at breathing. You'll love him."

"Uh huh, well I *do* love to breathe..."

The impoverished repartee didn't stop me from gourmandizing every inch of available flesh on this deposed god. But that was where we left it. Nick made reference to this Joey Bimbo whenever things began getting heated, and spoke of the chaste joys of tantra as though it were a pyramid scheme that I should sign onto immediately. I chalked it all up to cosmic retaliation for my evasion of him five years before. Nick went off to cuddle with Auntie Em before dinner and left me like strapped Odysseus to jack off watching the hurricane-force winds and rains that pelted against the picture windows and the poor beleaguered heliconias, ti, and banana bushes just outside.

After the splendid grub, the goddesses and gods regrouped once again in the intimate confines of the Jacuzzi. The evening winds had now picked up, sprays of rain assaulted us, and I discovered one of the more interesting of the local phenomena: most any evening at approximately this same time, roving saucer-shaped "ships" came lolling overhead, checked out the local action, passed into the area of the sea just beyond where the luscious dark canyon opened onto the rocky shores, and hovered there, out on the moon-lit surf, emanating their own strange lights, often well into the night.

The view through the regular partings in the clouds and the sheets of rain brought tears to my eyes. Garnish that with the heat of the bodies, the gorgeousness, the endemic nakedness, the freedom to touch, and the weather, which was of near-cataclysmic proportions; add to that the excitement of the incredible UFOs, which rolled right over the house, and then remained in fixed positions out in the ocean not over a mile away, taunting us with unearthly light plays into the wee hours. So, in our high, our euphoria, the happenstance discovery of sub-aquatic erections, the ships passing over, we let out one great and wailing cry of recognition, astonishment, and pure joy. This bliss, this enthusiasm, continued most every night for the two weeks that I was there. The saucers split after about the first week, the weather cleared and the mood changed, but the night-magic of the island was perpetual as the bouquet of bodies and energies revolved and indiscriminately traded places in that black and frothing pool.

Then Doug arrived, a slight gentleman who was not to be in our video "shorts" at all, but who was already slated as the star of the *Men in Love* film.

Doug was a cute little blond thing. I mean *cute* in the way that implies a calculated degree of earthiness that sets him apart from more traditional beauties. He was cute and homely in the way that one might expect of a Tom Sawyer or a Huck Finn: country, dowdy even when immaculately groomed, the sort of neighbor's child that one might encounter in an abandoned shed and return to every afternoon for the best blowjob in the neighborhood.

Doug had been an actor in LA, done some bit parts, slept around, played around, when he met and fell in love with Guy, his husband. He said to hell with Hollywood and flew off with Mr Right to begin a new life on the even scarier cliffs just down the muddy road from Lauri's *Tantrarama*. They had built a grand and largely glass white cathedral that looked down over a several-hundred-foot stone drop-off into the crashing cauldron of their own private bay—a bay, which, according to Doug, was the frequent host to these spacecraft, which often simply hover there whirring on the water through the night and on into the next morning—odd neighbors, to be sure, but it beats the hell out of TV.

"We raise cut flowers to be shipped to the mainland," Doug told me in our first conversation. "And Guy does real estate all over the island. Then Emerald asked me if I would star in their film!" He grew glassy-eyed, "It just goes to show you, that if you truly follow your heart, the Goddess will give you everything you need..."

My attention waned.

That second evening we had gathered for a brief meeting of the minds to ask questions and to express our feelings and projections about this inchoate and *vague* project. But more, Auntie Em was there to lead us through a "ritual," with the assistance of a bowl full of tablets known as Ecstasy, a lot of incense, crystals, bells and related New Age bric-a-brac.

There were other residents who showed up for the ceremony, a sexy (and straight) local dude who was to eventually score the films, two large and porpoise-like Swiss women who led tantric workshops with dolphins, Doug's Guy, and a plethora of miscellaneous faeries not unknown to Auntie Em's magical canopy bed. Again, I was faced with the dilemma of doing a strong psychotropic substance (I had never done Ecstasy, but had enough background information to ascertain the potency and nature of its trip—I had always been curious about it) and of attempting to relate to a room full of people, many of whom would be on the same substance.

Most everyone indulged. Emerald rang some chimes, said some inane prayers to this island goddess or that, and we started coming "on," losing our positions in the original circle and migrating into our own island realities.

Some five years earlier I had been coerced into doing the *est* weekend by Jo and Peter, who thought it the most powerful and cosmic experience on the planet. The entire weekend could be summed up in my experience of the introductory night, in which we were "led" verbally through a meditation of "expanding" outside the body to encompass the chair, the people sitting next to you, the room, the hotel, the city, state, country, planet, and on out into the universe. Well, believing that I was actually supposed to *do* all of this, I went on out there, veritably screaming and laughing with nirvanic Oneness as I experienced myself as the Divine in all of my Glorious Creation. When I was brought back to, I found the "leader" in a snit of anxiety as he attempted to dissuade me from doing the weekend. That's when it dawned on me, *They don't want you to experience enlightenment (none of them have), they simply want you to say that you have experienced enlightenment* (which is, in fact, all that *est* proved to be). The leader, of course, assumed that I was on drugs, which I was not, nor had been for four or five years, and/or he was, frankly, *envious*. This could be used to illustrate the schism between church and true mystics throughout the ages, no less applicable now in our world of New Age god-wannabes:

Up until now, Scott the producer had been impressed with me for what he saw as my spiritual prowess—the gurus, the yoga, the channeling, the whole crystal gamut. Scott, however, having been born on Christmas Day—I was Thanksgiving—had a very well-developed Messianic complex, perhaps as acute as mine. Consequently, when I started writhing in unabashed ecstasy, and the group formed a circle around me, vicariously enjoying my bliss and copping handfuls of the shakti that was flying out of my head, my heart chakra, and out of the tips of my fingers and toes, Scott immediately went through a change that subsequently marred the way that we were to relate from that point on. He ended up going outside with one or two of the household ladies, while Auntie Em led the procession around my bepassioned body. I looked at Emerald as he held me and I saw that he was my lover, as all wo/men were my lovers, and I laughed and kissed with him and with anyone that was within point-blank range.

When the evening at last began to lose its focus, Emerald became possessive of me and led me off to the sanctuary of his master suite. I wouldn't've fought *any*thing or any*body* at that time, and was happy for the solitude and the peace of his room, his celestial smile, his sparkling jade eyes.

We relished sensual pleasures all night as he was the all-responsive and surrendered goddess in my arms, beneath my torso, playing with feathers and with crystal wands about my titties, stomach, and testicles.

"Precious lover," he cooed and crooned in his womanly voice, "come and live here with me forever."

"I already have," I giggled, "I already will; I already do."

The next day was still too wet to do any of the scheduled outdoor shooting, so Emmy walked me over to his adjacent land across the forest valley. We played with his exquisite golden macaw, Mango, who jostled along until she was swept up in a wind which she rode from one end of the canyon to another, tree to tree, accompanied by her wild and capricious yells. Emerald showed me the spot where he desired to build me, his lover, a house in which to come and live with him. We ate guavas and passionfruits from out of the trees and off of the forest floor. It was all so perfect, and I felt, once again, like I was at *home*. Emerald's bed became my bed and I moved all my belongings out of my dormitory room and into his suite in the main house. All the Tantrarama staff became immediately both wary of me, as the possible new "mistress," and yet instinctively appreciative of my courtesies and helpfulness.

I fell into the pattern—every night after the cook had split—of creating huge trays of fresh banana and pineapple bread from fruit picked just outside the front doors. This upgraded my rating with everyone by about 600 percent, as only food (even more than sex) can do.

"I was thinking," Emerald said, smiling between mouthfuls, "I have to pop down to Bali after the shoot to check out some possible real estate situations. How would you like to join me?"

Bali had for some time been my first priority of places to visit. For over a year, whenever discussions arose about the future, I had grown accustomed to saying that I was, as a point in fact, moving to Bali (even though I had never been there). *This* was an easy *Yes*. I had money from the film, with which Emerald immediately purchased a ticket, and we were all set. *This* was *ecstasy*.

At last the videos began, starting with some beach scenes on the opposite side of the island where there was eternally sun. We still had no script.

The shooting went relatively well, actually, with the exception of constant equipment problems, the meticulosities of our photographer divas, surprise rain attacks, and the like. But it was invariably fun, the gents were lusty and playful, our cameraladies a joy. Then the drugs started wearing off.

I began to perceive Emerald as a self-possessed megalomaniac with only a token regard for the feelings and needs of his employees. He began seeing me as a nuisance and an intrusion on his privacy, his business life, and the regular trail of boys that would otherwise be occupying his bed. We had no more sex, spoke cautiously lest hard words ensue, and basically were behaving as though we had been married for thirty years. It had been three days since the Ecstasy.

Other relationships were smooth, though I began to understand something about the nature of the project that I could foresee as an intrinsic liability. Impresario Scott's undefined script was less spiritually invoked than the result of drug-induced irresponsibility. Scott would request the wisdom of Emerald or of Richard, our two illustrious producers, who would spout their own smoky directions like "Do what you feel like doing" or "It'll all work out, just shoot." And when, whilst filming, a director or a producer was the most needed, they were invariably off somewhere indulging in home-grown *paco lolo* and/or getting it on with some lovely island child or tantrica. So we ate; I got so fat off the waiting and the cuisine that I was embarrassed to finally do my scenes at all. I wrote, I read; we did local beaches. It was a wondrous time, even though we weren't sure to what avail.

As Doug hung with us, I became more and more attracted to not only his swell-guy-next-door demeanor, but his wholesome and neo-flowerchild persona. But he too was a chronic stoner, presenting certain blocks in the communication that I was unwilling to toke up to overcome. His Guy was hot for me as well, so I began receiving invitations to join them at their pad, but it was always stated such as *for some weed and to watch the game on TV*—gosh, not my idea of a good time.

At last, a week into it, the eminent Ona Zee arrived, straightway from accepting her trophy as Best Adult-Film Actress of 1989 in Vegas. I was to play with Ona in a half-hour tape entitled *Full-Body Orgasm for Women*.

Ona was beautiful, soft, round, with full white skin and long dark hair which she pulled up on top of her head and let fall in a cascade down her back. With her subtle makeup—not garish or whorey as I might've expected from a porn queen—she reminded me of a dark and voluptuous Barbara Eden in *I Dream of Jeannie*. "Hey, you're some kind of fox yourself," she reciprocated. We immediately took sanctuary in our sobriety. Ona had been through drugs, alcohol and all the trappings that her career enticed. She had since chilled out, met a Native American tantric master, and learned *that* technique of auto-eroticism and ecstasy-related breathing. Much to the chagrin of the adult-film industry, Ona then began producing her own films (*My Dinner with Andrea*) about said techniques, in a business which professes the liberation of the female through her sexuality but which has a vested interest in maintaining the notion that such sexuality is always dependent on a good man around the house—or at least a good woman. (Why do they think she's named *Ona*?)

"We have many things to talk about," she winked at me as she picked up the stack of my books that were decking the coffee table before us. I was looking forward to her... techniques.

Because Ona was on a shorter schedule than the rest of us, we essentially dropped all other projects and started work on the *Full-Body Orgasm* tape. Thanks to our new director, charming and competent Barbara, the tape was simple, direct, and rather clean. It goes through Ona's personal purifications and processes for readying herself for the sexual/spiritual encounter. Someone suggested that I be shaved to distinguish me from the me of the other films, and we taped an impromptu bathroom scene in which Ona did the honors— they put an overlay track on later in which Ona gives a brief interpretation on the nature and importance of "trust."

It was fun, and funny, and we decided at that moment, rather than pretend or "act" that we were some fictional relationship, that we would merely be Ona Zee and Gavin Geoffrey, two porno stars who had been hired to do this film about "tantra" together. From that point on the taping truly flowed. There was a scene in which we simply sat at a table and discussed what we liked and didn't like about sex, about each other, about this film—an invaluable notion of "clearing" unresolved issues and setting up parameters for the love-allowing process.

"I don't like to be treated rough," she told me, "I like to be caressed, softly, like a feather... yes... just like that..." (I was wafting my fingers over the undersides of her arms.)

"Me too, Ona, I don't like to be pinched, slapped, or bitten—especially my tits. I liked to be rubbed, deeply massaged, kissed..."

And then we had the sex scenes.

All through the filming, we were advised that it was perfectly kosher to

210 • In the Flesh

either engage in functional sex, or simulate, whichever happened naturally. As it was, there were always so many interruptions of equipment and "assistants" that maintaining a sexual flow would've been practically impossible. For the breathing and the body orgasms, however, everything *was* set up in advance. "We're just going to do our trip," Ona warned, "one time. And you guys catch it as best you can..."

I discovered that I was a natural at these tantric breathing methods, though I found that, as per my nature, the catharsis and the bliss were transcendent, and not necessarily even inclusive of the sexuality we were supposed to be evincing. Nevertheless, everything came out well on camera, so to speak. We had a splendid time, I learned a great deal, and the eventual product was not at all bad considering what little we had to work with (scriptwise), how little time we had, and the chintzy shooting ratio with which we were dealing.

Ona and I parted friends. She had me immediately slated to costar with her in some low-budget horror films/videos that she and her husband desired to produce (*Landlady from Hell* and other sure-fire classics—I'm still waiting); she and Leo got to be buddies upon her return to LA, in my absence, and Leo and I later joined Ona and her husband for another award ceremony at which she reigned queen.

The last short had been redesigned (now that the idea of a *concept* had proven expedient) around me as the poet (myself) engaging in quiet and fantastical reminiscences about men, love, and gentle encounters.

The nature of the tape, *Sacred Passion and Ecstasy*, was to provide a general, sensual presentation of male-to-male intimacy, not focusing on specific genital or climactic contact, as a sort of antidote to the crass and dry bang-bang media with which the industry is imbrued in these paranoid, reactionary, and AIDS-ridden times. I think.

As in the previous tape, I was to dramatize the preparations and rituals involving the nurturing of my own sacred body. There were brief and whimsical encounters with a local boy or two (I even got laid!), and there were ritualistic encounters with Emerald, which, setting our differences aside, brought back the excitement and elation that we had initially felt with one another while on Ecstasy.

It's hard to be objective about this particular film, but it does seem to be generally lacking in intent, content, sensuality, instruction, or even wholesome sexuality, any one of which would have been okay had that been a *focus*. The end product never really teaches you anything, or provides much to fantasize about *or* jack off to. Besides which, I was fat.

Hawaii ended, the filming was wrapped, auf Wiedersehens were bidden, and late the next evening my antipathy Emerald and I were to be off to Bali. On the one hand, I believe we were both dreading these jointly purchased tickets; on the other hand, both of us were joyous at the prospect of the exotic wilds of Indonesia.

Emerald had business to tend to, and I was free in the entr'acte to wander around, swim, play with the bird, and witness the arrival of some of the next batch of the house's guests, mostly older women attending a five-day women's yoga retreat. "Aloha," one of these broads accosted me at the entrance to the establishment's outdoor communal shower/garden. She was a potent-looking, ruddy-faced-but-handsome woman of some sixty years, I guessed, with a frazzled ponytail of what appeared to be authentic blonde hair, little or no makeup, and a simple Hawaiian-style jumpsuit.

"Aloha back," I stood there in my dripping everything. "Here for the retreat?"

"Yes, and you?"

"Doing some films on tantra. We're just wrapping. I'm heading out tomorrow for Bali..."

"First time?"

"Yeah—though I've been telling everybody for a year I was moving to Bali. Now I can see what all my hyperbole's been about."

"Oh you'll love it!"

I couldn't say what the attraction was, but I liked this lady right off. She was hip, wise, open—not just another self-abused old hen.

"And how'd the filming go?"

"Nothing a little less marijuana wouldn't've helped."

"Oh dear. What are the films for?"

"Sort of affirmative fluff for the starving fey audiences. Something other than gonad crunching, and yet beyond the permafrost that AIDS is instilling..."

She enticed me to expound upon my theories about the disease and its unnecessary perpetration by a murderous/suicidal society and an oligarchal pharmaceutical industry, the AMA as the medical CIA, ragging on at length (as I do) about cures, drugs, and the plutocratic anti-shamans of the medi-world versus real heroes such as Earl Rice. By the time I was dressed and ready to head out, she had written down the names of Dr Rice and his reticulose. That was that; I went about my wistful ruminations. It wasn't until I returned home from Bali that I received an excited telephone call from Earl, hailing that I had had this encounter with Doris Duke, and how impressed she had been by me. I responded that I didn't know who that was, but from what little I could remember, she had seemed like a kind and robust soul, and I hoped that her kid or whoever would be inclined to do the reticulose and would become well.

Earl panted that Ms Duke was, next to the Queen, the wealthiest woman on the planet. I later found myself playing host to a couple of East Coast homo friends of hers who *did* come out to do Earl's drug, stayed at the gallery, and even bought a couple of paintings. Sadly, Ms Duke has since died of very questionable circumstances. But the one handsome young friend that I remain in contact with is doing excellently.

❦ ❦ ❦

Bali was now less than two days away. Emerald and I left the wet side of the island to attend some activities that he was involved with on the beachier side, where he and two womenfriends had a small New Age enterprise leading boat trips between the islands to encounter whales and dolphins. That evening I saw a film the three had produced of the gentle giants swimming, playing and cavorting to their natural songs (although synthesizers were used to multiply, enhance and overlay the shrill-to-sonorous sounds). We were instructed both before and during the film of certain movements and rhythms that even we, upon dry land, could emulate, breathing included, to bring about a consciousness and an awareness of and shared by our aquatic cousins.

As the film progressed, and we were all involved in our own undulations and deep breathing, I again found that I was overcome with the reality of memories, empathies and experiences of the ocean and of these loving spiritual creatures. When I was a child of seven or eight I had consciously paddled out into the ocean on my inflatable rubber raft, as always to get as far away from my dreaded mother as possible, possibly to terminate this life and join that rich and electric water world. By the time I heard the screaming and looked back to see the ranting and waving of the lifeguard and my mother on shore far away, and realized that everyone had been evacuated from the water and that I was all alone, I became completely engulfed by the laughing, singing and "partying" of a host of hundreds of these shimmering silver water-people. I experienced an ecstasy as they acknowledged me, shared a laugh, spat water, and then dove on.

The lifeguard was pissed and exhausted by the time I had met him halfway; he thought he would lose his job if had I been eaten alive. This was South Carolina; it was 1963; people didn't know about things like the grace of whales and dolphins, and that I was safer with them than I ever would be with any of the two-legged hominids on the beach.

Now, I sobbed and shook as the others in the screening room undulated by and embraced me. I cried for the plight of the whales and the dolphins; the fact that Saint Germain had said that they have already decided as a whole that they would become extinct and move on into other dimensions. I cried for my life on this planet without them, and the probability that I would not be going with them.

The next day I went out to meet and dance with our massive gray friends. After an hour or so of travel we began sighting and pursuing the huge leathery fins and tails that spouted out of the choppy surf. Our excitement was unbridled as we shouted and cheered at our benevolent cousins, imploring their presence, their power, and their beingness to surround us. All at once we *were* surrounded: fins and tails were jackknifing on every side of the forty-foot rig. The engines were killed, we dropped anchor, and wasted not a moment in flinging ourselves in among them.

Despite the fact that my lungs are shallow and much out of condition for swimming, I found the body movements and natural undulations came quite freely, directing me simply and exquisitely through the waters without much use of my arms and hands. All around me was the booming of these comely creatures, penetrating not only through my ears but, via the surrounding waters, through my bones and the drum of my epidermis. It was devastating, like the womb, rushing with the vastness of inescapable sounds that are life itself; not merely approaching me as an observer, but embracing and devouring my every cell as participant and fellow traveler in this great unending sea.

Weeping in the ocean is redundant. Rather, at-oneness with that Divine Tear, as a saline creature, became my experience; the Ocean herself was my emotion, and that is all that I experienced.

I never touched the whales, despite my desire to do so, but merely basked in their divine presence for that brief period before they took off to other playgrounds. It was, again, all I could do to not simply go off with them, even if that had involved leaving this form to the depths and whisking along merely as a thought on someone's tail.

Emerald and I had come to a nonverbal understanding that Bali would be great, that Emerald would not be plagued with the hysteria of house and film, and that we would simply be relaxed and carefree in that awesome and bountiful place. I decided that, given Emerald's disposition, it would be best simply to concede to his whims and to set aside my own needs and desires for later gratification. Given the extraordinary opportunity of a guided run through yet another Fantasy Island Paradise, it was certainly well within my reason to practice emotional restraint, covert and overt peacemaking. Even on the gruelingly long flight to Indonesia, I found it quite natural to allow Emmy the entire row of our seats on which to lie down and nap—it was immediately obvious that he was not about to offer me this boon—while I sprawled out on the floor for a dismal and debilitating twelve-hour rumble.

Auntie Em is a born member of a rather secretive worldwide bunch of philanthropists known as the "Dough-Nuts"—for their mass wealth and their continual contributions and assistance to charitable (*nutty*) causes, invariably left-wing, PC, New Age, or ecologically oriented. While traveling, we continually collided with other members of this jet-life set. Which reminded me of one good reason for the accumulation of wealth: that these elite members of the world society were not only charming, literate, and articulate, but emanate the consciousness that comes from assimilating the great experiences of scores of conflicting religions, cuisines, sexual habits, music, art and politics. How can anyone possibly say that they understand Christianity without also exposing themselves to the tenets of Buddhism, Hinduism, Islam? They might say that they understand it on "faith," but what is faith, ultimately, but ignorance of God? With Emmy I encountered individuals whose faith was in wisdom, experience, nature, humanity.

In the Honolulu Airport, while hurrying to our Garuda dock, Emerald was hailed by a gentleman named Utne, publisher and creator of the *Utne Reader*. One night in Bali (Ubud), at what is considered the safest of local eating establishments, we inadvertently shared a table with a fascinating gentleman, Lawrence, who, along with his brother, had created and narrated the brilliant British series *Ring of Fire*, and who wowed us with even more harrowing tales of drifting the uncharted South Pacific and close encounters of the "primitive" kind with head hunters, cannibals and canoeing bands of prehistoric pirates (reminded me of West Hollywood).

Bali was hot, heavy. It was the rainy season, a time that I had been warned by some to avoid and by others to be sure and not miss. As it was, I cannot imagine a more pleasant Bali than that drippy, dense and olfactory feast-of-a-land that swallowed us.

The lowland streets are filled with tourists and tradespeople, and Emerald quickly hastened us through them, stopping only at a few points that he knew good for certain items that he desired for the rest of our trip. He had insisted that his hired driver take us inland to Ubud for merely a fraction of what the dude had initially suggested. This was my first lesson in Balinese economics.

The people are small, brown, dark-eyed, rarely gray, even at advanced ages, *never* fat (anyone fat was either an American, or possibly one of the dreaded Aussies that are so ill-thought-of by both locals and tourists alike for their brashness, their drunkenness and violence—the Balinese are never drunk). Like most Asians, the women can be exquisite; the men, though rarely of my personal taste, are generally at least fit, even well into their years. We saw scores of gorgeously calved elders, clad only in their colorful native skirts, trekking the rice-paddy walls in sandaled feet, with massive baskets of sweet-potato greens on their heads, rippling stomachs betraying nary an ounce of excess flab.

Ubud was enchanting, as had been the terrifying taxi ride up the mountains to this center of all crafts and arts of the island. Trees were laden with bouquets of ferns, vines and bromeliads; temples abounded everywhere; great stone figures and pyramids were enshrouded in moss and tropical flora.

The domesticated lands of Bali are all ribbed in paddies that skirt the hills and mountains in every direction. All the water for the island seems to begin at the top, up in the ancient and long inactive volcanic crater, flowing down in rivers that veer into paddies, gullies, toilets, showers, and eventually canals that spew all their waste into the sea. Needless to say, Westerners are advised not to drink the native water. Still, there is a marvelous feeling of the water as the blood of the land, nourishing, cooling and cleansing the terra and its inhabitants as it races through intricate networks of veins and arteries.

Most meals were entirely untouchable for me, due to a deadly green salsa (or chutney) that few Western mouths can even pretend to tolerate. The substance of the meal was basically white rice and these native sweet-potato greens, neither of which have much flavor of their own; I found myself indulging in the constant partaking of the number-one island breakfast, banana crepes and bowls of fresh-cut mango and papaya—this, alongside the constant stream of boiled black pulverized coffee and sugar, a liquor which makes the mind-altering Turkish variety seem like Evian.

We stayed in what is referred to as a "home stay," a cozy little row of cottages set amid the rice paddies so thoroughly that the only route to the compound was the native one: the steep, slippery and five-inch-wide mud walls of the paddies themselves. One quickly learned the grace necessary to accommodate these walkways, even in the torrential downpours, to avoid sliding hip-deep into the paddies, riddled, we were warned, with both eels and a species of *very* lethal green snake.

Emmy's main intent in this visit was the acquisition of an agreeable piece of real estate—he actually wanted to move to Bali and to create a cross-cultural school of Balinese and Western arts. We spent a good deal of time trudging around mountains and pastoral river-valley land with local guides, the ever present swarms of children, and agents. It was a serendipitous way for me to get a local's perspective of the island. The natives were charming and, with the exception of the few hard-core business enthusiasts on the main city streets, seemed to have no association between *time* and *money.* They did what they did, which is what they had chosen and/or been taught to do, as a craft, as an enjoyment, as a part of life; and they received remuneration for their products, but only, it seemed, as an aside. It was fascinating to hang loose with the painters and the carvers and grok the totality, the holism, the lack of separation with which their lives seem imbued.

The same applied to their music, as they sang and chanted out in the rice paddies to the cadence of sticks and tin cans which hung on strings that stretched throughout the fields. They pulled on these strings to rattle the cans to scare away the birds that would otherwise alight to devour their crops. The explosive chanting that they did to the same end is borrowed from the songs of the local monkeys. I had professed "The Monkey Chant" to be my favorite piece of music on the planet ever since sitting endlessly in the rehearsal halls at Cal Arts where the Balinese musicians taught this timeless masterpiece to the students. But it was not a "piece," I now made the connection, it was *life.* This life began at sunrise, encompassed the entire island, and subsided only at dusk, when the birds were no longer a danger to the rice. "This is the most miraculous symphony ever written." I stood wet and naked at our glassless window.

"And it never stops," Emerald agreed. "At night the song is simply taken up by the geckos and the tree monkeys."

And there was the constant titter of tiny brown boys that knew and followed Emerald about from every direction.

Homosexuality, on Bali, is rarely, if ever, an issue. The odd two men or two women who live out their lives together seldom get so much as a glance from their neighbors. The general rule, however, is that as long as a man (or boy) has a wife (and especially a child), anything is acceptable.

Emerald, of course, made frequent mention of his wife back in Hawaii, and we were continually invited into the family compounds of these youths, whose families would warmly welcome us, as the spouse, mother and daughters prepared exquisite (if inedible) banquets.

But our most significant encounter was with a young American lad, Robert.

Robert was twenty-four, a successful model on the international scene (enough so that he needed to work only two or three times a year to support his Balinese lifestyle, and the incomparable house that he had constructed on a cliff overlooking a breathtaking mountain vista). Robert was also a "shaman," a stoned-out medicine man so prominent that even the island priests invited him in on any of their most sacred or difficult exorcisms or ceremonies. Timothy Leary, Stan Grof, and others had visited at various times. The locals were terrified of him—he continued to have his way with their daughters—frequently putting curses and ill omens against his door; but the priests respected him, feared him. And said curses were minimal, at most challenging, in their effect, as Robert laughingly retaliated with counter-curses and psychic blockades.

From Robert's open windows—there are no windows, actually, in Bali, they are simply open walls, with bamboo curtains to block gale winds—one looked down over a massive serpent of a river, a foreboding cave at one bend, verdant paddies that climbed up hills on every side. Huge papayas hung ripening just at arm's length. I looked out on his world and wept.

Inside, the precious house was all apainted in scenes and mystical symbols. Power objects and tools of divination abounded on every surface. A section of his puja table was fried from where, during a ritual to Yama or Kali, a lightning bolt had crossed through the open room and struck the deer-bone skulls that Robert was blessing. (He gave these to me.)

As we sat around a cluster of candles in the dim evening light, we passed around a bottle of an elixir that the impious shaman had prepared for our awakening. A wine it was, containing innumerable bitter herbs and essences—when he listed, as one of the ingredients, fox dick, we immediately distracted him and set the bottle aside. Our stomachs churned for the rest of the night. But Robert's face and naked brown chest churned in my brain for weeks...

The plane ride back to Hawaii was less dreadful, as I elaborated in fantasy a possible future life in such a sensorium. I did not know what all these gems of images would amount to, but I knew the effect would be profound. Surely there is nothing more humbling than to truly experience a world that is so totally alien to one's own.

My brief segue on Maui allowed for further reflection, as well as a moment alone with Doug, during which I was able to express my desires to get to know him better. I had that chance four months later when I was flown up to San Francisco by Scott to do some looping on our soundtrack, as well as to attend the opening of the *Men in Love* film at the San Francisco Lesbian and Gay Film Festival (a small consolation for the fact that I had not, as originally promised, been included in the piece).

Doug and I (sans Guy) immediately took it upon ourselves to arrange for a single bed in a private room at Lauri's Tiburon estate. We didn't stop touching for more than a moment, in the jacuzzi, shower, on walks along the bay. Eventually we shared a futon at the home of fellow *Men in Love* veterans Bruce and Joe back in San Francisco for the festival itself.

It was also the weekend of the 1989 Gay Pride Parade, and we cruised arm-over-arm through the swarms of histrionic and half-clad women and men, marching just briefly in the parade with the NAMBLA contingent (if only to protest the festering PC pox against the group). People would stop us en route, to photograph us together or to cop an autograph, people who knew me from my films, my books, or my readings and people who had just seen Doug in *Men in Love*.

His smells became a part of me, his smile the answer to all my questions; it was as though we had been raised and groomed for this weekend, these exquisite four days of love before I headed back down to Leo, and he back to Maui and his Guy.

Doug and I did stay in touch for a year or two, but I have never returned to Maui, depite the invitations to do so. I encountered Nick a year or so later when he slipped between Tom Bianchi's sheets, still warm from my visits—he apparently once again has ejaculations. And Emerald I have heard not a boo from, though I fully anticipate a future hike through Bali, and the vision of Auntie Em in the art center he has created, surrounded by a scarcely-clad gaggle of smiling brown girls and boys.

DAD

*The truth is not
divisible by opinions.*

The first pure communication that my dad and I ever really enjoyed, as adults, was when I informed him, at seventeen, that I was a flagrant Homo-American. He admitted that it didn't surprise him (I had been living with my first husband Dalton since my fifteenth birthday), and that he loved me no matter what I was or did.

He went on to explain that he was loath to live with my mother, that home life had become intolerable. And that the very same year that I had left home, that Mom hit menopause, and that my brother got sent up as the town's first drug bust, he had asked for a divorce. Mom, of course, having all the men in her life turn away from her at once, rather than asking herself *Why*, turned the other cheek to face an abstract Jesus (the only man who would have her at that point). But the divorce didn't happen, and since then life with her had been hell.

In a family of polite WASP amenities, to hear my dad speak this way was news indeed, and it became the turning point in our newfound adult relationship.

Dad was a staunch Republican, fighting the elusive commies to the end. And, being by nature conservative, Dad always felt obliged to confront my bold and rash "radical" actions with pre-fab didacts and rueful admonishment. Yet he would in his heart go *with me* on my excursions and crash courses through life. I was Dad's eyes in the world, as I have been to so many of my stay-at-home friends.

Dad, of course, would have no ability to ingest much of the perverse fodder of my life, especially after miring myself in Hollywood, gurus, disco drugs, the Seventies; but we always touched tone on the important notes, and at times shared a bona fide soul-felt understanding. When the LSD sessions began bringing up their worlds of buried material, I simply disclosed to Dad the most skeletal theories of rebirthing and consequent reactivating of rudimentary consciousness and psychic material. That was sufficient for him, and he was fascinated to hear about my childhood remembrances, especially when it got to the details about my mother's affair, which he had only suspected and had never been able to substantiate. "I was never able to talk to anybody about this," he told me, "because I never could prove anything."

But he and I both concurred upon who the suitor was. "And you guys never loved each other after that?" I asked.

"Well, it was never the same..."

"*Did* you ever love each other?"

"I loved your mother."

"And that's why you stayed together?"

"We stayed together because of you guys. Things were different than they are today."

"Well we're gone now, Dad. We're on our own."

This was when I encouraged Dad to get out of the house, in 1983, and he moved into a quaint carriage cottage on the estate of some old friends of his. He immediately discovered the joys of being an attractive single man in an environment in which most of his peers had already had heart attacks, cancer, and the like, leaving behind swarms of horny widows. Fortunately for Dad he liked women his own age, and he found himself opting to play the field, dating a new woman most every night of the week and dropping them like a hot tomato when they began harboring any notion of permanence or exclusivity.

Even though Dad was the president of one of the oldest and most respected real estate companies in Asheville, North Carolina, people simply were not moving to Asheville (every time a census was taken, the city was obliged to expand its boundaries into the rural areas in order to keep from *losing* population). Besides which, Dad hated real estate and was consequently a rotten salesperson. A few years back, during an earlier economic crunch, having sold their house and paid off my mother, he was unable to come up with the $300 for the rent of his bachelor pad. This was during a period when I was still turning tricks, so I was able to help him out. This was a splendid turn of events that not all children get to come to, and it drew us into another bond of intimacy. Dad experienced that bit of vulnerability with me; the conservative teetered, just a mite.

By and by Dad met a miraculous woman named Bessie, a good Republican just on the rebound from being subverted out of her golden years of marriage by a case of blatant infidelity, which she did not stand for. She was alone for the first time ever, angry, and fit pickins for my dad. It was precious seeing Dad, at that age, spanking a woman's fanny and paddling around their love nest after her like a forlorn child. Bessie had money, which didn't hurt their retirement/honeymoon any. She also funded Bhakti Books' inception, paying for the publication of both *Pagan Love Songs* and *The Naked Poet* without ever seeing either of them—Dad requested that she not, being aware of the genre of my writings; and Bessie, being Bessie, simply had faith in me. "I *know* that you wouldn't do anything that was harmful or *wrong*. But I'd never go against your father's wishes," she assured me.

Not much more than a year into the relationship Dad began slipping. No one knew why. Bessie had the forbearance of a saint with him. Dad didn't get better, and over the next two years Bessie grew more and more in command of household matters, eventually even having to monitor his cigarette smoking, lest he simply drop the lighted butt on the carpet or the seat of his divan. It was a shame, and from what I knew of this—intuiting things only, as Bessie, ever southern, kept only the brightest face forward with me at all times—I was pissed at Dad for blowing this platinum opportunity to be with such a sweet and loving, gracious woman.

I have since come to deduce that my father really didn't want to go on with life. He was tired, and Bessie, paradigm of saintliness that she was, was really too good for him to have continued with at that point without having to make some radical leaps himself, which his conservative nature simply forbade. A year with Bessie was like an eternity with one of the Goddess' own devis, and made Dad simply want to fall further into the arms of Heaven. He did, and as he did he became more and more the child, requiring the constant and adoring attention of this beguiling nouvelle *mother.*

Bessie at last admitted to me that problems were arising, at least after I quizzed her about Dad's lack of coherence in phone conversations. Then one day she called me up and explained that Dad was in the hospital. "I think you better get here at once," she said bravely. "We'll pay for the flight."

I checked with Leonardo, who had been anxious to see the mountains from which I had sprung. It was autumn there, and we both took advantage of Bessie's hospitality.

Dad, when I arrived at his room, looked like he was already dead; I had never seen anything so pitiable that was still breathing. Four varieties of cancer and an undefined dementia had devoured his life and his brain within weeks.

"May I be alone with him?" I asked Bessie and the private nurse. I was choking and I felt as though I was in the womb of a burning building.

"Dad," I said, taking his limp lolling head in my hands, "I know that you're dying. And I know that you know that you're dying. And I know that these women will continue to pretend you alive until you are actually dead. But I want you to know that it's all right with me that you die. I want you to know that I'll take care of Bessie. Everything will be all right here. I love you."

My eyes stung, yet they watched him with suspicion, half expecting an argument to ensue. Instead his eyes rolled up and he heaved a great sigh that I was certain would be his last. In between some babbling, he managed to get out the name of my brother.

"I'll get hold of Mark as soon as I can. We'll get him here," I assured him.

Dad smiled again, sighed, and then resumed his incoherence, as though it took too much effort to keep his conscious mind within his body.

Bessie came back in and we set about the business of feeding, changing his IV's and the like.

I held my dad's heavy head and fed him baby food from a jar.

❦ ❦ ❦

Leonardo and I had a great time in Dad and Bessie's grand and posh Biltmore Forest home. Bessie spent the nights in the hospital, so we were able to sleep together, making sure that the beds in both bedrooms were askew by morning. We were both reading new Anne Rice novels, and spent a great deal of time writing in our journals, or photographing and fucking in and around the Oriental garden and hot tub.

One morning Dalton drove up from Winston-Salem and we did a day at the nearby Biltmore House, the gross and aged Vanderbilt home that is the largest single-family dwelling on this continent. Bitchin' gardens and greenhouse. And it is always amusing to put together the current husband with an earlier model and sit back as they dish and compare notes.

The next morning Bessie arrived home early to find me butt-naked in Leonardo's bed. We never could decide whether she simply was too cool to worry about it, or so innocent that she, in fact, merely believed us to be having an early morning chitchat. "I'll get the coffee started," was all she said.

Leonardo fell in love with Bessie as much as I had.

Leo also came back to California with a singular comment about elite southern society: he picked up the word "nice" (pronounced *nas*) which can be applied to almost any subject, and relates to the fact that southern gentlefolk simply *will not* see anything that offends them or doesn't fit into their etiquette book. He drove me crazy for weeks, going "Weeell, isn't that *nas*! How *nas*! I think that's *soo nas*. Isn't this *nas...*?"

The daytimes spent with Dad were tedium exemplified, with my reflections and his babblings, my babblings and his reflections, and the exception of increasingly rare moments of lucidity when he would make some profound remark or gesture in my direction. His favorite was "Well, Hello!" as if noticing you for the first time. Once, out of the blue, "Say, have you killed any deer?"

Another time he interrupted our messy feeding, swallowed, cleared his throat, and sang out the rousing line "Mine eyes have seen the glory of the coming of the Lord!" then went right back into his muttering. His pitch was flawless; I had never before heard him sing.

I commented to Leo that it seemed as though the Republican were dead already, that what was left at last was this simple spiritual being that I had loved even before my life had begun. I kept expecting the Republican to re-emerge and rankle me. But other than the hunting line, not a modicum seemed to be left. In fact, worlds that my dad would have always denied the existence of he was now living in. At one point I felt the presence of my dad's dad, and smelled the unmistakable waft of Royal Copenhagen that the loving gentleman always wore and that I have smelled intermittently since his death, whenever I could feel him near.

"Hey Dad," I caught him between his blithering, "your daddy's here, can you see him?" He squinted his eyes and struggled, shaking his head *no*, but I reiterated that his dad was there. "He's come to take you home with him."

At that moment his eyes closed and he started weeping. He tried to hold out his hand to his father, but his arms were both cuffed to the bed. He simply fell back onto his pillow and left his body to its murmuring. The Royal Copenhagen disappeared as he and Granddaddy went off into the ethers, in hunt of the Heavenly Herd.

Leonardo commented, on a visit, "Your dad has pretty feet, just like yours." He showed up next time with my camera and took photos of the two of us, Dad oblivious.

By the time we left Asheville, Dad was rarely cognizant. We had gotten hold of Mark and he was on his way. I grieved for Bessie, cheated out of the time she deserved with the man she loved; but her strength seemed boundless. She continues to tell me what a blessing those three years were to her; that Dad taught her the meaning of unconditional love.

I went back again for the funeral services, only for Bessie's sake. I had no remorse over Dad's demise; his illness had allowed us the most quality time that we had ever spent with one another.

Bessie and I located a flying buddy of Dad's who took his ashes up and scattered them over Mount Pisgah, as he had requested. And I realized that his final act was probably the most creative act of his life, and perhaps the only illegal thing that he had ever participated in.

The Republican was dead.

RACE

It isn't enough to know the answers,
one must forget the questions.

Among the finer accomplishments of Studio LEONARDOGAVINCI was a program of evening "readings." These consisted of the dramatic interpretations of actor Larry Maraviglia, poets Jonathan Williams and Tom Meyer, the naked meanderings of yours truly, and the palpably ubiquitous lust, love, fire and humor of poetic sadhu James Broughton.

As we all know, poetry readings can be some of the driest, most apoplectic and humiliating experiences known. When obliged to attend, I've learned to bring a pad of paper and writing instrument with which to scribble notes to myself, poems, or just draw dirty pictures. Anything to avoid yawning or tittering with the neighbors. But when Master Broughton began one night in 1988, the entire studio went into a hush. As the seventy-five-year-old saint disseminated, softly, thoughtfully, we found ourselves alternately guffawing and weeping from the evocations. Some of LA's all-time jaded queens were there dabbing handkerchiefs and blowing their fat old noses. It was awesome.

And when he was through, after numerous encores, the room en masse encircled the bard, hugged, and had a good cry and laugh. It was not sad—his work is light and humorous. It was overwhelming: the simplicity, the pulchritude and the humility with which he approached his craft (and us).

Then, when the readings were finis, when the art shows were sworn off and the end to our lease was in sight, we were approached by the newly formed LA branch of the National Leather Association, a group that specializes in the introduction, monitoring and education of leather, bondage and other "kink." We were dubious, at first, neither Leo nor I interested in the least in anything that this demimonde stood for or had to offer. But when the cognoscenti showed up (on time!) and began educating *us* about their purpose, we were both immediate converts.

They spoke little about leather, which both Leo and myself, as animal advocates and practical vegetarians, found neither socially nor sexually appealing. There was *a lot* spoken about "trust," about "pushing one's limits" and the emotional/spiritual "benefits" of pain. But more important than what was said was the sincerity, sobriety, and the openness of the members themselves—these were all extraordinary individuals. Far from the maladjusted, clandestine sex leeches that we had anticipated, these were strong, secure, professional and inordinately intelligent folk, some of whom were overtly same-sex oriented, some of whom were not, some of whom seemed to have few limitations left in the sexual arena whatsoever.

Most impressive were the women, vibrantly sexy creatures, vested with their innate power and strength. We were especially taken by a svelte and dark Latin vamp, poured into a red leather mini-outfit, wielding the legs of death and a matching set of don't-fuck-with-mama spiked heels. Also a boyish diva with a bleached-out punk flattop, uncountable earrings, and arms and shoulders adorned in a pantheon of radiant tattoos.

But I—*Can we not guess?*—fell turgidly in love with the leader of the pack, the regional chairperson, most-coveted turnkey and local demagogue, Master Race Bannon.

Now Leo and I had not signed the official divorce papers at this time, pending, possibly, the final barring of the studio doors. Or perhaps it was simply that we were maintaining an estranged closeness in the event of dire horniness. But feelings were tense and occasionally quite raw, so it did seem prudent to maintain some semblance of discretion around the dude.

But when I caught sight of Race, the goddesses of discretion fell to their callused knees. My balls in a vice, I took the first opportunity available to confront him vis-à-vis. "I want to know what you know," I said, "and I want you to teach me."

He smiled from one little ear to another, his topaz blue eyes looking diligently within me. "Yes. I would like that."

As soon as the two of us could schedule an encounter we did.

I drove out to the Valley to a small house on a rather innocuous middle-class street, parked my car in the drive and was let into the front room through a steel guard door.

No sooner was the door latched behind us than we were at each other's mouths, faces, necks; our clothes fell to the floor and we tossed into a waiting sofa, locked in each other's clutches as though the walls were about to tumble down upon us.

Testosterone always seeks its own level. I couldn't get enough of this man's sex, his puissance, his radiant aura; *this* was a master par excellence—a master of sexuality.

His face wasn't essentially handsome, but it was beautiful. His physique wasn't flawless (at least above the waist), but it was perfect. Whatever it was, this was the most sexually powerful man I had experienced since Vince. Yet, unlike Vince, Race had the understanding of his sexuality to accompany the physical aplomb. I was determined to find out just what made his clock tick.

We exploded. Race confessed to me his obsession with bearded and long-haired men (rare among his peculiar subspecies), that I was his erotic ideal. But more, he knew that I was a man of awareness, that I would challenge him, and that I could reward him with my own ability to learn. He had my books; he said that he had admired my words and my beauty for years.

His legs were strong, irrefutable as they wrapped about me; his arms could salve any emotional bruise. His genitals were without compromise, just slightly larger than mine, his dick hard at a moment's breath. And his *butt*...!

I would have that butt. And I told him so.

"You can have it baby," he said, "if you can earn it."

I was tied by my wrists to an overhead rod that ran the length of his ex-garage "playroom." My ankles were bound at either end of a thick wooden dowel. I was naked in a flittering candlelight; the sonorous drone of Jean-Michel Jarre created an infernal surreality.

The Master removed his own clothes, slowly for me to enjoy, kissing me as each article fell to the floor, until he stood there naked, akimbo, exquisite in every detail. He didn't blindfold me, but ordered my eyes shut.

Then he began.

The first and most constant sensation was that of his lips against mine, that almost familial warm kiss that fed me like a bottle.

"Just remember," he said, "all that I will ever do to you is make love to you. I am here to fulfill *your* fantasies. I will never let pain come to you unless it is the pain that I want you to feel. You are beautiful and I love you. Now I am going to make love to you."

He began with a vibrating prong that he moved about my legs, genitals, and anus. The sensation was a teasing pleasure, but this was too easy and I experienced fear of what I knew must surely follow.

"Relax," he kept saying, "let go, go with it, give it to me, give me your pain, your love." It was as though he were reiterating the words of Big Mama from times before when she pressed me into her eternal bosom in the effort to bring me to enlightenment.

I submitted, and the pleasure seared through me in waves that caused me to tug at my bonds. I had to hold them with my hands to avoid the ropes tearing my wrists.

Then the pleasure was over. *That* pleasure. His kiss returned. "Keep your eyes closed," he ordered. I did.

I heard the pop and whir of an electrical device being turned on.

"Open your eyes. Look," he said.

I saw him touching a tiny glass dome to his chest, which created a burst of blue flames that sparked into the salt-and-pepper fur, then went silent. When he pulled it away again the sparks shot back out and it seemed as though his chest sizzled. I knew what would happen next, that he was simply showing his novitiate that the machine was not lethal, that it was merely a toy, a tool of his heart.

He reached out to me and the blue light popped against my flesh until he had made contact. It hurt. It hurt as he dragged the rod back and forth above my skin, my abdomen, touching my nipples, the head of my cock, my scrotum.

Then I understood: *I was supposed to react!*

And I did. Starting with a whimper, as he encouraged me. "Come on baby, let me have it."

He stepped against me and I broke down, pressing my face into his shoulder. *Daddy save me, protect me from this pain. Protect me from all pain!* And I sobbed as I saw the doctor pull me from my hideaway and spank me for no reason, cut my dick, cut the umbilicus. The years of spanking and offhand abuse. And the love that I always maintained for that man, that father that meant more to me than any god in any heaven. And that was *Race.* This man that I wanted to make happy more than I even desired to be happy myself. Even if that meant extreme pain to my own person. *I was his.*

Again I felt his salivating kiss on my tear-wet face. He was licking the salt from his subdued quarry, drying me with his daddy breath. I could taste the acrid aromas of his sweating nakedness, and feel the pressure of his rigid column, excited by my tears and my release.

"This will only be on you for five minutes," he said while inserting a cold leather knob into my mouth, fastening it at the nape under my hair.

"I am going to give you fifty of these," he said as he held up a black whip of many thongs.

The saliva ran uncontrollably in my mouth and it seemed that I had little ability to swallow. I aimed my face toward the ceiling in an effort to allow gravity to pull the spit down my throat as I contracted it to keep from choking.

"One," he struck me very gently. "Two," a bit harder. "Three. Four. Five..."

It was easy at first. A game. But I knew the lashes would grow in intensity. That's the way Race worked, gradually, steadily, building in trust, in power. I didn't cry. The tears would have drowned me with that damned thing in my mouth. I was relieved when he had reached his *fifty*, but even more relieved when he finally removed the leather nipple. He took a cheekful of water from a plastic bottle and fed it into my mouth. *Then* I wept.

He untied my hands and I wept more while he held me.

"Let me have it," he kept saying, "give it to Daddy."

I realized that I was disappointed that he had untied me.

We chatted while he was unlashing my feet. He pulled me down on top of him on the floor and we rested in peaceful *ecstase*, forgetting the pain, our demanding dicks—the complete erasure of all that was outside of this room—just *being*.

He corrected a popular myth that I, like so many others, have always maintained about the S&M community, that, in fact, it was nothing but a bunch of callous and tired old queens who needed a barrage of tools and equipment to register any physical sensations whatsoever through their gnarly old hides. Race explained that, in fact, the experienced "bottom" (or *masochist*) relates to pain much more acutely than does the average person, and that, as they become more centered in their "craft," the pain becomes such that the brush of a feather—under the proper circumstances—is experienced like the gash of a razor. And yet imagine the people who swing on ropes by hooks pierced through their tits and their flesh; they, he insisted, in their *sankalpa*, are hypersensate to degrees of absolute cosmic bliss. By contrast, the trained "top" is one who is sensitized to the care and needs of the person for whom he is "giving" the pain/pleasure/sensation, with stipulatory rules of care, conduct and etiquette so strict that one infraction can have her/him banished from the professional leather circuit forever.

"It is the master, in fact," he whispered as though revealing a forbidden arcane apothegm, "that is the ultimate slave. It is the master's duty to serve his ward."

I thought of Jesus on the stake. I felt my vesical muscles contract and my gut ignite with the revelation.

He then ordered my eyes closed again.

"This is what I consider the most important form of bondage," he said, pulling my legs and my arms out straight by my sides. No restraints. "Don't move. Keep your eyes closed. I'll be right back."

He was gone for only a moment before he told me to open my eyes again; I saw him place a lighted candle upon my chest. The illumination on his face that should have made him look strange and monster-like in fact made him all the more lovely. I knew what would follow.

He took the candle above me again and let fall one drop of wax. I winced.

He dropped another on another part of me. And continued until the hot wax was raining like a storm all over me, burning my balls, my ram, everywhere but my face.

I detached from my body, as is my habit when I am in pain, and he reprimanded me. "You're cheating, stay with me!"

I came back. I felt the pain. I started screaming and he sank down on top of me, glued to my body by the torrid paraffin; he made love to me, with his words, with his breath, with the drumming of his heart.

And afterward, when he had peeled off the desiccated wax and showered me clean, he pulled me down on top of him again and allowed me to possess him inside. But it was as though that were a different person altogether, as though I were a different person as well. Oh, it was splendid, being inside him, watching that big and beautiful man give himself to me as would an ingenue; but these were two different people, different Race, another Gavin, somehow less multidimensional, like shadow puppets that we were watching upon his bedroom wall. Beautiful, in all its complexity, alive with the smells, the sounds, and all the warmth of this kingdom; but we were just two men then, enjoying love, allowing our sex to be satisfied. The Being that had stirred my soul with his games, his words and his devices was infinitely richer. Race Bannon, my urban shaman.

The kink and bondage gallery show was an unmitigated success. The art was poignant, proficient and evocative; but most impressive were the dozen or more "living sculptures."

Because of the nature of the show, and the "models" who were placed in positions of extreme vulnerability about the place, the audience was invitation-only, carefully selected from friends and friends of friends for their discreet and mature participation in the evening. I must say that I have never seen such a controlled, circumspect, and yet *inspired* group of people. It is very humbling to be in the presence of women and men who are unable to speak, unable to move, unable even to see their admirers.

There was one large redheaded woman, unattractive by most standards—your basic Gary Larson housewife—who had her slaves drag in some half-dozen cages, chairs, boxes and slings in which they were, during the course of the evening, confined. Race informed me that she was one of the most famous sadists in the world. "She has over fifty slaves who have all signed contracts to be hers for life. She had just been a mother from Orange County some seven years ago. She never has sex with her slaves, except for the one little man in the sling—that's her husband..."

A gentleman—the publisher of *Drummer* magazine—constructed a sculpture of three naked musclemen, tied together by their arms and their feet in a giant Atlas-esque tripod; when he was finished with the bonding he placed a huge inflatable globe on their heads. Fascinating.

Ona was there, with her husband Frank; a friend that I had met through Ona, porn star Sharon Kane, arrived with a girlfriend, the two of them wearing little but black nylons and a few selectively placed thongs.

There were ladies and gentlemen hanging from our rafters in slings, swings and spiderweb nets of all kinds. But *I* missed a great many of the presentations: *I was Race's art.*

On a plywood platform Race had me laid out, naked except for a small swatch of felt over my dick and across my eyes. I was not allowed to speak unless he gave me permission. Then he began the bondage.

With a fine red silk cord he began to wrap me, back and forth against tacks that he was placing in the sides of the wood; as he tied me in this fastidious Lilliputian web, he chatted with the visitors to the exhibit about the nature of bondage, the nature of trust and relationship.

Friends—Steven, Ona, Jamie, even Leo—bent down to me and gushed with emotion. Few were used to ever seeing Brother GAVCO in a position of such humility, such potential debasement, beyond even what the naked readings might have evinced. I couldn't see their faces, but I felt the tears that fell on my skin.

For two hours I was in the master's hands, aware of the supervision of his aquiline eyes, imagining his hot glands pressing down upon my face. Occasionally he would ask me if I were in any discomfort and I would simply shake my head and he would continue with his artful swathing.

No one else was allowed to touch me without his permission, for my safety and my comfort; he would frequently bend over me with a mouthful of champagne/*prasadam*, kissing its contents into my thirsting throat.

By the time I was manumitted and Race began making preparations to string up and display a lovely lady that he also played with, I was alerted that there was a problem at the door.

It turned out to be the fire marshal, complaining that we had no permit for operation, as well as that we had well exceeded the fifty-person capacity allowed for such a structure—yes, we must've had 350 at least...

We remonstrated with the guys, sweet-talked them, eliciting time, even showing them around the room full of whirling Barbarella-style mobiles, captive caryatids, the flogging, the piercing, even tattooing which was taking place. They certainly had never busted a party like ours before; they too were abashed by the impeccable vibes of both audience and demonstrators, by the honest attention that was being paid to every sensual nuance. And by the time they finally had to insist that we must stop, it was only a half-hour short of the slated climax anyway. No one seemed to object, really. We had all been sated.

I saw Race several times after that, always with new and renewed magic and edification, and always storming with the same turgid template of unqualified lust. Sometimes we would have sex after the playroom experience, sometimes we would just fall asleep holding each other.

Then one night, after a week of both being "too busy" to find time to make an appointment, Race finally squeezed me between professional gigs. I had begun to realize that I was growing rather attached to this gentleman, this coveted virtuoso whom I could never in any effect possess.

Race *was* a professional, he traveled around the country giving lectures and demonstrations on the techniques and comprehensive theory behind bondage, sado-masochism, the leather community (in between his regular "job" of corporate computer analysis and systems management, and the how-to manuals that he wrote on these subjects).

And as I wandered into his bedroom ahead of him I came upon the ad that he kept regularly placed in the *Advocate*, circled in pen beside his terminal: "Leatherman," "topman," "master of bondage and discipline..."

Not unlike the ads that I had once maintained in that very same paper, just from a different perspective. Well, what comes around goes around.

I can't say that I didn't know about the ads, about Race's regular clients—he frequently discussed them; he rarely if ever had sex with them. He had told me that I was unique among all his clients, friends and loves, that I was the most beautiful, his ideal, the only man that *ever* fucked *him*. Besides, he saw me for free. Now, with no prelude, he led me into the back, where he placed me face down upon a large padded table. He bound my arms and my feet to the corners of the bench and lodged a handkerchief in my mouth. Then he began to whip me, informing me that I had a hundred strokes coming to me.

They started out easy, as usual, and then progressed in their strength and their fervor. "I'm going to make you break," he said, and he kept on counting.

But the alchemy had been broken. *I* could not. I couldn't let him have me this way, right now, no matter what drubbings he might've inflicted. Half of me wanted to, and I sought for the opium of his perspiration in the air. I recalled all his gallantries and the invincible union that our body parts could create at their best. I could not open myself. I imagined him raping me, taking me by force and obliging my sentiments to comply.

But he would not. He would follow his procedure. There was nothing to do but hold my ground, shivering with the stings, until of his own accord he was finished.

He tried running a vibrator around my sphincter, impaling me with several small objects, something that I previously would've applauded him doing. But still I didn't respond. I reread his ad in my mind; I imagined myself a paying client.

He stopped. He untied me in silence and then sat across from me on a large wooden bed.

"I'm sorry," he said, "if that hurt you too much. I thought you would break. I should've stopped when I saw that you were resisting. I'm sorry if I hurt you."

"It didn't hurt," I lied. "I'm just... not quite here. You wanna try again?"

"No." He stood up and took my hands; he was crying. "Let's go lie down."

We lay together for a while in silent continence, or rambling on about not much of anything. We were both exhausted; he rattled off some dispassionate theories about pain and repression that simply didn't mean anything to me.

By and by I excused myself; Race had an early day and I just wanted to leave. I never mentioned my response to seeing his ad (he had clearly left it there for me to see); I never mentioned the fact that I had developed such an attachment to him.

It was all very convoluted, of course, and I had simply clammed up, annulled my responses, rather than merely utilizing his services for my own pleasure/enlightenment. I was not "being here now"—oh, how we are confined by our own defenses!

Besides, I had by this time decided to leave LA. I knew that Race's designs to visit me in the mountains and tie me to tree and fence would never happen. He had his world, and I had mine. I wasn't sad. Just tired.

"I'm sorry," he repeated, "that I hurt you." He thought it had been the flogging.

LITTLE BEAR

*It is the perception of annihilation
that screams forth my existence.*

A friend of Steven's, Lori, the West Coast representative for *Playgirl*, wanted to do a fantasy sequence with a long-haired man, a masked girl, and a snake. Steven made the sets, I had the snake and the hair, and we secured the services of a sultry little waitress from Catherine's. It was a sin to hide the darling's face, but Lori wanted every woman in America to be able to imagine herself in the girl's place.

After that "exposure" I was cajoled, by Jeri, the sister of a friend, to be the only white model for her all-black agency, Ebonaire. I was immediately scheduled to dance at a massive African-American fashion show at one of the big airport hotels. In between the furs and the evening attire, I came out arrayed in a minuscule fragment of black spandex, balancing Rio, the nine-foot porn-star python, dancing seductively to a disco rhythm. As the large, bejeweled matrons in the six front rows screamed and veritably catapulted through the aisles to the rear of the room, I arabesqued Rio above my head and performed a round of tongualingus (ophidian-style) for the shrieking and cheering crowd. Rio loved the attention.

I carpentered the fantastical sets that Steven had designed for a dance performance by Remy Charlip at the Museum of Contemporary Art, as well as designing and building my own sets for a play that would have made Merlin chuckle, *Artie and Gwen* (a modern-day appreciation of the Camelot tale).

But high on the list of my spate of creative output was a resurgence of lyric and songwriting. I was attempting, for the twelfth-odd time, to initiate a relationship with Gary Jeske, the wiry young artisan whom I had housed with upon my reentry to Twinkle City, who I now believed was between marriages. We did manage to have one or two rather kinesthetic nights of consultation/consummation/copulation before the ex du jour showed up and ransacked the apartment, slashing all of Gary's canvases and spraypainting pert obscenities on the walls—I was lucky to have missed the debacle. They made up, broke up again—ad nauseam. I kept trying. Jeske always played dumb, but I didn't buy it. I was certain there was *some*thing there just waiting to be brought out. Besides which, he had a bonny white ass.

"I love you Jeske."

"Gosh—gee—thanks Gav..."

Then one day *he* called *me* for a surprise date to a soirée at a friend's apartment. He had given this buddy, David Francis, copies of my books, the friend was instantly impressed, and I was asked if I would read at the party—the get-together was in *my* honor. Of course I said yes—I detest reading poems, but it goes with the turf. Besides, I wanted another pop at the Polish potatoes. David Francis turned out to be utterly charming, and his guests equally so. They politely encouraged me to go on and on reading beyond all propriety. It was an intelligent and sympathetic audience unlike any that I had ever had; I felt as though *they* were reading *me*.

Then David began feeling me out with regards to music. I told him about my one recorded song—he had Sam Harris's first album, but not the second. We made a date to get together (sans audience) to play demos, as well as to talk about the possibilities of writing together. That, I then discovered, had been the intention of the whole evening; the party was just a ruse. David was a famous (at least in Memphis) concert pianist, choir leader, composer; he had fallen out with his ex-lyricist/partner, and he loved my poetry. He also had a profound bubble butt and the greatest set of basset-hound eyebrows.

The evening was over. And guess what? The Jeske stayed with David! I thought it had been *our* date. I would've stayed with David myself, or *both*, had I been invited. Silly me!

But David and I began creating songs (even as he and Jeske moved in together); we demoed one, then another; some significant publishers went crazy for the songs—"Surest hit I've heard in three years!"—and they were delivered firsthand to Natalie Cole, Patti LaBelle, the Pointers. *Nada*; nothing. Raves from the "help"; jack shit from the stars. Was it a curse?

Then David was hired to create a score for an animated film being put together by Ralph Edwards Studios. I was employed as lyricist. It was a beautiful story about a baby cow that essentially gets enlightened for her good deeds. Major fucking tearjerker. We spent the next year in and out of the studio completing ten songs for the production. They gave us some advances to augment our inspiration, and lots of strokes. I unethically played our prospective hits for several top agents. Bob Knight at Paramount's Famous Music started crying before the chorus of our number-one hit, "When I Fly," even played. He looked across his desk and shook his head. "This is a big big hit," he said.

"I know," I said.

"Streisand would kill for this," he said.

"I know," I said, "but it's not available."

He broke my heart. The package was put on hold for six years; a deal was finally struck, at which point all our songs were rewritten by their newly hired narrator, Randy Travis. Another curse?

I concentrated on painting and my life with Steven, with Leonardo. *The Naked Poet* was released.

I did regular in-the-buff readings at the A Different Light bookstores in LA and in San Francisco, enamored of the boss honcho there, Richard Labonté, a Santa Claus of a hippie, a festive faerie, an easy hug.

Helga came back into my world with now-regular dance attacks on Catch

One. In our inglorious attire and disco cruise-control mode, we'd turn heads all night long. Steven fell hysterically in love with her; "She's a dude," he kept shrilling, "and she's fabulous!" He shot the two of us regularly—we montaged all kinds of sets and fantasies. Helga hasn't a bad angle, which is why Helmut and Steven love her so; the *camera* loves her; she is every frame a goddess.

Then we were visited by Samantha. Samantha is Steven's other favorite model; his books are filled with her. Like Steven, she spent years in the association of Salvador Dalí. Samantha was Dalí's confidant for well over a decade; they played house together, spoke in a bird language all their own. Gala, Dalí's life partner, hated Samantha and threw knives and plates of food—but then the nettlesome Gala apparently threw knives and plates of food at everybody, especially Salvador. Steven said that Dalí's one true romance was with the poet Federico García Lorca; but, coveting money above amore, Dalí allowed Gala to move into the picture (dumping her own poet husband), take over finances, and subsequently create Dalí's career. They lived in separate castles and only affected the great romance, coming together for formal dinners and state occasions, where they would invariably end up spitting across the table at one another. Samantha frequently got it right on the nose.

Samantha always sat next to Dalí; she would wear dildos up her skirt and invite Dalí's hands to wander during the meal. They were playmates. She spent years roving around by herself, the great white goddess, through the jungles of South America, befriending bush people, trekking out with the men, then beating clothes on stones with the women. She did time for something in maximum security, shooting junk the whole time, had a mélange of marriages, male and female.

Now she was residing in Yosemite, living naked on the land, raising a menagerie of birds and dogs, feeding the drought-stricken deer. She is an artist, a surrealist.

We intended to introduce Samantha and Helga.

"Samantha will rip Helga's clothes right off her and throw her in bed," Steven screamed.

"Helga will adore Samantha. But not that way," I said.

"You don't know Samantha," Steven insisted.

"You don't know Helga!"

They fell absolutely in love—platonically; Helga went off to visit Sammy, where she fell in love with the Sierra Mountains. She took the nest egg that she had been laying for years and plunked the money down on a thirty-two-acre hill just downwind from Samantha.

I was intrigued.

The Beverly neighborhood was a hellish one, replete with illegal refugees of every stripe, gangs, bag people, *santeria* shops and the scary Christian publishing company next door. The week before I moved in with Steven, someone had fired a wild shot through the wall of what was to become my bedroom. The previous roomie, an already unfortunately Nervous Nelly, was watching a favorite old movie at the time the bullet passed through the wall and into the TV, blowing the contraption up. He left the next day.

Despite this boding tale, I moved in—I didn't *have* a TV.

Little Bear and Marlene, my precious felines, both had moved in with me and were faring well. Upon receiving my key, I did what I first do in any new dwelling; I dragged in all of my plants, cuttings, bulbs, even trees that traveled with me, and went right to work setting up the garden. The studio had been a quintessential Twenties farmhouse onto which, in the Forties, someone had dropped a three-thousand-square-foot pretzel factory. So when you stepped out of our back door, you actually stepped *into* the factory. The side of this barn was a huge sliding wooden door that opened up onto a quaint bouquet of weeds, then farther onto a vacant lot. I wasted no time erecting a chain-link fence around what was most likely our territory, tacking down stolen industrial wooden pallets for a verandah, then planting my little heart out with enough vines and rapidly growing tropicals to all but obliterate the filthy vacant lot and the cacophonous intersection beyond. So, besides the mired and cumulative five thousand square feet of house and studio, the "kids" had this marvelous dainty patio and weed bed in which to claw, hide-and-seek, and loll in the sun.

Then one day Little Bear didn't come home. My best friend and most constant bedmate for six years; I felt hollow, to have no body to bury, to grieve over. I searched the neighborhood daily, but I didn't feel his presence. That very same week our noble governor signed into effect a morose law that made it illegal to eat cats and dogs in the state of California. I was sick, heartbroken. I pictured him eviscerated on a lab table at UCLA, or worse, a zombie in a cage with microbes and wires hanging out of his skull, his butt and his eye sockets. I suspiciously eyeballed any itinerant Asian women shuffling about carrying sacks or baskets.

I cased the two local pounds, but I slept at night knowing that it was no use. I could hear him bouncing through his broken window, feel his fur against my face in the darkness; Marlene began sleeping with me for the first time in years.

The pounds were dreadful—places I have always avoided. Then one day I cracked: I purchased two of the hundreds of kittens that were screaming in their disinfected cages—Quan Yin and Yang. The next day I went back for two other boogers that had haunted my dreams that night—Sponge Muffin and Big Tao. I knew that they would not take Little Bear's place, or allay my grieving, but that they would sure as hell provide a good distraction.

But Little Bear's shadow still plagued me. And all too soon the new monsters would start roaming outside. I didn't want them on the street. I didn't want them in that rotten neighborhood. I didn't want *me* in that rotten neighborhood. I wanted to see the little bunny-hoppers scampering through misty meadows, chasing deer, gophers, snowflakes.

It was time to leave LA.

PAUL

No garden is complete
without a gopher.

Once the decision to rout my way out of LA had been reached, I immediately turned against the city; all signs pointed away. I began getting extremely restless with Steven and the Studio. It wasn't that Steven was a bad roommate, per se, but he did manage to pack down a fifth of cheap vermouth a night, and burn cigarettes like a two-legged Detroit. He was a quiet drunk, all in all, but the smoking became inexcusable, unavoidable and most uncomfortable.

Steven was never disrespectful or overtly uncaring of either the pets or of my areas and belongings; quite the contrary. He was just spaced out. And besides all that, I simply *wanted to be a monk again.* I was now very serious about my painting, very intent on beginning this book, and I basically just craved time alone, to have some quiet, reflection, to breathe some *clean* air, rediscover myself as me-without-someone-else-always-there.

Painting had come into its own while I was at the Beverly address. I began using the hi-tech name I had chosen for my music publishing company, GAVCO, knowing already too many Gavins to feel that that would be a good handle, and never having felt any particular ties to the family name that always seemed to imply my father, or his father before him.

One of the few LA painters that I had any genuine interest in, Andre Miripolsky, came in one day on other errands and ended up buying the first painting sold of my new work; he later bought another, and another. An art-dealer friend of Steven's traded me a huge Calder silkscreen for one of my canvases (I had always wanted a Calder). And finally my buddy Macy swooped by and purchased the huge "Noah's Return" canvas (a five-by-eight-foot depiction of a flying saucer dropping down to Earth to pick up the awaiting pairs of animals). This availed me the finances to begin contemplating a change in location.

Besides, a queen's a queen, and no castle needs more than one.

I went north to visit Samantha, to see her land, Yosemite, and to visit Miss Helga's Mountain, to see what these two divine devis were cooking up.

Helga was rarely around; she had purchased her mountain, but now she was back in Santa Barbara, working overtime as a postwoman to pay the place off, to put in a road, a well, eventually a trailer, then a house. It would take time. Samantha, however, was the definitive hostess. She and her roommate Ed (old-timer, chased flying saucers in Japan for the army in the Forties; Fifties and Sixties was an engineer for NASA, for the first Apollo flights, for nuclear bombs; now turned to real estate, sold Helga her land) would make every provision for my entertainment and edification re: the park and surrounding area. We cooked and dined, watched videos, played with animals, sloshed through the rains and snows over nebulous parcels of mountain property, homes for sale, or just areas of the park and other local natural highlights. I was treated like a king (instead of a queen); I frankly relished getting to know Sammy.

I had been offered a fair chunk of money, as a loan, from Bessie, to buy a house and get out of the city. It was a way, I thought, of eventually doubling my income through real estate investment, and ultimately repaying the dear for the substantial wad of money for which I was already obliged. She wasn't rich, Bessie, just generous, and the amount that could be proffered would buy precious little in LA, had I so desired, and precious nothing on Kauai, which was where I truly wanted to be. Yosemite, though, seemed to be the great undiscovered Shangri-La in California, sure to boom up as the white flight continued away from LA, SF and other urban wastelands.

And it *was* beautiful, magical in many ways. Not to mention the proximity of my two favorite dames, the goddesses Helga and Samantha. We walked Helga's Mountain ("Rock Steady") in her absence, made a list of several viable chunks of land on which I could perform a similar transformation (do a trailer for a while, survive a winter or two, get to know the deer, the coons, the buzzards, bobcats). Then we found a comely cabin, tucked in some trees between mossy clusters of granite boulders, lush meadows, and, best of all, its own pond, *with ducks!* The fourteen acres were sprawled neatly upon the high meadow cleavage of Helga's and Samantha's mountains—what could be more cosmically correct? Besides, I've always loved ducks. I wanted the place.

Into the gallery walked a gentleman who browsed around, left, came back, browsed around some more, and purchased one of my paintings. His name was Michael Gregg Michaud. He went on to buy more than two dozen pieces from me. He also hung out incessantly. He was obviously lonely, bored, and would do most anything for companionship—though he seemed to genuinely appreciate my work. He also had a vast collection of Dalí, Chagall, Peter Max, and had just purchased an original Cocteau—I could be among worse company.

Michael was peculiar, to say the very least. Leonardo couldn't abide him, and would invariably ask me to lead him away at the end of the day lest he just sit indefinitely. I can't say that I liked him either. In fact, I had an immediate dislike of Michael from the word go. But then, Michael does that to everyone, ostensibly to turn people off before they have a chance to turn on him. Still, when someone buys your work, you are at the very least courteous to them—when you're broke—and besides, I was a sitting duck.

Michael began showing up daily with a panoply of Thai take-out, Häagen Dazs for dessert, libraries of magazine articles about art, auction catalogues, even original pieces that he was acquiring—anything to hold my attention, excuse the visit, and provide a lead into a conversation. I have rarely encountered a more socially misfit person. Michael was thirty-three—some six months younger than me—with thriving dark hair and bottle-thick glasses. He always wore blousy white shirts and baggy trousers from Fred Segal's that were an effort to conceal his lack of a figure but had the effect of simply making him all the more frumpy. Michael had spent the last six years of Mae West's life with her. They were constant buddies, and eventually Michael ended up with daily nursing duties, from Miss West's morning colonics to her evening ice baths and breast rubs. He became one of her regular escorts to openings, dinners, and her infamous Friday-night seances at the beach house. He also ended up with priceless collections of Mae's astonishing writings, and fan letters from everyone from Streisand to Fellini, Warhol to Jimmy Carter; amazing correspondence that spanned decades between the diva and Kinsey (who wrote her regularly for advice on assorted sexual topics); letters from Fellini imploring her to star in his films; letters from Dalí after she returned each artwork he gave her. Also in his possession were dozens of radio plays that have never been performed; her original film scripts (she wrote them all), even a scrap of paper on which, through a series of scratchings and doodles, the love goddess coined that most-famed fiat, *Why don't you come up and see me sometime?*

He came to tell me about her many loves and rows, from the regular overnight visits of OJ Simpson to the putting-in-his-place of William Randolph Hearst that all but terminated her early stage career. Michael's dissertations on the lady led me to perceive her as one of the greatest minds of this century, and certainly the most astonishingly liberated woman in modern herstory (but that's the book that Michael needs to write...).

Upon Mae West's death, Michael related how he ended up as lover to/caretaker of Joe Dallesandro. For three years Michael (unwittingly for most of it) supported Joe's junk habit, held his head over the toilet while he vomited, wiped his butt for him, continually concealed his whereabouts from his beloathed exploiter, Andy Warhol, and slept tenuously beside the icon while he shivered and sweated through his DTs.

Michael *has* written this book: *Joe*. He took me to meet Joe just briefly one day, but the demi-superstar, now married, sober, and ensconced in a cushy little off-Melrose bungalow, was laconic and obviously put out by the unannounced call.

He was also buddy-buddy with a number of the Beverly Hills art hierarchy, regularly purchasing their wares and attending the most exclusive shows. We began schmoozing and opening-hopping together. I was hyped, and Michael was overjoyed to have a date to some of these bravura bashes; he became sworn to the furthering of my career. "Hanson's is the way to go," he assured me. "Hanson carries Max and Kostabi; they're the hippest gallery, and one of the most successful—we won't show them the penis series right off the bat—but the hummingbird series is splendid." (Michael owned ten of these.) Coincidentally, we discovered that one of the salesladies at Hanson's had come to the UNcensored show and purchased a piece of mine. It was a huge ejaculating penis—but never mind, the director of the gallery, Mr Rae, said that my portfolio was the finest he had seen from an up-and-coming, took it personally to Hanson at the Sausalito headquarters, and came back swearing that Hanson was most impressed and would purchase a dozen or so pieces to "try me out."

We also, for PR's sake, gifted pieces to Janet Leigh, Beatrice Wood, Patty Duke, Stephen King, Anne Lindbergh, Dr Seuss, and numerous other brand-name friends of Mikey's. Kirk Douglas purchased a painted vase for his wife; I already had pieces in the collections of Bear and others of the Hollywood set.

We went on to schedule shows at Michael Himovitz Gallery in Sacramento, William White Gallery in Eugene, Oregon, Galeria D'Art Carlos Lozano in Cadaques, Spain. My large and grinning skeletal homage to Nancy Reagan, "Just Say Yes," was thrown out of a show at Pierce College ("This is a *Republican* school...!"). And we came up with a line of GAVCO T-shirts that have done quite well at Fred Segal's and other hoity-toity boutiques. We also began both bronze editions and printmaking to reach a more extended audience (Michael said that he used to help Dallesandro run off fake Warhols, which they sold up and down Rodeo for a fortune...).

"Does this mean we're married now?" Michael asked me one evening over lemon sorbet.

"Sure doll, as long as we don't have to sleep together..."

"Oh," he sighed, "we must be *really* married."

Michael has proved invaluable to both my art education as well as my previously elusive career, yet the emotional issues of love and sexuality have been the continual barbs in our wire.

Which gives way to the next factor, that as I began making decisions and commotions about leaving LA in my wake, Michael began desperately participating with me in the search, as well as the endeavor to head out of town. And so it came to pass, after a lovely snow-enshrouded trip together to visit Sammy and check out the frozen turf, that Michael, a real estate mogul from years back, against the advice of everyone who knows either one of us, decided to invest with me in this exquisite ponded estate ("Little Bear Acres").

During our acquisition, Michael went to see a lady known as Sandy the Psychic that Jamie Lee and a number of his star friends recommended. Sandy told him many things of note, but as much, she talked about me. Finally she said to him, "You just better have this person call me."

So I called, then went to see Sandy the Psychic out in her little prefab home somewhere in the wilds of Simi Valley. I was late, however, due to the shock of discovering that my Jeep had been vandalized, my camera and light meter stolen, the angle window busted. Sandy reprimanded me immediately, shaking her chubby forefinger at me, "You shoulda come to see me yesterday, I would've told you it was gonna get hit." She said, "Leave the angle window alone, and don't leave anything in the car, because the same kids'll be back one more time before you leave town."

Sandy was a large Jewish lady with that bleached blonde hair that looks like a loaf of Canter's braided eggbread, too much makeup, a house full of candles, a quaint crystal or two, a Buddha, assorted Christian saints—the usual psychic condo-stuffers. She could've been cast as the augur in any Hollywood reel. She told me about many people that I knew or would soon meet. She had remembered me from our last lifetime together as indigenous Americans in the Arizona/New Mexico area; my name had been simply "Eagle" she said. She whispered that I was very worried about "Paul." I said that I didn't know any *Pauls* that I should worry about. She changed the subject as though she had mentioned something that was, perhaps, taboo.

Every card that she turned up implied money. Money money money. *Where was it?* "Don't worry," she said, "you'll be richer than God, off your paintings, your music, any art that you set your mind on. *Don't limit yourself!*" (Where had I heard *that* before?) She said I'd soon sign an auspicious contract for art with a handsome middle-aged man with darkish hair (Hanson?). She presaged I would fill the coffers while traveling and speaking, here and abroad. A Japanese woman would have much to do with this—perhaps Hawaiian.

She fretted that my health was being compromised by what she thought was cigarette smoke, that it was affecting my circulatory system and liver, that I needed fresh air and water. Then she saw Steven, who she said was developing cancer as a result of his smoking. She backed up my stance of avoiding marijuana users for psychic reasons.

She mentioned my friend (and fellow samnyasin) Charles, "a tall and slender black or Indian man," by name (Charles is one-quarter Cherokee). That he would be spending time with me up in the mountains. She got goosebumps on her arms and said that this was a great boon, that this was a very old soul indeed. She liked him a lot.

Spirituality, she said, would never be my problem. I would continue to go through many profound changes; everything would be finished this lifetime.

"Spirituality and money," she reiterated, "are with you all this lifetime. Stop being *afraid*, stop worrying, you will have it all! The move to Mariposa is very blessed indeed. You will prosper there."

She didn't mention Michael. I didn't ask. She said my mother was coming down with the flu; she said I'd tell off Samantha for something, Jamie Herlihy and Leo as well.

"Watch your words," she added, "people don't understand you sometimes and your words hurt them. Preface yourself with *I care about you*, then you can say anything that you like."

That was that; the half hour was up. The next day I called Mom, who was just coming down with the flu; three days later my car got hit again—but there was nothing there to take...

I never asked her about love.

Then I met Paul.

I found a piece of paper in my office that bore the name *Paul* by an address and a scribbled note from me which said, simply, "cute." He had been at the A Different Light reading as well, and I asked, as I always do, for people who desired to be on my mailing list to please give me their name and address. After the reading, I received a brochure in the mail for a Jungian dream-analysis group, led by Paul Chirumbolo, which also included an obtuse and heady, but colorful poem. I put the two together, and was intrigued.

I called the man and we chatted freely about channeling, shamanism, negativity as self-fulfilling prophesy, "allowing love" as opposed to "making love," "facing the answer" versus "seeking the answer"; about drag queens as one of the greatest shamanistic forces in creation; about the current rage of PC-babble, "assimilationists," about sex, fame, and the evils of Hollywood. I had no image of what the bloke looked like, but I seemed definitely to be looking for something tasty to either take with me to the mountains, or some memento to leave behind. We set up a dinner for the next evening.

Paul had fascinating stories. From being completely demolished in a head-on collision, to two years with a very radical Urok Indian shaman. From six months living and writing under the frustrated advances of Franco Zeffirelli in Italy, to being threatened at gunpoint by a jealous Rudolf Nureyev in the wee hours of the morning with a certain lead dancer for the Italian Ballet tucked between his sheets.

He read my tarot cards for the first three hours; after a fine Nicaraguan meal at the local Restaurant Managua, I cornered him on the couch. It had just started to rain, a three-day storm expected. His ribs and knees, having all been shattered in the accident some thirteen years ago, were feeling the weather. I offered him a massage that he would've accepted except for his Thai boyfriend picking him up at 5AM to go to the flower mart.

He was smooth, delicate, lithe; purebred Italian, with a master's in clinical psychology, specializing in Jungian dream analysis. Obviously stopped traffic as a youth. He smoked cigarettes, drank coffee, and had breath worse than mine (I've always liked angels with bad breath, it makes the etheric seem somehow more tangible).

It was 1AM when I quit stroking his eyebrows and spanked him off to bed. We had long kisses, embrace, and sighs at the door. The rain began pouring.

Three days later he had had a dream about me. We arranged to meet again that night.

I removed his clothes, then mine, and put him naked beneath me upon his waterbed; I massaged him for some four hours touching every bone, tendon, ligament and muscle. I experienced his auto accident as though it had happened to me; and I felt him healing. I knew him as though I had been inside him, working my way out through the arteries, the follicles, the sweat upon his chest. Full of desire. Full of love. He accepted my *love*, but not my sexuality. He held me in the kitchen afterward, having put back on his clothes, and I knew by his calculated stoniness that I had lost, that he had opted for his boyfriend; his embrace was warm, but final. He noted that my eyes were sad.

He had told me earlier, after the Thai dinner that he had prepared for us, that he had been honest with his friend, that he was confused to have this gorgeous and accomplished poet call him out of the blue, make a pass at him. All I could advise is that he follow his heart. Mine had already gone too far—I was beyond decisions. I had fallen in love. I would've given up Yosemite; I would've given anything.

I called him the next morning at his job. "Lest there be any ambiguity, dude, I love you and I have every desire to pursue a relationship. And if such should become appropriate, at any future now moment, do please let me know."

"You've made that clear, Gav. And thank you, I certainly will." He seemed quite thoughtful, sincere.

And I slept with him on my mind, our brief emotional interpenetrations, his languid penis, soft brown nipples, celadon eyes, the annular hollows of his armpits which seemed to fold all the way inside him; his nervous laugh, the canine teeth that were a bit too long, giving him an evilish, otherworldly appearance; sweet round ass, pliable beneath my palms like the halves of a living heart that had been cleft in two.

Paul, like l'enfant terrible Craigele, had made a point of having been sexually abused as a child. In their respective adulthoods there remained much wariness and Weltschmerz. I did not have the answers to give them, but in my mind I raped them both.

It never gets easier, not being able to have what we desire the most. But then, I told myself, poets are just here to *write about* relationships, not to *have* them. I just wanted to go away.

I called up Austin.

This was just the time at which Steven and I had our massive last bash, an art show/opening of our latest work. Ellen Burstyn was the unofficial hostess; Gavin Danker on the bar (with fangs); everyone came. Even Paul, though I hardly had time to speak to him and was unaware when he left.

Austin, though, hung around later, and I asked if we could have a date. He was completely taken aback, but he smiled and said sure. Austin was a gorgeous child, a frequent model of Steven's, with clear slate-colored eyes, soft pink lips, and the most spectacular chest hair, forming a perfect eagle, the cupreous wings of which embroidered both breasts, the head pointing upward into the hollow of his neck, the tail crossing down over his belly, pubic spinney, and onto the sturdy limb on which the bird was perched.

He was terrified of me when I showed up at his Hollywood apartment. He kept offering me shots of Scotch, which I refused, then downing them himself. I could see from the start that we would find little to talk about— he *wasn't* Paul—and *he* was aware of the same. But once I got us naked and into his bed, our hands and mouths did the rapping and the evening made at least some semblance of sense.

Sex wasn't comfortable either, though my aesthetic appreciations knew no bounds; still, we saw each other off and on, even chatted daily on the phone for the next couple of weeks.

What the experience did conclude was that Austin would move into the studio and take my place. This was perfect: Austin was an aspiring artist (did frivolous sort of fashion art on clothing), he was soft and gentle, beautiful, and he drank and smoked.

And that was that. I had been worried about who would take my place and put up with Steven; now it was settled, everybody was thrilled. And though Austin and I continued, I believe, to covet one another's bodies, the words were never there to expedite the consummation. Yet he would sleep in my bed—without me.

GAVIN

Love is the simplest
of all solutions.

As I write this chapter, the Nineties have come and all but gone. My five years in the woods of Yosemite eventually led me to the foggy coasts of West Marin and a series of four Advaitic teachers who would bring me to the cessation of all my questions.

On the whole, the Nineties were as bland and as white-bread as the Eighties had been, with few notable highlights. Andrew Martinez walked naked through the streets of Berkeley; Camille Paglia arose to attempt to free us from misandrous moral crusaders posing as feminists; Sinéad O'Connor tore up a picture of the pope on national television. But our idolatrous media so soon tires of iconoclasts.

In August of 1996, Binti, a female gorilla in a zoo in Brookfield, Illinois, rescued, cradled, and handed up to the guards a three-year-old child that had fallen into her concrete domain. On the very same day, a boy scout troup in Yosemite stoned to death a bear cub caught rifling through their belongings. The media reported both of these in the same paper, yet neglected to make any connection.

Comet Hale-Bopp wowed us all with its effulgent display; and on January 23, 1997, a particular planetary conjunction was hailed by many to be the official beginning of the Aquarian Age, a time of near-instantaneous completion of the old and manifestation of the new.

According to the ancient Mayan calendar, the world lasts only until the year 2012. Given the current rate of ecological devastation, I wonder how we can hang on that long. In any event, having witnessed the deaths of dozens of lovers, friends, and compatriots, I have come to see that there is no time to waste.

Over the last years I have been made aware of the deaths of Vince Romano, Al Petersen, Dave, Jerry Ragni, Tom Eyen, Jimmy Barron, Peter Allen, Flip, John Preston, Larry Kert, John Krause, Steven, Raymond, Austin, Jeske, and other lovers and friends not mentioned here. Given the friends whom I know are surviving their once-illness through natural and holistic means, I do not attribute the deaths of the others to AIDS at all, but to useless and lethal drugs (under the avaricious auspices of the AMA, FDA, Glaxo-Wellcome...), the cowardly, ignorant and homicidal doctors who prescribe them, and a medical empire and propaganda machine so heinously wealthy and all-powerful that its critics are deemed heretics.

Just as I was completing the chapter about him, my early buddy Craig was found decapitated beside a railroad track in Santa Barbara at three o'clock one morning, his pockets full of cocaine and money. The police said there had been a scuffle, but that there were no suspects—friends related that he had been talking about suicide just the night before. He was one of the few homos I knew who had not had any contact with AIDS.

Jamie Herlihy killed himself because he had AIDS, because he was aging, and because he was terrified to become a burden to anyone.

Michael and Samantha began their own line of greeting cards. Michael has recently become West Coast editor of the official Salvador Dalí newsletter, though he spends most of his time with Tippi Hedren on her Shambala Preserve, helping out with the funding and feeding of her ninety-some refugee cougars, leopards, tigers, and lions. As per Sandy the Psychic's pronouncement, Samantha and I are no longer on speaking terms.

Big Mama has, at last, married her sidekick Ananda. They are both employed in the corporate world.

My first husband, David Dalton—who recently aptly described me as "a doorman for his cats"—has abandoned the farm in North Carolina and moved to within a quarter block of where I had once lived with Raymond in San Francisco. He is just putting the finishing touches on his first novel, *The Crippled Collie of Haight Street.*

Philip Littell's libretto for *Dangerous Liaisons* had its premier two years ago at the San Francisco Opera House. Next in line for him is *A Streetcar Named Desire,* with music by André Previn.

Shari Famous is now Shari Famous Foos—Mrs Rhino Records. Watch for future GAVCO recordings!

Race Bannon has begun a very successful publishing company and has most recently brought out my massive pan-sexual anthology of kinky verse, *Between the Cracks.*

Bear's official biography has been released; I reportedly am not mentioned.

In the Flesh, originally scheduled as a Penguin release in 1993, was crunched by Hollywood lawyers, compliments of the Bear, Sam, and Dolly. I have moved from the invitation list to the hit list.

One day I received a phone call from Sam. "So, I hear you've written a book about me."

"No, Sam, why would I do that? I've written a book about me. You are merely a character in my life—one of hundreds—and I don't believe I'm unflattering."

"All the same," he retorted, "you don't have the right to tell *my* story."

"I'm not telling *your* story, Sam, I'm telling mine."

"But it's just from *your* perspective."

"Of course it's from *my* perspective. I'm a writer; that's the whole point.

I'm subjective, I'm herstorically inaccurate, and I'm full of bias, prejudices and loopiness, which are the only things that make my story—or life in this otherwise pabulum society—interesting."

"And what does that do to me?"

"Write your *own* book!"

"And what about Bear? Don't you think this could hurt his career?"

"Somehow I find the concept of *my* jeopardizing the careers of *either* of you guys just plain ludicrous."

"Look, if I want to come out, I'll *out* myself!"

"I thought you already had?"

"That's my business."

"I saw it in *Esquire*. Besides, Sam, I'm not *outing* anybody. As if there were anything to be outed *from* or *to*. I don't mean to purport anything about *any*body's sexuality. Who cares! I just talk about the sex, and love, that I've had. And whom with. People can draw whatever conclusions they wish..."

I called up Bianchi, who was wallowing in his recent successes as head photographer of the buffed and fluffed.

"Tommy, dearest, did you by any teensy-weensy little chance mention anything to Ms G about my book?"

"*She* called *me*."

"And what did *she* say?"

"She asked if I knew anything about your book."

"What did *you* say?"

"I said I knew that I was in it. Sam asked me how that made me feel, to have you writing about me."

"And...?" I persuaded.

"And I said I didn't care what you said about me, as long as you said I had a big dick. That'll at least piss off my enemies!"

"Did Sam laugh?"

"He tried to."

"Poor Sam."

"Yes. We should all be so poor!"

"Love you, Tom."

(Did I mention that Tom has a formidable cock...?)

I have recapitulated a number of lovers in this saga, but they have really been too numerous to mention. I cherish every one, though to attempt to capture the meaning of each encounter upon the evolution of my soul is the complete despair of prose. In the inexorable beauty of Yosemite, I had the time, the space, and the solitude for self-reflection, and to recall and appreciate the unfolding of the myth that I am, thanks to my friends, my gurus, and the many blessed naked saints.

And as I've reminisced, my only regrets in all of the sacred encounters that I have had were but the loves that I have missed because I was too wary, too righteous, too proud to just say *Yes*. Pride, after all, is the only sin.

I remember Braum, Colt model, six-foot-four two-hundred-and-twenty-pound German, brilliant classical pianist, who used to tie our genitals together with scratchy leather straps, put steel balls up my rectum and ride me around on the back of his motorcycle.

I recall an even bigger gentleman (six-eight!) who was the revered baritone-bass for the Seattle Opera Company, always a featured vocalist in their Ring Cycle; climbing aboard him was like saddle-backing a rhino.

I dated a few times, at Ona's instigation, the beautiful young porn star named Sharon Kane. Sharon was my age and had made over three hundred films. She disappeared to have her face and tits tightened and I have yet to see the latest product.

I spent an evening or two with Michael Feinstein, largely involved in trying to convince him that nobody gave a shit about Gershwin any more, that if he wanted any kind of *real* career he had better start to do his *own* thing (so much for *my* prescience).

There were two or more Marlboro men. Off and on I played with Tom Eyen, back when he was still writing *Mary Hartman Mary Hartman* (sordid soirées in Louise Lasser's backyard hot tub). I also had an encounter with Jerry Ragni, one of the most significant lyrical geniuses of our century.

I remember Richard Montoya, Ann-Margret's sexy Spaniard dance captain (used to growl like a wolf under his breath and make my hair—and everything else—stand on end).

I also summon to mind that splendid bodybuilder on Haight Street who took me up to his flat one evening (pre-AIDS) and had me fuck him (sans condom) even after I told him that I had the clap, just because it was his birthday and he wanted this stranger in him.

And Big Bob, who had a thirteen-inch penis and coveted my affections because I was indifferent to the thing (he had a sweet butt).

I remember Fredy Burger—half Italian/quarter German/quarter Peruvian-Quechua—serving up sizzling *chorizo* and *huevos grande*. What we lacked linguistically we made up for with body language.

And that saucy young Sicilian, David Lopatin: David was secretary/escort/adopted son to Zsa Zsa. They used to fight like lovers; David would jerk his phone out of the wall, Zsa Zsa would call me up crying for hours—as David lay in my bed with a pillow over his face—begging me to tell him *zat she vas sorry, darlink*, to tell him to *plees come back to Mama*.

But as blessed as any of these were all the nameless or name-forgotten passersby, one-nighters or weekend specials; the Ganymedes I collapsed with beneath a sink in a disco john, and the *Sakyamunis* (Silent Buddhas) who were nothing other than fleshly forms in a steaming *Sunyata* (Void) with no light or voices.

Even as I write about them, I am unlocking the door on each and every cage, setting all the canaries free that they might opt to fly with or without me into the reaches of memories still to be. I stand divested, the Naked Poet at last.

I love being alone, and have realized finally that *I* am the Center of the Universe. And in this consummation of Self I have not made a million dollars, or been discovered by Gus van Sant, but I have learned the distinctions between crows and ravens, buzzards and vultures, and can confront a mountain lion in the shadows without question or fear.

Sci-Fi author Orson Scott Card instructs us, "We are the stories we tell about ourselves." But I have come to see that I am none of the things I have written about, all of which memory changes and rearranges at its convenience. Nor am I even that fickle one who tells the tale, for he too creates a new story for every mood of the day.

I had a vision one night recently while sitting in a crowded and chattery room, waiting for a concert to begin. I experienced all of us as paper puppets on sticks, the breeze blowing through us making us to rattle and quiver. We, of course, believe ourselves to be singing and dancing. But we are merely rattling in the wind.

I have become less interested in the arrogant display of puppetry, and more interested in This Wind Which Animates. And the subtle ways in which this Wind manifests in the flesh.

So I petition all lovers past, those whom I have overlooked, and those who are yet to be wrapped inside my arms; all my relations, dancing within this eternal satin ball of stars:

May we dance always and only in love.

Peace and poems,
Gavin Geoffrey Dillard